Current Thought in Musicology

Symposia in the Arts and the Humanities, No. 4
Sponsored by the College of Humanities
and the College of Fine Arts
The University of Texas at Austin

Current Thought in Musicology
Edited by John W. Grubbs
With the Assistance of Rebecca A. Baltzer, Gilbert L.
Blount, and Leeman Perkins

University of Texas Press, Austin and London

Library of Congress Cataloging in Publication Data

Main entry under title:

Current thought in musicology.

Symposia in the arts and the humanities; no. 4
Includes index.
Grubbs, J. W. Introduction.—Seeger, C. Tractatus
esthetico-semioticus; model of the systems of human
communication.—Hamm, C. The ecstatic and the
didactic; a pattern in American music. [etc.]
1. Musicology—Addresses, essays, lectures.
2. Music—History and criticism—Addresses, essays,
lectures. I. Grubbs, John W., 1927–
II. Series.
ML3797.1.C87   780'.01   75-29245
ISBN 0-292-71017-8

Designed by David Mortimore & Eje Wray

Second Printing, 1977

Contents

61486

Introduction

In the spring semesters of 1968, 1969, and 1971, a series
of seminars entitled "Current Thought in Musicology"
was offered to graduate music majors at the University of
Texas at Austin. Each of these seminars, organized and
supervised by the musicology faculty, included twelve
distinguished speakers (or a total of thirty-six) and was
designed to offer to the music students and faculty of
the University of Texas a wide spectrum of "current
thought" on the study of music and related subjects as
evidenced in a variety of disciplines. Just what kind of
spectrum was involved and what "current thought" in
musicology was provided may best be seen in the following list of participants and titles:

Spring Semester 1968

The Problem of Acculturation
Klaus Wachsmann

Music, Speech, and Man as Communicatory Systems
Charles Seeger

Current Views in Eighteenth-Century Style Criticism
Leonard Ratner

The Origin of the Madrigal
James Haar

Viola da Gamba:
Lecture Recitals
Eva Heinitz

**The Impact of the Enlightenment on the Artistic
Concepts of J. S. Bach**
Karl Geiringer

Leonardo da Vinci as a Musician
Emanuel Winternitz

The Study of Musical Behavior, Musicology, or
Anthropomusicology?
Frank Ll. Harrison

Structural Analysis by Computers
Allen Forte

John W. Grubbs

Adventures in the Romantic Sonata
William Newman

The Limitations of the Computer in Musicological
Research
Franklin Zimmerman

The Musicologist and the Library of Congress
Harold Spivacke

Spring Semester 1969

Perspectives in Musicological Publications
Frederick Freedman

The Musical Theory of the Renaissance from
Tinctoris to Coclico
Albert Seay

Modes of Musical Explanation
Claude V. Palisca

Classic and Romantic:
Factors in Stylistic Change
Leon Plantinga

The Norms of Style
Mantle Hood

Hamburg Opera before Keiser:
A Confluence of Baroque Operatic Styles
George Buelow

New Directions in American Studies
Ralph T. Daniel

The Use of Historical Constructs as Tools for Criticism
Leo Treitler

New Directions in Aufführungspraxis
Frederick Neumann

Introduction

The Library of the Mind:
Observations on the Relationship between Musical
Scholarship and Bibliography
Vincent Duckles

John W. Grubbs

Taken in their entirety, the titles of these lectures suggest
the use of the term *musicology* in its broadest and nar-
rowest senses, involving historical musicology, systematic
musicology, and ethnomusicology; focusing on topics
ranging from the Middle Ages to the twentieth century
from such standpoints as composer, genre, instruments,
performance practice, theory, aesthetics, criticism, style,
and analysis; and revealing musicology's growing awareness of its need to utilize other disciplines, such as art
history, linguistics, sociology, and anthropology. I think
it is also fair to say that the spectrum of "thought"
about what was going on or remained to be done in
musicology represents not only that which was "current" at the time of the seminars but also that which is
"current" (from the Latin *currens*, "running") for the
1970's in general.

Although it was apparent to us from the beginning
(i.e., in the academic year 1967–1968) that a useful publication might ensue from the topics presented in the
seminars, it was not until the seminar of 1971 that we
were able to make the necessary arrangements for a
book of essays. The result is the present publication,
which includes essays, often with revisions in content
and title, by nine of the twelve speakers who participated
in our spring 1971 seminar series.

There are so many ways in which the order of the essays could be arranged—each with convincing logic—that
we eventually decided to present them to the reader in
the same order of succession that they were presented
to us. Moreover, this "natural order," as it were, offers
us a particularly meaningful introduction and conclusion.
In what we may regard as a "keynote address," Charles
Seeger presents us with a remarkable twentieth-century
treatise on "communication among men" and constructs
"a model of the contexts in which the study of art and
artifacture may best be pursued." And after we have
explored the wealth of information in the fascinating
topics by Charles Hamm, Elliott Carter, Howard Brown,
Lewis Lockwood, Daniel Heartz, Gilbert Chase, and Gil-

bert Reaney, we are challenged by Vincent Duckle's intriguing essay, "The Library of the Mind," to contemplate what value the previous material may have to us as individual scholars. The important and courageous moment for the scholar, he reminds us, is when he shuts his books, marking "the throwing away of crutches . . . a readiness to proceed on one's own." The library of our minds houses the most important bibliography we will ever assemble.

Introduction

I am deeply gratified to see, at long last, the publication of this fine collection of essays. And I wish to express my sincere gratitude to the many persons who have made this publication possible: the authors, who have been most generous in offering their time and abilities; the Department of Music and its former chairman, Dr. Robert E. Bays; the College of Fine Arts and its dean, Mr. Peter Garvie; and those responsible for the generous funds that were awarded to cover publication costs, including Dr. Peter Flawn, then vice-president for academic affairs, Dr. T. A. Griffy, then associate dean, and Dr. Donald B. Goodall, then acting dean of the College of Fine Arts. With the help of the latter, part of the fund was obtained from the NDEA Title IV Program, O.E., no. 2, and matching funds were transferred to the College of Fine Arts College-Wide Development Fund.

John W. Grubbs

Current Thought in Musicology

Tractatus Esthetico-Semioticus:
Model of the Systems of Human Communication
Charles Seeger

One

*What one cannot speak of may long have been drawn,
carved, sung, or danced.*

This essay outlines a general theory in accord with which
the communicatory systems—that is, the arts and crafts—
of man and their cultivation in their common physical
and cultural context may be presented with least distor-
tion by the inescapable bias of the system in which the
presentation is made—the art of speech. Both theory and
model are speech constructs. But, except for speech, the
arts and crafts and their compositional processes are not
speech constructs. Their names are; but, except for
speech, they do not name themselves. Speech names them;
that is, we name them by means of speech, for that is
the only way in which we can name, relate names in sentences, relate the named among themselves by means of
more names, and relate the relations among the names
to the relations among the named.

As is speech itself, all systems of communication
known to us, both nonhuman and human, are known
directly to us as are we ourselves to ourselves. To the
extent we hold, in speech presentation, that this knowledge is real, to that extent we can say that we are real
and that they, their compositional processes, and what
these communicate are real. We have the "working" metaphysics of "common sense"—an epistemology; an ontol-
ogy, a cosmology, and an ethology, or ethics (axiology,
theory of value)—for we imply that it is worthwhile saying so. The more adept we are in the compositional process of speech, the more elaborate and extended the
reality.

But speech is a many-edged tool. We do *not* know,
can*not* say, or find *not* worth saying at least as much as
we *do* know, *can* say, or find worthwhile saying. Of whatever we say, we can say the opposite. Or we can qualify
it. And we can find that much of such saying may seem
equally worthwhile. Thus, we have developed an indeter-

minate number of ways of saying things and of realities. The tendency has been for each user to propose or take for granted that one way of speaking is better than another and that his reality is *the* reality.

To avoid such simplism, we may distinguish three principal modes of speech usage. All the above ways of speaking are variants, or hybrids, of these modes. The first, general, discursive, is the mode of "common sense" and its more sophisticated versions, sometimes referred to as "uncommon sense." The second and third are specialized—one is belletristic, poetic, mystical, and the other, logical, mathematical, scientific.

Each specialized mode can be said to produce its own characteristic reality. Treatment of reality in the discursive mode varies between the extremes of adherence to a particular reality of a specialized mode and either the skeptic's denial of reality as factual and valuable, or verbal protestation of one reality with behavior that is in accord with another.

The boundaries of the modes vary. Those of the discoursive shade off gradually into the domains of the specialized. The boundary between the logical and mystical modes is fairly sharp as far as individual users of them are aware, but below the threshold of awareness the boundary is very easily crossed.

The relative coverage of the total potentiality of speech by the three modes is probably still far from complete. Since there is no conceivable unit of measurement, their relative coverage may be considered equal, as visually represented in figure 1, with each mode covering half the total area. The following steps explain figure 1:

1. The heavy-lined square *xy* is a skeletal model (visual) of the total communicatory potential of the speech compositional process viewed as the maximal unit of form of that process.

Figure 1. Two-dimensional visual projection of the coverage of the total communicatory potentiality of speech by the three principal modes of usage, in its four simple transformations that are possible in the compositional processes of all principal systems of communication among men. See text for explanation of symbols.

Charles Seeger

2

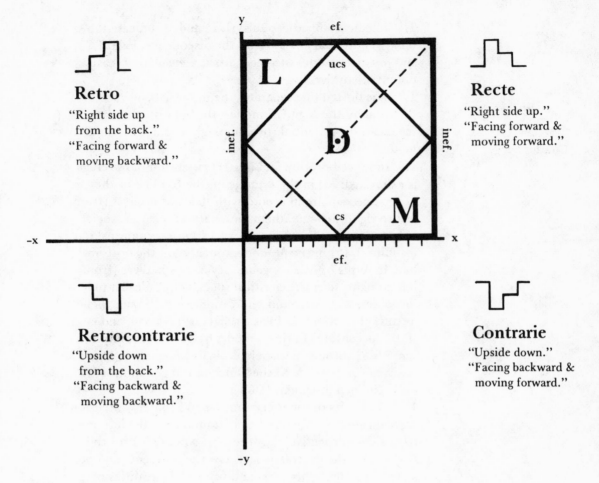

Retro

"Right side up
from the back."
"Facing forward &
moving backward."

Recte

"Right side up."
"Facing forward &
moving forward."

Retrocontrarie

"Upside down
from the back."
"Facing backward &
moving backward."

Contrarie

"Upside down."
"Facing backward &
moving forward."

1.1. The heavy-lined capitals, D, L, and M indicate the relative potential coverage by the discoursive, logical, and mystical modes of speech usage viewed as at least potentially universal.

1.2. The dotted line separates the potential coverage of the total by the L and M modes; the light-lined square separates the potential (overlapping) coverage by the D mode.

1.3. Inner elaboration and (outer) extension of coverage is calibrated: (a) in the L mode on the top line of the heavy-lined square in accord with fields of interest (from left to right, logic, mathematics, natural sciences, social sciences, communicatory theory, esthetics, empirical philosophies); (b) in the M mode, roughly, on the bottom line, in terms of literary genre, style, or whatever (from left to right, scientistic-critical speculation, idealist philosophies, scientistic and impressionistic criticisms, belle-lettres, poetics, mythologies, religious, mystical, and ecstatic speech); (c) in the D mode, by general common sense (CS) through a vaguely definable hierarchy of increasing competence to the "uncommon common sense" of disciplined judgment (UCS).

1.4. The limits of inner elaboration and (outer) extension are indicated: (a) for the L and M modes by the left and right sides, respectively, of the large square; (b) for the D mode by the central dot ($\cdot$). For time present—and possibly, if not probably, past and future—the realities of the L and M modes may be taken as ineffable (*inef.*); the reality of the D mode, as variably both effable (*ef.*) and ineffable, depending upon focus of attention and distance from the central dot. Often as not, opposite realities are professed and acted upon by one and the same person.

2. The stenogram at the right of the large square stands entirely arbitrarily for the unit of esthetic-semiotic form of each of the several systems of communication among men—tactile, visual, and auditory, including speech. Thus, a fourfold transformation of the unit can be modeled upon the axes of two-dimensional coordinates uniformly for all systems.

2.1. The positive axes upon which the large square is projected are extended to indicate three other projections: two, half-positive, half-negative; one, wholly negative. The compositional processes of all systems except speech employ all four of these projections, or transformations, as integral elements of both their esthetics and their semiotics. In the speech-compositional process, the transformations lie at the base of the elaborate and extended panorama of conceptualization found in nearly all languages. Thus, for an elementary example, we could represent concepts of antimatter, antitime, and, for all I know, antispace-time, as $x -y$, $y -x$ and $-x -y$, respectively; but, except for amusement, we do not spend much time using palindromes ($x -y$), and it is impossible to pronounce words upside down or backwards and upside down. The absurdity of the attempt can be shown by such simple verbal transformations as are found in transformational linguistic trees:

Doctor gave Bill a pill
Bill gave Doctor a pill
Pill gave Doctor a Bill
Pill Bill Doctor gave a, etc.

The esthetics are fully transformable, 120 in all, but the semiotics of 118 are nonsense. If given four esthetic units of form as commonly met with in the compositional process of any other art or craft, it is not difficult to find analogous transformations that are traditional components of their compositional processes, few or none of them semiotic nonsense.

2.2. In the present model, the names of the four transformations are borrowed from musicology (*Recte, Contrarie,* etc.); the words below them are borrowed from visual and tactile systems.

3. The square is, therefore, the exclusive speech variant of the stenogram; but it is in its terms that we may try to speak of any or all the others. Therefore, the undertaking to align the compositional process of speech with that of any other system is subject to severe strain simply upon technical grounds, in that speech is the only one of the lot that is ineluctably symbolic at its base: its esthetics symbolize, *represent*, its semiotics. The rest *present* theirs. We are in a position precisely the opposite of Lord Rayleigh when the lady told him she had enjoyed his lecture on electricity but that he had not told her what electricity was. Lord R., sotto voce: "I wish I knew." By virtue of our being adept in the compositional process

of the system being talked about, we know but we cannot say.

The provenience of these three modes and their realities is uncertain—a matter for speculation in prehistory. A highly developed discoursive mode was, however, existent in the writings of Plato, Aristotle, and their contemporaries. The farthest reaches of both specialized realities were open to discourse in their "uncommon sense" and led to proposals for resolution of many of the incompatibilities and contradictions among the lot. But, long before the present writing, the logical and mystical modes became set up separately as mutually exclusive opposites. Most users of each still try to keep them so. And successfully, in that the writings of both are often incomprehensible to each other and to nonspecialists. But, in spite of their contradictoriness, they are ineluctably interdependent and complementary: the logical, on the one hand, depends upon the mystical for an unspoken assumption that the unlimited pursuit of knowledge of fact is worthwhile—that is, valuable—for which there is no logical or scientific evidence whatever and which is inconsistent with all the other carefully reasoned assumptions of the mode; on the other hand, the mystical mode depends upon the logical for the apparatus of the lexicon, the grammar, and the syntax required for reference to the highest values, as, for example, the name "Tao" in the first line of the *Tao Tê Ching* (a prime example of the mystical mode) is not the name of the Tao. The result— the great philosophical joke of all time—is the twentieth-century discovery, through the principles of complementarity, indeterminism, and uncertainty (not to speak of Planck's constant, of which I have minimal, perhaps no, understanding), that the ultimate reality of the physical universe is still just as ineffable as the ultimate realities of the Vedas, the sayings of Buddha, and the *Tao Tê Ching*. The one says, "Although hopeless, it is worth trying"; the other, "Because it's hopeless, there's no use trying." Both, I believe, are in error: the logical, on account of the uncriticized assumption of worthwhileness, which may be leading to serious damage of the biosphere; the mystical, because of its indoctrination of enormous populations with verbal mystification with the result that, until modern times, the class of adepts in speech was

Charles Seeger

6

kept in positions of undisputed economic, political, and social power.

The present undertaking is written in the discoursive mode of speech usage. The core of this mode is the critique. It is the particular job of the critique to try to resolve the contradictions of the two specialized modes, to show their complementarity, and to construct a unitary speech concept of reality that takes into account the realities of the full roster of communicatory systems other than speech.

I owe the title, the idea for the epigraph at the head, and something of the outer form of the essay to my contemporary Ludwig Wittgenstein. Until about 1960, when work on this essay began, I had put him down as but one more logical positivist. I knew him only through his *Tractatus Logico-Philosophicus*, which, in spite of the admirable austerity of its literary style, showed only too plainly that he was imprisoned in the linguistic solipsism of traditional philosophy—the attempt to view speech solely from the inside, as it were, from the viewpoint of the adept in speech alone, to make it hoist itself by its own boot straps—although he came closer to escaping from this linguocentric predicament than any other writer known to me. Had he been as adept in another system of communication as in speech, he might very well have cast the turnabout that he made in his *Philosophical Investigations* under just such a title as mine and achieved an approximation of the objectivity toward speech as a tool that he sought but thought possible only in a perfect language, which he admitted must be an impossibility.

The moot question is: But, supposing that we might look at speech objectively from the viewpoint of another system of communication, how could it be expressed except in speech?

Admittedly, the case itself is a speech construct. It has not been distinguished nor is it conceivably distinguishable in terms of the compositional process of any other system. The very conception "viewpoint of another system" is itself a speech construct. The question becomes, then, two-pronged: first, To what extent can the compositional processes of two systems, one of them speech, be operated simultaneously by one person adept in both and be reported upon in speech? and, second, To what extent may the two compositional processes operate independently or interdependently not only above but also below the threshold of our awareness?

Talking about what one is doing or about something entirely unrelated to it while making music, painting a picture, dancing, making love, fighting, whittling, or working on a conveyor belt is common practice. Keeping in mind the knowledge of what one was doing in such activities is quite another matter. To the extent, however, that we believe and give evidence that we can do this, we may then review in terms of speech what is said by ourselves or by others about it. To the extent that we can generalize such review, we can begin to lay the base of a critique of the speech compositional process with reference to the compositional process of another system. Such a critique of speech is not to be confused with linguistics, which strives to be a science; nor with philosophy, except in the broadest sense of that term as comprehending all serious concern with anything. It is simply an inquiry into the reliability and usefulness of one system of communication in its relation to another. If it barges into the domain of philosophy, it is not the first time in history that nonphilosophical writing has done so. Anyway, philosophy has barged into the domains of other systems of communication so often and with such arrogant dilettantism that the present is no case for the pot to call the kettle black.

Such a critique as I propose will be, then, a speech construct but one of a special kind: an alignment of two compositional processes in as nearly identical terms as possible and then a comparison of two speech reports of two kinds of knowledge—a two-way task.

There is ample precedence for such procedure in the natural sciences. Ordinary language becomes less and less adequate. Too many words in common use are ambiguous. Abandonment of some, redefinition of others, invention of neologisms, and more careful construction have led to the formation of metalanguages. One begins most conveniently and economically with the distinction of analogues, proceeds next to homologues, and advances to heterologues. Analogues and homologues are affirmative.

Analogues are distinguished and expressed mainly in terms of abstract and empirical concepts with adjectival qualification naming (1) the sensory medium (tactility, vision, audition) or (2) the particular traditional systems (music, dance, painting, sculpture, artifacture, etc.). Such concepts are those that, within the limits of similarity and difference characteristic of analogy, can be considered factors in the respective compositional processes in alignment: knowledge, understanding, thought, feeling, imagination, perceptuality, conceptuality, space, time, structure, function, fact, value, form, logic, intelligence, and so forth. For example, depending upon the system aligned with speech, we must accept the reality of graphic, artifactural, and musical concepts and concepts of the dance and other kinds of corporeal movement.

Homologues are distinguished and expressed in both conceptual and perceptual terms that can be used without qualification of medium or particular system, as, for example: causality, teleology, determinism, purpose; long, short, high, low, fast, slow, straight, curved, and simple arithmetical functions, such as plus, equal, and minus.

Heterologues are distinguished and expressed in terms of negation: systems other than speech do not name, do not contradict, and operate in ways that speech does not.

Some words are to be avoided—for example, *meaning*. It is highly ambiguous. It is almost impossible to divest it of speech bias and involves us with the enigma of the meaning of meaning. Some other words are to be handled with special care: as, for example, *mind*. It sometimes refers simply to silent verbalization or the repertory of the funded verbalization of a person, a culture or a period in a culture, an age or sex group, and so forth. If not used to comprehend operation of the compositional processes of the whole roster of communicatory systems, it had better be avoided.

Throughout this kind of enterprise, one finds oneself dealing with two different aspects of a system of communication: on the one hand, its potentialities, on the other, its actual role and function in a given spacial and temporal context. There is no reason to believe the potentials of the various systems are other than equal; but the actualities of the case are very difficult to isolate and vary enormously. In the present essay, we are dealing primarily with potentialities. Elsewhere, I shall hope to deal with the concrete state of affairs among the various systems in the Western world of the 1970's. I will still be

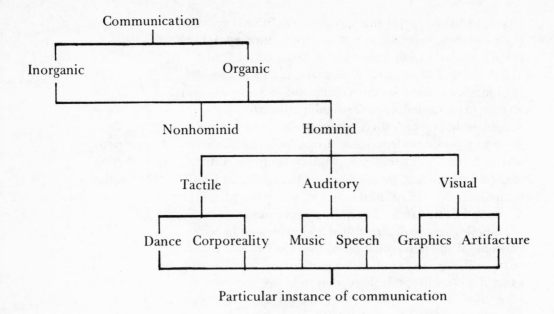

Figure 2. "Genealogy" of the concept communication.

looking at the product of the speech compositional process as an object, from the outside. But the later attempt will be to try to pry off the lid of the linguocentric predicament and to look with the eyes of another system upon what is inside this seemingly most powerful but easily misused tool.

I must beg forbearance of the drastic simplism of some titles, especially numbers 9 and 25. There seemed to be no other way of avoiding entanglement in one or another of the many different ways of referring to the results of the inner functioning of human behavior.

To aid the reader in threading his way from the abstract concept of Title 1 to the concrete percept of Title 33, I append a genealogical tree of the family "human communication" (fig. 2) and a summary of titles.

1. Communication
2. Attention
3. System
4. Society
5. Semiotics

Tractatus Esthetico-Semioticus

1. **Communication**: in this present context, a string of graphic (visual) items of attention (letters) that stands for, represents, refers to, symbolizes, or whatever a string of vocal (auditory) items of attention that has been admitted to the lexicon of the English language as a word by a consensus of the carriers of the sociocultural tradition of that language because it has been found to have been convenient and economical—perhaps appropriate— to regard its utterance as the name of another item of attention that has seemed to have been worthwhile, that is, valuable enough to be paid this attention.

1.1. The item of attention named ("communication," the named) is a concept definable as "transmission of energy."

a. Transmission of energy varies in form and intensity. Form is a structural concept; intensity, a functional concept.

b. With respect to form, energy is transmitted from one material source to others, as, for example: from a hot furnace to a piece of cold iron introduced into it; from a source of light to the chemical composition of a sensitive film; from a source of sound to the pane of glass that is broken. Similarly, a blow or handshake, a gesture, a word or a tune, transmit energy from and to live but not dead bodies.

c. With respect to intensity, a transmission of energy may leave unaffected a potential receiver or transform it to varying extents. Ultimately, transformation may destroy a receiver as an item of attention.

d. Transmission of energy may be regarded equally as a chain of many links (structures) or a stream of many strands (functions).

1.2. The act of writing or uttering the word *communication* is an exercise of a person's born appetite to live and his culturally trained capacity for doing the work of producing and receiving products of auditory communication that accord with the tradition of speech of which it is an example: the act is a speech act.

a. The sound of a word is regarded here as its structure; the name, as its function; the word itself, as an item of attention, a symbol standing for what it symbolizes, the named.

1.3. A speech act relates items of attention: (*a*) names to named, (*b*) names to names (as in sentences, by grammar, syntax, logic, rhetoric), (*c*) named to named (as in various modes of speech usage from mathematics and logic to common and uncommon sense, to poetics and mystical utterance), (*d*) in more complex sentences, by relating the relations among names to the relations among the named.

a. Relating is considered here as connecting two items of attention (names or named) that can be regarded as connectible.

1.4. The speech act is regarded as endosemantic (in a broader sense, endosemiotic) to the extent that the items of attention named and related are names and relations of names, that is, are items of attention intrinsic to speech communication; it is regarded as ectosemantic (ectosemiotic) to the extent that the items of attention named and related are not speech acts; that is, they are items of attention extrinsic to speech communication.

a. Except in linguistics and linguisticslike speech, the named are not words, although their names are words.

1.5. The endosemantically named are named and related

both by man-made rules of traditional speech compositional procedures (phonation, lexicon, grammar, syntax,
logic, rhetoric), which channel the energy transmitted in
doing the work of speaking, and by the natural laws of
transmission of energy.

1.6. The ectosemantically named are named and the
names are related by the same man-made rules but are
themselves related by natural laws.

2. **Attention**: in this particular context, a word that
names the focusing of the awareness inherent in the
living organism's appetite for living.

2.1. Attention occurs variably by communicatory impact upon the organism from without, which is factual,
and by impulse from within (*a*) to receive it, (*b*) to re-
act and, possibly, to return it, which is valuable.

a. Both awareness and attention are psychobiological
categories, analogues of the logical category "distinction" and the critical-mystical, "choice." As preconditions of acts of speech, they are among an aggregate of
other preconditions of communication, many of which
are so extensively researched and so controversial in
their epistemological and metaphysical implications that
no one man can comprehend them all. The concern in
the present undertaking is that, to the best of ability,
they be recognized and borne in mind as preconditions.
Their continually developing conceptualization and the
evidence of new experimentation relevant to it should
be sought in specialized literature of the various scholarly disciplines concerned.

b. Of the two categories (or concepts), that of awareness
is the more comprehensive and, so, the more complex.
There are many gradients between the conscious and the
unconscious. Even specialists quarrel over what is what.
Nonspecialists do well to keep off the grass. The only
comment offered here is that what is awareness in other
than speech communication may be so far from being
susceptible to naming and relating of names as not to be
regarded as awareness when one is talking about it. As
any musician, dancer, painter, sculptor, master craftsman, fighter, lover, or leader of men surely knows by
direct experience, there are moments and even protracted
periods of them when the communicatory activity is in-
tense but without verbalization whatever. And, upon re-

flection, one knows that it is difficult or impossible to say much about them. One is prone to say that one "was unaware what one was doing"—one was *fuera de sí* "outside oneself"—yet there are probably no occasions when one is more aware of what one is doing. One is merely not "speech aware."

2.2. The items of attention named by speech may or may not be items of attention in other systems of means of communication.

3. **System**: an item of attention regarded as a unit, a one, a singularity, a Gestalt.

3.1. Systems comprise components that may be regarded as systems; thus, every system is to be regarded as a component (species) of another system (genus) or other systems (genera) and, as itself a genus, every system is to be considered as comprising other systems that are its species.

3.2. Every system may be regarded equally in terms of structure and in terms of function.

3.3. Structure comprehends configuration of the capacity for work as spatial and static; *a* structure comprehends a discrete formation, a shape, a storage of energy as matter.

3.4. Function comprehends configuration of the capacity for work as temporal and dynamic; *a* function comprehends a discrete transmission of energy.

3.5. Structures are to be regarded as patterns of functions; functions, as traits of structures.

3.6. Two comprehensive systems of speech communication have been constructed by and have become embedded in the traditions of the English and cognate (and probably most other) languages: the one, endosemantic, of names and relations of names, the universe of discourse; the other, ectosemantic, of the named and the relations among the named, the physical (phenomenal) universe.

a. A universe is a system that names the most, or nearly the most, comprehensive conception of the content of a taxonomy or hierarchy of systems. (N.B. A taxonomy is regarded as an ordering of ectosemantic systems, as, for example, of the physical [phenomenal] universe, here regarded as primarily factual; a hierarchy is regarded as an ordering of endosemantic systems, as, for example, the universe of [speech] discourse, here regarded as primarily valuative.)

3.7. To the extent it names and relates the names and named of the physical universe, the universe of discourse comprehends the physical universe; to the extent the universe of discourse names and relates itself qua sound or cultural phenomenon, as here and in linguistics and linguisticlike speech, the physical universe comprehends the universe of discourse.

3.8. Systems are of two main kinds: organic and inorganic.

a. Systems are continually in communication with other systems, sometimes destroying them, sometimes mutually interacting, sometimes neutral toward each other.

3.9. Organic systems are disposed by the interconnection of their components (organs) to maintain and develop this interconnection and, so, to continue to exist as discrete organisms and to reproduce themselves to the extent of their capacities to withstand and exploit communication from other systems.

a. We cannot say that inorganic systems are not so disposed; but neither can we say that they are. The distribution throughout the physical universe of atoms of elements and molecules of compounds exhibits various degrees of congruence and the formation of collectives with continuity, that is, maintenance of separate onenesses. To the best of present knowledge, no borderline between the inorganic and the organic has been defined.

b. To regard the readiness of a drop of water to crystallize at a certain temperature and pressure qua appetite would appear quixotic; but the present context contemplates a uniform connectedness of inorganic and organic communication as readily as it does that of the nonhominid and hominid. And it is felt that the teleology of the case, heretofore mainly the concern of mystics, religious teachers, and poets, can be and is being brought to a stage of verbalization that might eventually convert it from an antonym of the causative (deterministic) rationality of science to a complement expressible in mathematical terms—perhaps a series of imaginary numbers.

c. The more diversified and elaborate the communicatory capacities of a species (the higher in the evolutionary scale), the more its individual members seek others of its kind near in space and time for mutual support in withstanding and exploiting communication from other systems.

4. **Society:** in this particular context (lest the reader forget), a string of graphic (visual) items of attention that stands for a string of vocal (auditory) items of attention that is admitted to the lexicon of the English language as a word, because, by a consensus of the carriers of the sociocultural tradition of that language, its utterance names an item of attention—a distinction worthwhile, that is, valuable enough, to be paid the attention.

4.1. The item of attention named ("society," the named) is a concept that names a class of items of attention that are societies.

a. We do not speak of a concentration of inorganic atoms or molecules as "a society," but the fact that gold, diamonds, water, hydrogen, planets, suns, galaxies, and so forth are found in concentrations throughout the physical universe is worth noting in the present context.

4.2. A society is a generalization (empirical concept) of the total ongoing enactment of the funded communicatory activity of an organic collectivity learned (inherited) by its members from their ancestors, cultivated and transmitted to their descendants by the individual members that are intimately juxtaposed in time and space.

a. The item of attention named by the term *ongoing enactment* is an empirical concept of a class of behavioral patterns—tactile, auditory, or visual—of the individual members of society. *An* ongoing enactment names a percept of a particular instance of such behavior.

4.3. Societies are of two main kinds: nonhominid and hominid.

4.4. Hominid societies tend to be regarded by their members as quasi-organic, with "organs" interconnected in ways analogous to the interconnection of the bodily organs of the individual human being and, like him, withstanding and exploiting communication from inorganic systems and other societies from without and for diversification and elaboration of communication within.

a. Societies are formed in accord with the structural patterns of man's own physiology and tend to be regarded by men as "living" along the functional lines of the organisms that form them.

5. **Semiotics:** in general, the speech study of communication by members of a society living in that society—

in this particular, communication among men as a system.

5.1. As a named item of attention in the physical universe, communication among men is through three media, or channels, and only three: audition, vision, and tactility (gustation and olfaction being regarded as tactile).

5.2. It is economical and convenient to name communication among men as comprising six systems, or means, of communication: speech and music (auditory); graphics and artifacture (visual); and dance and corporeality (tactile).

a. "Graphics" refers to all visual communication in two dimensions; "artifacture," to all visual communication in three dimensions.

5.3. Evidence of the congruence and incongruence of the communicational processes of the lot is both copious and vague; they seem to act variably in independence of and interdependence with each other. Eventually, here, artifacture may be broken down into sculpture, architecture, and articles of use; corporeality, into combat and copulation (direct) and cybernetics (indirect); speech and music, into speech, song, and (instrumental) music. The borderlines of all six or nine systems are shadowy. There is dance in swordplay and hand and posture dance in speaking and music making; it is sometimes hard to determine the difference between fighting and love-making.

a. Direction of this network of communicatory systems by a "mind" or other central ordering capability is to be regarded here as a strictly mystical conception.

5.4. The extent to which homologues, analogues, and heterologues can be found among these systems is a prime concern of semiotics.

5.5. There is no reason to believe that *potentially* any one of the six or nine communicatory systems is more (or less) necessary for or valuable to man than another.

5.6. The semiotics of speech has been the most extensively studied and has been given the specialized name "semantics"; that of the other systems has received little or no study and no special names. Use of the terms *musical semantics* and *semantics of the dance* or of gesture, graphics, sculpture, or architecture should be restricted to speech analogues in the semiotics of other such systems, or to speech compositional processes associated—

17

by tradition or individual initiative—with their respective compositional processes.

5.7. Historically, speech has been more deliberately and extensively organized than other communicatory systems and, as a rule, has been depended upon in social relations in most cultures; but the possibility of an overdependence upon it and of a consequent underdevelopment of the other systems is one that we must examine.

5.8. Semiotics is above all a comparative study, but it faces two major hazards: (1) it is conducted in terms of the compositional process of only one of the systems of communication that it compares; and (2) speech is the only system that names, though both tactile and visual systems can "point to."

6. **Linguistic bias**: a characteristic of all speech communication.

a. The concern of semiotics—indeed, of all use of language—is the extent to which this bias must be admitted and the ways in which it may be avoided, tempered, or compensated for or accepted.

6.1. Use of the several modes of speech usage of the English and cognate languages can be located upon a parameter of speech semantic variance whose limits are, respectively, avoidance of this bias and acceptance of it. Such a parameter may be represented on figure 1 as stretching from the left side of the large square, as the avoidance limit, to the right side, as the acceptance limit.

6.2. Like any other study in the humanities, semiotics varies with the viewing of its item(s) of attention.

6.3. To the extent that it deals (ectosemantically) with named items of attention in the physical universe, that is, with facts heard, seen, or touched, semiotics is to be pursued with scientistic, if not scientific, methods; to the extent that it deals (endosemantically) with named items of attention of the axiological universe, it is to be pursued with critical methods.

6.4. Semiotics is to be regarded, therefore, as a normative study, half scientific or scientistic and half critical.

a. Since no way of effecting a perfect balance between the two methods seems to exist or to be in prospect at present, some semiotic studies will be more scientific than critical and some, more critical than scientific. The relationship of the two should by all means be kept in view. However, the contexts of a study may recommend imbalance; for they must be seen to be not only systematic (synchronic) but also historic (diachronic), and any semiotic communication automatically takes its place in the system of history and the history of systems, that is, in context.

7. **Method**: in the context of serious study, development of the compositional processes of speech communication with maximal and equal attention to the limitations of its potentialities and the liabilities inherent in the traditional overreliance upon its usefulness in sociocultural affairs.

7.1. Scientific methods are determinist, causative, and humanly regarded as outer directed; critical methods are creative, teleological, and humanly regarded as inner directed.

a. Scientific methods are concerned primarily with production of speech judgments relative to systems of fact. For example, based upon one's general experience of living and talking—and especially upon that of one's predecessors—one constructs a piece of speech referent to a system the order of whose components and relations with other relevant systems is not known or is believed to be incorrectly or inadequately known. The piece relates the fewest, most comprehensive, and most abstract names relevant to the case in the most succinctly expressed order. The more rigorously endosemantic, the better. This is a theory, a system of names and relations of names. Next, it is submitted to verification by check against a sufficient number of named items of attention in the case. If the order of the names (the theory) is found to correspond to the order discovered among the named, the theory is considered verified. A single exception in the ectosemantic system may imperil verification of the endosemantic system. The essence of scientific method(s) is: (1) a presumption of perfect order among the named and potentially nameable, and (2) an attempt to create an order among the names—a model that corresponds to the order among the named.

b. Critical methods are concerned primarily with speech judgments relative to systems of value. Based upon experience analogous to that of the user of scientific method, one has formed early in one's life a belief in one or

19

several higher values. The value may not be named or even nameable. Its relations with lower values may be variably ordered or unordered. But it constitutes a posture incorporated deeply, perhaps unchangeably, in the human organism—a posture that relates, to extents we may be only partially or totally unaware of, one's knowledge and one's ignorance, one's beliefs and disbeliefs, one's individual appetite (want) and the social discipline (ought), and so forth. Construction of a piece of speech referent to such a posture is also a system of names, a theory. It requires an economy of verbiage similar to that of any scientific theory. The essence of critical method(s) is: (1) a presumption of chaos among named, potentially nameable, and unnameable values, and (2) an attempt to create an order or model, not of the disorder, but of the values that could be a guide for conduct in the context of the disorder.

c. Each method conceives an overall system that comprehends an unlimited number of subsystems. But the procedures are each other's opposites. The scientific theory is verified by checking against facts; the critical theory is verified by checking lower values against higher values.

d. In general, scientific knowledge is never final or absolute; critical knowledge is always final and absolute. In particular cases, scientific judgment may be final and absolute; critical judgment may not be.

e. Science and criticism are best regarded here as complementary and coextensive.

7.2. The accord between natural law and man-made values may vary among the six or nine principal systems of communication, within each of these systems, and with time, place, and individual-social relations.

a. There is no common measure for this variance.

b. Natural law is to be regarded as assuming both a rigorous determinism with respect to the (endosemantic) ordering of the names of the (ectosemantically) named and an equally rigorous limitation upon the extent (1) of the nameability of man's awareness of the ectosemantically named, (2) of his awareness of the full roster of causes and effects, (3) of the reliability of the logical (and any other) mode of speech usage, and (4) of the reliability of speech communication as a whole.

c. Man-made rule is to be regarded as based upon acceptance of these limitations as a condition for the forma-

Charles Seeger

tion of sociocultural traditions of communication that impose upon individual carriers of the culture an obligation to act in accord with them but that cannot prevent modification, even contravention, of them.

d. The formation of sociocultural rules and conformance to them, and modification or contravention of them are mainly end oriented (teleological), though often expressed in pseudodeterministic verbiage.

e. Individual conformance, modification, or contravention of tradition is variously punished, tolerated, or rewarded.

8. **Message**: in general, viewed as a structure, a discrete transformation of matter in space, that is, an object; viewed as a function, a discrete transformation of energy in time, an event.

8.1. As a structure, a message has form; as a function, intensity.

8.2. Individual members of most organic systems communicate among themselves in production of messages by acts that are functional, consisting of direct auditory, visual, or tactile stimulation of their receivers. The message is an act of corporeal (tactile) communication, even when transmitted by visual or auditory media.

8.3. Individual members of some of the higher organic species, particularly man, communicate among themselves by production of messages that are material structures that function quasi-independently of their producers and, in some cases, even of the traditions in which they were originally cast.

8.4. To the extent that humanly produced messages are auditory, visual, and tactile, they are phenomena in the physical, phenomenal universe—that is, they are factual and obey natural law; to the extent that they are ordered in terms of human sociocultural traditions, they obey man-made rules.

8.5. Production and reception of humanly produced messages is effected by a psychobiological process about which specialists in this field are constantly revealing new knowledge that must be sought in their professional reports and digests. Whatever is said in such contexts as the present will probably need revision by the time it is in print. However, the need here is not to try to relate in detail what the latest discoveries say the psychobiologi-

21

cal process is and how it functions but to explain that something of the sort does function and to note its importance as a precondition for a general semiotics.

a. The process, long debated by philosophy and by diverse sciences, seems to show a very complex interdependence between production and reception of messages, their funding in memory and transformation in the continuing give-and-take of individual initiative and collective judgment. In the course of the inheritance, cultivation, and transmission of the traditions they spring from, they are either forgotten or remembered and incorporated with others of their kind in the continual changing and growing of those traditions.

8.6. The process is here referred to solely for present convenience and economy as the "communicatory syndrome."

Charles Seeger

9. **The communicatory syndrome:** a two-way, reciprocative mode of human appetitive behavior, both afferent and efferent.

9.1. On the afferent path, the appetite of the receiver for reception of a message as a sense stimulus transforms the message into a sense datum for him; on the efferent path, the appetite of the producer for production of a message as a sense datum transforms the message into a sense stimulus for him as well as for actual or potential receivers.

a. Upon the lowest level of abstraction—convention—we may outline the afferent path as sensation-perception-cognition-conation and the efferent as conation-affection ("feeling")-imagination-sensation.

b. Except for the reduction (convenient and economical simplification) of this initial, lowest level, purely propositional view of the syndrome, it is wise from the beginning of its consideration to regard it—as one should regard all parameters of speech semantic variance—as capable of more subtle symbolization than that of a single track, upon which traffic moves only in one direction—theirs. Communicatory traffic is rarely simple. The same can be said of its production and reception. Multitrack, multidirectional traffic moving in all directions simultaneously—even up and down, above and below ground, and crossways, with thousands of blithely ignored signs and signals—is more characteristic of the living organism, as well as of the social "organism" conceived in its likeness.

22

c. The syndrome is, above all, relational. In operation, both producer and receiver relate the aggregate of messages that constitute, for them, their environment. They relate the messages to themselves and select from among them the one or more to which they attend and fund in memory for immediate, delayed, or no action.

9.2. The communicatory syndrome is aggressive and appetitive with respect to reception of messages and is rarely so passive as not to respond with production of a message of its own, potential if not overt, except to items of minimal attention.

10. **Reception of messages, I**: the meeting of the efferent, outgoing energy (appetite) of a receiver and the afferent, incoming stimulus of the message sets up a reversal of the syndrome from sensation to conation or from conation to sensation, as the case may be.

10.1. The energy exerted in the act of reception and its dispersal among the components of the message may vary from minimal to maximal regardless of the energy exerted by the producer in the production of the message and its dispersal among its components and vice versa.

10.2. The more energy exerted by the attention, that is, the more appetitive and preferential it is in isolating one message from others ("noise"), the more complete may be the reversal of the syndrome and the nearer the overt production, by the receiver, of a message of his own. Conversely, the more energy exerted by the stimulus as opposed to the energy of the appetite to receive it, the less likelihood of production of a message by the receiver, if, indeed, any such results at all.

10.3. All activity of the syndrome is conditioned by its previous activity in both directions; it is quite impossible to show, either ontogenetically or phylogenetically, that, in general, activity in either direction is the prime mover of activity in the other.

a. In concrete instances, either the stimulus or the appetite may appear to outweigh the other.

11. **Reception of messages, II**: the sensory and perceptual phases of the communicatory syndrome are difficult to distinguish from each other and may most conveniently and economically be regarded as together comprehending the *esthetics* of the message. The cognitive and

conative phases are more easily distinguished, but the distinction is deceptive only too often, for each is a condition for the other, so that it is also convenient and economical to regard them as together comprehending the *semiotics* of the message. Similarly, in the production of messages, the conative and affective phases of the syndrome may be regarded as comprehending the semiotics of the message, and the imaginative and sensory may be regarded as the esthetics of the message.

12. **Esthetics and semiotics of messages, I**: all messages that communicate sufficient energy to receive esthetic attention are received with semiotic attention.

12.1. "Esthetic attention" refers to sufficient appetite, that is, exertion of energy, on the part of a receiver to permit reception of a message.

a. The appetite is a hunger, a value-seeking, for the sense datum by a living human being. It is an intentionality in that it may do something with the sense datum. This intentionality is one limit of the parameter of speech semantic variance, whose other limit is an extensionality that has been formed by experience funded in memory—a memory that sense data result from sense stimuli and that, by reversing the process, sense data can be extensionalized as sense stimuli so as to repeat an old or create a new message. Hence, the build-up of a phenomenal universe of which the producer of the message is also a component. By the same process, the phenomenal universe becomes intentionalized (verbalized) in an axiological universe of speech discourse that the producer uses.

12.2. "Semiotic attention" refers to sufficient appetite on the part of a receiver of a message to effect its more or less extensive integration (1) with previously received messages funded in memory, (2) with factual and valuable behavior—thus, for him to become aware of the correspondence, interconnections, and relatedness among the components of the message (endosemantic reference), and (3) between these and the other repertories in the environment involved in production and reception of the message (ectosemiotic reference).

13. **Esthetics and semiotics of messages, II**: the esthetics of the message comprehends the converting of the energy of the sense stimulus (a physical fact) into the energy

of the sense datum (a physiological fact) by the appetite
of the syndrome; the semiotics of the message comprehends the relating of the sense datum by this same appetite (1) to other sense data funded in the behavioral capacity of the receiver, and (2) to the receiver himself as
an entity that strives to be and to continue to be himself
in a society of other such organisms bound by a common
culture in a common environment to common patterns
of behavior (traditions) with respect to the communicatory syndrome.

a. The study of the esthetics of the message, of the communicatory systems, and of communication is, therefore,
to be envisaged as the semiotics of the esthetics with
which messages are received. Since both the study and
what is studied by it are conventionally named by the
same word, ambiguity may be avoided by capitalization
of the first letter of the word when it names the study—
thus, *Esthetics*.

b. A comprehensive Esthetics is not to be confused with
the "criticism of taste" or "philosophy of the beautiful"—
a specialized branch or species of the comprehensive
study conventionally known as "aesthetics."* Since this
study and what is studied by it are also conventionally
named by one and the same word, ambiguity may be
avoided by capitalization of the first letter of the word
when it names the study—thus, *Aesthetics*.

c. A comprehensive Esthetics will distinguish two main
classes of communicatory behavior: (1) afferent-efferent,
conditioned, factive, and (2) efferent-afferent, preferential, valuative.

d. All classes of communicatory behavior are to be regarded as behavior of individual human beings. Like a
culture, an esthetics is carried by individuals and, like a
culture, an esthetics, to the extent that it is a facet of a
culture, evolves by the participation of individuals in a
society.

14. **Esthetic and esthetic-semiotic messages, I**: messages
are of two kinds; the one, esthetic, originates by nonhuman agency, given *to* man, as it were, through his inclusion as an element or bundle of elements in the same repertory as the message, that is, the physical universe of
the senses; the other, esthetic-semiotic, originates by human agency, given *by* man, through his production of

messages that are objects in the physical universe but with attributes that are characteristic of a traditional repertory of human communication of his own invention.

14.1. There is a two-way relationship between these repertories: esthetically, that is, physically, the former comprehends the latter; semiotically, the latter comprehends the former.

15. **Esthetic and esthetic-semiotic messages, II**: esthetic-semiotic messages resemble esthetic messages in that both are material objects and behavioral functions whose components are drawn from the raw elements of the grand repertory of the physical universe but differ from them in that these components are manipulated by the techniques of repertories marked with the communicatory syndrome of man and are arranged in the esthetic-semiotic message in accord with these techniques and the traditional modes of employing them in communication in varied sociocultural contexts.

15.1. Esthetic messages originate with neither feeling nor valuation but are always received by the appetite of human receivers with both feeling and valuation.

15.2. Because the feeling and valuation with which the esthetic-semiotic message is received so often seems to correspond more or less closely with the feeling and valuation with which it has been produced, it is convenient but misleading to say that the message "communicates" the feeling and valuation.

a. Both feeling and valuing seem to be factors throughout the whole span of the communicatory syndrome. To the best of present understanding, it is not clear whether they may, should, or must be treated as one or as two.

b. Both feeling and valuing are hierarchical. At "lower" levels, both can be reasoned about in terms of causality; the "higher" the levels, the less in terms of causality (because of our ignorance) and the more—and, finally, solely—in terms of teleology (because of our feeling).

c. Cultural and social values—especially as expressed in the past—are susceptible to objective analysis, as are also past expressions of private, individual values, to the extent that these are variants of sociocultural norms. Otherwise, they are largely matters for conjecture. But much valuing takes place, as does feeling, largely below thresholds and above the lintels of speech awareness and often instantaneously, without verbal deliberation.

d. Feeling, on the other hand, is still for the most part a matter for rational conjecture; yet there is no factor in the syndrome of which the receiver and the producer of messages may be more certain, for it comprehends not only the distinctions of the afferent sensation of the stimulus but also varied awareness of the steps in the communicatory syndrome leading up to the discriminations of the efferent-conative drive (appetite for action).

e. Feeling seems to underlie valuing; and valuing, feeling. Surely, formulation of a theory of feeling is a task proper to the psychobiological and social sciences; of valuing, to these sciences together with musicology, linguistics, philosophy, Esthetics, and communicatory theory. Search for a general theory of value or feeling seems, however, to be overlaid, at least for the present, by copious production of specialized theories.

f. Meanwhile, without a general theory of value and feeling, many disciplines other than those responsible for its formation have the choice of either shutting up shop or making do the best they can, for they cannot operate without assumptions implicit or explicit or rules of thumb for ignoring them—and perhaps unconsciously acting as if they were self-evident.

16. **Valuation of messages, I**: valuation is the behavior, or the function of the behavior, of a producer or receiver of messages that relates the message to him, that relates him to what is not him, that equally reflects and molds his cognition and his conation, and that mediates between what he knows and does not know, between what he feels and does not feel, between what he is and what he ought to be, between his etiology and his teleology, between necessity and free will, and between the manifold pressures inward upon him by the determinism of his environment and the more or less unified pressure outward upon that environment by his own determination to be and to continue to be himself.

16.1. Valuation is of two main kinds: one is of the esthetics of the message, which, though socially trained, is mainly individual, inner-directed behavior; the other is of the semiotics of the message, which, though individually expressed, is mainly social, outer-directed behavior.

16.2. Valuation of the esthetics of messages has ruled,

over the course of time, the selection of the natural, raw materials for most efficient channeling of messages into the sensory and perceptual phases of the communicatory syndrome. For the most part, these materials are not used for communicatory purposes without manipulation to make them suitable for those purposes.

16.3. Valuation of the semiotics of messages has been joined by social man with valuation of their esthetics in a continuing refinement, elaboration, and manipulation of the natural, raw materials for inclusion as elements in the repertories of various traditions of communicatory behavior.

a. The natural, raw materials available for repertories of communicatory behavior—clay and stone, gut and skin, wood and metal, sounds and sights, the human body it- self—may be regarded as existing either independently of man's conative behavior or in relationships to him other than communicatory and may exhibit behavior of their own, peculiar to them.

16.4. In submitting to manipulation by man in his com- municatory behavior, each raw material affords him cer- tain potentialities and imposes certain limitations. Apart from man, the raw material affords no semiotic potenti- alities.

17. **Materials of messages—raw and manipulated**: a tradi- tional repertory of esthetic-semiotic communicatory be- havior consists of (1) a funded aggregate or reservoir of manipulated, traditional materials, and (2) an assemblage of techniques of combining, interconnecting, and form- ing them in discrete units or products. (A nontraditional repertory consists of raw materials alone, with natural, built-in variance of form and behavior.)

17.1. The characteristic esthetic behaviors of the natural, raw materials persist variously in the behavior of the tradi- tional, manipulated materials. Although refined and elabor- ated, the behaviors of the manipulated materials are still functions of the physical, material object that is the es- thetic-semiotic message and, so, can be quantified as can the functions of any other natural, raw material in the repertory that is the physical universe.

18. **Tradition as a repertory of communicatory behavior**: traditional repertory of esthetic-semiotic communicatory

behavior is a repository of the funded values of its builders, inheritors, cultivators, and transmitters.

18.1. Messages whose components have been drawn from a traditional repertory constitute, in their reception, discipline in the factual and valuable behavior characteristics of the culture that has built and maintained the repertory, subject only (1) to the abilities of their producers to reenact these in terms of the potential continuity and variance, that is, growth, of the culture and of the repertory concerned, and (2) to the appetite and ability of the receiver(s) to receive these messages.

19. **Valuation of messages, II**: the characteristic behavior of man to valuate messages received by him is carried over into valuation of messages produced by him. Through the refinement and elaboration of the communicatory techniques of a traditional repertory of esthetic-semiotic communication, messages can be qualified, that is, valued, by him in producing them. It is to varying extents worthwhile for him to exert the energy necessary to produce them and to produce them in a certain way at a certain time.

a. Qualification of the esthetics of an esthetic-semiotic message is understood to comprise equally (1) valuation of the inner relationships among the components of the messages, (2) valuation of the outer relationships of the message as a whole, both to the producer and to the context in which the message is produced, and (3) valuation of the relations of these two.

b. Qualification of the semiotics of an esthetic-semiotic message can be developed as a technique of critical study. It is most precise in estimation of the relative dispersal of energy among the components of the message, of their relative integration or interconnection in the whole, and of the relationships of this whole to the environmental continuum of its producer and receiver(s).

c. To what extent, if any, the semiotics of the esthetic-semiotic message can be quantified is an open question.

20. **Estimation of the variance of esthetic-semiotic messages**: variance of the esthetic-semiotic message with respect to the quantity of energy expended and the quality of its dispersal among the traditional materials and techniques of a communicatory repertory can at best be esti-

29

mated in terms no more precise than increase (+), decrease (−), invariance (=), or absence (0).

21. Structure and function: the esthetics and the semiotics of the esthetic-semiotic message are to be regarded equally in terms of structure and function.

21.1. In terms of structure, both the esthetics and the semiotics of the esthetic-semiotic message consist of the phenomenology of the physical repertory from which the aggregate raw materials (elements) that are its components are drawn; in terms of function, they consist of the axiology of the cultural repertory or tradition from which the manipulated materials are drawn.

a. This implies that the student will rely principally upon physics and biology in dealing with the rawness of the materials of the message and upon a specialized discipline—a critique—devoted to a particular communicatory repertory in dealing with the manipulatedness of the materials.

22. Embodiment, signification, representation, symbolization, implication, metaphor, and disembodiment: the relationship between the esthetics and the semiotics of the esthetic-semiotic message varies over, along, or upon a parameter defined in terms of connectedness and disconnectedness, upon which seven structural pattern types, or functional areas, may be distinguished.

22.1. Embodiment refers to maximal correspondence (connectedness, even fusion) of the esthetics and the semiotics of the message and its endo- and ectosemiotics. Music, pure mathematics, and tactile systems—dance and direct corporeality—of communication are the paradigms.

22.2. Signification refers to use of signs. It is not to be confused with symbolization (use of symbols). A sign resembles the item of attention it stands for; a symbol does not. Gesture, much corporeal movement, and artifacture are paradigms.

22.3. Representation means that the message mimics a referent, that is, portrays the elements of one repertory in terms of the elements of another. Drawing, painting, and sculpture are paradigms.

22.4. Symbolization refers to a compositional device for overcoming the disconnectedness (1) between the esthetics and the semiotics, and (2) between the endosemiotics of a communicatory system. The outstanding paradigm is speech. The connectedness we handle so glibly between sound and name, name and named, might, in the earliest history of the development of some languages, have been onomatopoetic; but, to the best of present judgment, it is now and for a long time has been utterly random and arbitrary. The device fools only the unwary. And custom, habit, and convenience encourage unwariness.

a. Confusion, or even identification, of name with named and of definition of the name with description of the named is characteristic of the discoursive mode of speech, especially of the common, garden variety known as "common sense." Until a discrepancy, potential or alleged, is spoken of, it is considered fussy, tricky, or a waste of time to bother with the distinction. In the more refined and studied varieties of "uncommon common sense," the philosophical problem raised in the nominalist-realist controversy has bedeviled Western thought since the late Middle Ages and has been newly emphasized by twentieth-century logical positivism. In the present undertaking the case is regarded less as a problem and more as a dilemma of the linguocentric predicament in which both horns are (it is hoped) given equal attention.

b. The earliest recognition of the dilemma seems to have been in the teachings of the few great religious writings that have come down to us, as, for example, in the Rig-Veda and the *Tao Tê Ching*. These are frankly in the mystical mode of speech usage. As long as a person speaks and acts in accord with the parameter of speech semantic variance covered by this mode of usage, he can, with apparent success, lead the life of a hermit, an ambulant holy man, or a sedentary sage. One stops talking. Speech is illusory.

c. Twentieth-century recognition of the problem or dilemma by atomic physicists and astronomers has led us, by refinement of the logical-mathematical mode of usage, to the principles of complementarity, indeterminacy, and uncertainty, showing that, for science, the dilemma or problem is still there. We are thus, in the 1970's, living with no less than three principal realities, each of which propagates (verbally) ever new subrealities, all equally plausible, verbally speaking, for there is no other way of speaking.

31

22.5. Implication refers to a logically necessary, specific involvement of a semiotic reference that is not incorporated in the esthetics of an esthetic-semiotic message; that is, it is separated, disembodied with respect to the esthetics but not with respect to the semiotics of the message, for these are inseparable from the aggregate semiotics funded in the traditions of a culture, a sampling of which is funded in the memory of each carrier of these traditions. Implication, strict to relaxed (suggestion), may characterize all means of communication.

22.6. Metaphor refers to a specific but logically unnecessary (speech) semantic reference that is incorporated in the esthetics of an esthetic-semiotic message; that is, it is disembodied with respect to the semiotics but not with respect to the esthetics of the message. Poetic speech is the paradigm.

22.7. Disembodiment refers to maximal esthetic separation of endo- and ectosemantic speech reference in the message, as, for example, in the speech of mystical reverie and ecstatic vision in which there may not even be pretense that the esthetics of the message corresponds to any other esthetic (factual) object, and there may be little or no endosemantic lexical, grammatical, syntactical, or logical form—so little, indeed, that the referent is "beyond words."

23. **Tactility, audition, and vision, I**: all human communicatory behavior is, in a broad sense, tactile.

23.1. The concept of a single comprehensive repertory of tactility, though not so named, is as old as written history and has been enshrined in the concept of appearance, as opposed to reality.

23.2. Both ordinary common sense and the literate, or uncommon, sense of the humanities customarily distinguish reality in terms of five repertories, one for each of the five senses: tactility (as touch), olfaction, gustation, audition, and vision.

a. For economy and convenience in this particular, olfaction and gustation can be considered as inner-surface touch. (Other kinds of inner-surface touch—respiratory, digestive, or whatever—need not be considered at this point.)

b. With social assistance, organic life is possible without vision or audition, or without both, but it is impossible without touch.

23.3. Repertories of gustation and olfaction are common and well known. In highly elaborated and diversified cultures they are extensively professionalized and industrialized.

23.4. No comprehensive repertory has been proposed for tactility as a whole, but many specialized repertories—magical, therapeutic, curative, and religious—are known.

23.5. Repertories of visual and auditory tactility have been highly organized for communicatory purposes in every known culture: visual, in two and three dimensions; and auditory, in speech and music.

24. **Tactility, audition, and vision, II**: it is to be doubted that any one channel of communication can serve alone in reception, except briefly, without involving others, or that any one message can involve all possible channels equally.

a. A stimulus to one sense cannot be a stimulus to another. For example, we cannot see a sound, a smell, a taste, a touch, or hear a color. We can see something that is sounding, smelling, tasting, or touching. It might be held that some messages that are stimuli to one sense can activate any one, two, three, or four other senses. But is this one or five messages?

25. **Afferent and efferent processes of the communicatory syndrome**: the interrelationship of the afferent (receptive) and efferent (productive) processes of the communicatory syndrome must be regarded from at least four different viewpoints.

25.1. First, a single, interlocking syndrome of afferent neurons leads from the sources of their stimuli to a single, unitary, cognitive-conative center in the brain (the classic "mind") largely or wholly independent of them and leads from this center back to the sources of the stimuli and to sources of other stimuli for possible action by the body of the receiver-producer of messages.

25.2. Second, five largely or wholly separate syndromes lead from the sources of their respective stimuli to five variably independent-interdependent parts of the brain and from these parts back to the sources of their respective stimuli and to sources of other stimuli for possible action by the body of the receiver-producer of messages.

25.3. Third, a single syndrome and its afferent and efferent functions constitute one more or less integrated whole in which the customary concepts of "senses" and "mind(s)" are to be viewed as never completely disconnected.

a. One of the implications of this view is that sensing is a kind of thinking and thinking a kind of sensing, with similar bivalence between knowing and feeling, perception and imagination, and other such pairs of concepts, whose empirical referents operate together, thus defining, as limits, various parameters of speech semantic variance in whose terms we endeavor to discourse about discourse.

25.4. Fourth, there is an indeterminate number of levels of attention upon which we may regard the operation of the communicatory syndrome.

a. Microbiological investigations now in progress may completely transform these merely common-sense views of the case.

26. **Craft products and art products, I**: esthetic-semiotic messages are of two principal classes: (1) in which the energy of the producer has traditionally been channeled into its esthetics, and (2) in which this energy has traditionally been channeled mainly into its semiotics.

a. To the first of these classes belong messages having to do with the survival, maintenance, and elaboration of man's individual being as a system in the physical (inorganic) and biological (organic) universe: protection, tools, weapons, food, clothing, and so forth. To the second class belong messages having to do with the survival, maintenance, and elaboration of man's culture in that same context.

b. Structurally, esthetic-semiotic messages of both classes are material products in space; functionally, they are acts that are events in time. It is customary, however, to regard some classes of such messages—especially simultaneous exchanges of them (combats, love affairs, military and managerial orders, whether obeyed or not—as acts or events only, forgetful that they are also products of the necessity or desirability of transmitting energy in some particular form.

27. **Craft products and art products, II**: esthetic-semiotic messages serving primarily esthetic ends, that is, to be "used up" by their receivers, may be classed as "craft

products" (artifacts); those serving primarily semiotic ends, that is, to be "used but not used up" by their receivers, as "art products" (works of art).

28. Craft products and art products, III: craft products serve their esthetic-communicatory ("to-be-used-up") ends primarily through the direct contact of the sense of touch of their receivers, that is, through their olfactory, gustatory, and surface (corporeal) tactility; art products, their semiotic-communicatory ("to-be-used-but-not-used-up") ends, primarily through the indirect contact of the tactile, visual, or auditory senses.

a. The dance is an exception to this proposition in that the dancer perceives his dance through his sense of touch, but a receiver of his communication, except in much collective dancing, receives it only visually.

29. Craft products and art products, IV: besides service of their primary functions, all craft products serve also a secondary semiotic-communicatory (value) function and all art products, a secondary esthetic-communicatory (use) function.

29.1. In both classes of product, the proportion of primary and secondary functions may vary from minimal to maximal; but the excess of a secondary over a primary function is to be regarded as exceptional and does not change the classificatory distinction between the classes of product.

a. In cases in which the communication function of a craft product exceeds its use function or the use function of an art product exceeds its communicatory function, there is an inversion of ends that results, in each case, in the product's not serving, or serving less characteristically, the function that defines the class to which it belongs.

b. Thus, we have chairs, kitchen utensils, even tools and appliances that have not or have but little served, or no longer serve, the touch (use) ends characteristic of their class and have scarcely been, if at all, sat in or worked with but have served mostly, or solely, visual communicatory ends and been mainly, or solely, looked at, as in museums.

c. Similarly, we have works of speech and music, paintings, sculptures, even architectural works, that have but little served the auditory and visual ends characteristic

35

of their class and have been rarely, if at all, listened to or looked at as communications of their producers but have served mostly, or solely, for touch (use) ends in directions for using can openers, advertising display, military commands, shelter for industrial development, and so forth.

d. Instances abound, also, of products that have been produced by their producers not so much to serve the functions defined by their class or subclass as to serve the functions of the opposite class—chairs designed *not* to be sat in, utensils *not* to be used but looked at, and music, literary works, paintings, sculptures, and even buildings that are designed more to advance the status or fill the pockets of their producers than to communicate.

e. Instances abound, also, of craft products with such low coefficients of either function that they are thrown away after one communicatory exposure, are "used up."

f. Historical and geographical distance and discovery of strangeness of cultural tradition or of traditions of social class can point up or compensate for either inversion or for inadequacy of use or communication function(s) by transposing the surviving or discovered product into another repertory or subrepertory, as, for example, by archaeological, culture-evolutionary, museum-esthetic, or other general or scholarly interest.

30. **Whole production, control production, preparatory production, intermediate production, and reproduction:** production of both craft and art products is of five main classes according to the extent to which their producers are involved in the whole or only in part of the production process.

30.1. Whole production consists typically in the performance of the whole process of production by a single producer all the way from the selection of the raw materials through their manipulation to the finished or end product.

a. In the twentieth-century Western world, whole production is increasingly rare. Only occasionally does a producer still find, select, and cut his reed, clean and dry it, bore finger holes, and play his flute to his beloved, or raise his sheep, shear their wool, wash, card, and dye it, spin his thread, weave his blanket, and wear it.

30.2. Control production consists in production of models, plans, patterns, blue prints, orchestral scores, written prose and poetry, mathematical formulas, memoranda, position papers, and other directives whereby the remaining production processes involving many producers of preparatory and intermediate products are directed.

30.3. Preparatory production consists in the gathering or cultivating of raw materials for manipulation by other producers, as, for example, in the mining of ore, the lumbering of forests, and the growing of cotton.

30.4. Intermediate production consists in the manipulation of raw or partly manipulated preparatory products for further manipulation by other producers, as, for example: conversion of ore (better reduction of ore) makes possible the smelting of pig iron, the milling of lumber, the shaping of building materials, the weaving of cloth, and the cutting and folding of it into the yardage on the dry goods store's shelves.

30.5. Reproduction may be manual but is increasingly by machine copying of a visible model or by following the directions of a verbal-graphic control product.

a. From whole production to reproduction, correspondence steadily decreases between the behavior of the manipulator of the raw or traditional materials and the behavior of the receiver in reception of the end product. Indeed, preparatory intermediate producers and reproducers may act at cross-purposes with respect to original and control producers as well as to receivers of end products.

31. **Variance in production—continuity and change**: production of both craft and art products varies according to the extent to which producers (1) have available to them fairly comprehensive and sufficiently strong evidence of the repertory whose materials, techniques, and functions they draw upon in production of their products, and (2) have the capacity to comprehend and to make use of the potentialities for growth inherent in this repertory and in the traditions of the culture of which they are carriers.

31.1. Production varies greatly with respect to both of these variables—namely, the external juncture in which producers exist and their internal capacities, on the one hand, to adapt to the juncture and, on the other, to exploit it.

31.2. Producers who excel in the esthetics of production become known as craftsmen; those who excel in the semiotics, as artists.

31.3. The most highly valued esthetic-semiotic products are those with high levels of both craftsmanship and artistry.

Charles Seeger

32. **Singularity as fact and value, I:** a particular end product that is conceded by a wide consensus of arbitrage to stand out above others of its class on account of the uniqueness of its inner organization and its communication of the highest values of the tradition of whose continuity and growth it is an enactment.

a. Producers of such end products are usually conceded to be both exceptional craftsmen and exceptional artists. In such cases there is little profit in the attempt to distinguish where the one ends and the other begins or to what extent the valuation of a product depends upon the tradition in which it is cast and upon the competence of a carrier of the tradition in perceiving the potentialities inherent in it.

33. **Singularity as fact and value, II:** the more elaborated and extended the tradition, the more numerous and varied may be the valuations of singularity among such end products and their producers.

Note

Oxford English Dictionary, s.v. "Æsthetic." "Æsthetic . . . also esthetic. [mod. ad. Gr. αἰσθητικ-ός, of or pertaining to αἰσθητά, things perceptible by the senses, things material (as opposed to νοητά, things thinkable or immaterial). . . . Applied in Germ. by Baumgarten (1750–58, *Æsthetica*) to 'criticism of taste' considered as a science or philosophy; against which, as a misuse of the word found in German only, protest was made by Kant (1781, *Crit. R. V.* 21), who applied the name, in accordance with the ancient distinction of αἰσθητά and νοητά, to 'the science which treats of the conditions of sensuous perception,' a sense retained in the Kantian philosophy, and found in English *c* 1800. But Baumgarten's use of *æsthetik* found popular acceptance, and appeared in Eng. after 1830, though its adoption was long opposed.

. . . Recent extravagances in the adoption of a sentimental archaism as the ideal of beauty have still further removed *æsthetic* and its derivatives from their etymological and purely philosophical meaning. . . .]"

The Ecstatic and the Didactic:
A Pattern in American Music
Charles Hamm

TWO

Some things happen over and over again. A historian
should be able to identify such persistent patterns and
make use of them to help illuminate events of the present when they can be seen as one more repetition of
such a pattern obscured by passions and murky rhetoric.
The intent of this paper is to identify such a pattern or
situation that has existed in American music from the
time of the Puritans.

A basic Puritan belief was that all a person needed to do
to lead a Christian life was to read the Bible and understand it. The Puritans attempted to strip away all the
things that had been added to the Christian religion and
to Christian life since the Bible had been written and to
base their society, their institutions, and their personal
lives on what they read in the Bible. As far as music was
concerned, what they read there was that singing should
be confined to the singing of psalms, and for a time this
was the only music they allowed. They also understood
the Bible to forbid the use of instruments in worship.
   These psalms were sung by having a leader sing one
phrase with the congregation repeating it after him.
Most people could not read music, and this was a way
for them to sing. Actually, it was a threefold process.
The minister would read one verse of a psalm, a precep-
tor would sing a line of music, and then the congregation
would repeat that musical phrase. This procedure would
be repeated for each line of each psalm, and, since some
psalms are very long, it took a while to get through
them.
   The music that was sung had been brought from England. There had been various publications of psalm tunes
in England, Scotland, and on the continent in Holland.
The preceptors at the various churches knew at least
some of these tunes and would select one in the proper
meter for each psalm. Over a period of time a certain
practice of singing these psalms grew up in this country.

41

Charles Hamm

We know what this practice was like only from what certain people wrote about it. Some descriptions are quite specific:

Where there is no rule, men's fancies (by which they are governed) are various; some effect a quavering flourish on one note, and others upon another which (because they are ignorant of true musick or melody) they account a grace to the tune; and while some affect a quicker motion others affect a slower and drawl out their notes beyond all reason; hence in congregations ensue jars and discords, which make singing rather resemble howling, and drawing out the notes to such lengths is the occasion of their tittering up and down as if the tunes were all composed of quavers, and make 'em resemble tunes to dance to.[1]

This is a derogatory account of the singing in the churches, but the passage is describing a type of heterophony, music quite different in sound from that which one sees when examining these tunes as they were notated. Several other accounts paint a similar picture:

. . . I have observed in many Places, one Man is upon this note, while another is a note before him, which produces something so hideous and disorderly as is beyond Expression bad. And the even, unaffected and smooth sounding the Notes, and the omission of those unnatural Quaverings and Turnings, will serve to prevent all that Discord and lengthy Tediousness which is so often a Fault in our singing of Psalms.[2]

I have but one more thing to observe, and that is, that the same Person who sets the Tune, and guides the Congregation in Singing commonly reads the Psalm, which is a task few are capable of performing well that in Singing two or three Staves, the Congregation falls from a cheerful pitch to downright *Grumbling*, and then some to relieve themselves mount an

Eighth above the rest. Others perhaps a Fourth
or Fifth, by which means the Singing appears
to be rather a confused Noise . . . than a decent and orderly Part of God's Worship.[3]

Tunes are now miserably tortured, and twisted,
and quavered, in some Churches, into an hor-
rid Medley of confused and discordant Noises;
much time is taken up in shaking out these
Tunes and Quavers, and besides no two men
in the Congregation quavering alike, or together, which sounds in the Ears of a Good
Judge like five hundred different Tunes
roared out at the Same Time.[4]

From such accounts we know there had grown up a practice of singing that resulted in very complex music, with
each person singing the same melody, free to embellish
it and even to improvise other notes. There are musics
in the world today in which the same sort of thing
takes place, and these have a great interest to musicologists. But this way of singing was anything but interesting and pleasing to some people at that time.
    In the early eighteenth century a group of people,
mostly in and around Boston, decided that such singing
was not the sort that should go on and decided to reform it. Cotton Mather, writing in 1721, said:

The Skill of *Regular Singing* is among the *Gifts*
of GOD unto the Children of Men, and by no
means unthankfully to the Neglected or De-
spised. For the Congregations, wherein 'tis
wanting, to recover a Regular Singing, would
be really a *Reformation*, and a Recovery out
of Apostacy, and what we may judge that
Heaven would be pleased withal. We ought
certainly to serve our GOD with our *Best*, and
Regular Singing, must needs be *Better* than
the confused Noise of a Wilderness. GOD *is
not for confusion in the Churches of the Saints;
but requires, Let all things be done decently.*[5]

The phrase "regular singing" meant singing from note,
rather than singing by ear. Books began to be published

43

in which music was written down and attempts were made to teach the people who had been singing by ear to look at a book and sing only those notes that were there and no others. The first of these was the ninth edition of the *Bay Psalm Book*, published in Boston in 1698 with thirteen two-part settings of psalm tunes. Then the Reverend John Tufts published his *An Introduction to the Singing of Psalm-Tunes* in 1721, Thomas Walter published *The Grounds and Rules of Musick Explained* in the same year, and the institution of "regular singing" was well under way.

The term *puritanical* is sometimes used in an inexact way today. The basic Puritan belief was that a group of principles or laws could be set up to solve any problem by reading the Bible and basing these laws or principles on it. Once set up, they were right and correct and must be followed. Where there were no laws to govern a given situation, they could and should be drawn up by a proper authority, one who understood how to do this according to what was said in the Bible. The very title of a dissertation by the Reverend Nathaniel Chauncey expresses this attitude: *Regular Singing Defended and Proved to be the Only True Way of Singing the Psalms of the Lord* (New London, 1728). Whatever pleasure the old style of singing gave was of no matter; whatever part it had played in strengthening the American churches was irrelevant. It had been proved to be incorrect according to the Scriptures, or at least by someone's interpretation of them; so it must be replaced by the "true" way of singing. The true way was the old way; those who had sung in the new way had been wrong ("It looks very unlikely to be the right way," writes the Reverend Chauncey, "because that young people fall in with it; they are not wont to be so forward for anything that is good"); it is the duty of those who know the right way to instruct those who do not. The music itself was intended to serve the function of instruction, not only in the art of music but in the Christian life as well. God is not for confusion in the churches, but requires that all things be done decently.

This first great controversy in American music sets the pattern for what was to follow. The names of the participants change, but the basic issues do not, nor does the rhetoric.

Andrew Law, born in Connecticut in 1749, attended
Rhode Island College, which later became Brown University. His personality was such that he was given a job of
checking the attendance of his fellow students at morning and evening prayers, and his classmates nicknamed
him "Domine." In 1777, after abortive attempts at being a minister, he decided that he would be a musician
instead and began publishing tune books, instruction
books in music, and musical magazines, most of them
designed for didactic and pedagogical purposes. His first
collections were similar to those published by many
other New England musicians of the time, containing a
number of tunes by William Billings and other American
composers. But his *Musical Primer*, published in 1793,
had an essay attacking American music, and from that
time on he printed more European music and less American. In 1803, for example, a new edition of the *Musical
Primer* had 105 pieces, 104 of them by European composers. The other piece was by Billings, but he put another name on it. He still thought it was a good piece,
but he did not want anyone to know that he was printing a piece by Billings. When he died in 1821, the obituary in the *Connecticut Courant* for July 17 read: "To
his correct taste and scientific improvements may be
ascribed much of that decent, solemn and chaste style
of singing so noticeable in so many of the American
churches. He led a life of obedience to religious impression."[6]

William Billings (1746–1800) was another sort of person. He was described by the Reverend William Bentley
thus: "He was a singular man, of moderate size, short of
one leg, with one eye, without any address, and with an
uncommon negligence of person. Still he spoke and sang
and thought as a man above the common abilities."[7] His
New-England Psalm-Singer of 1770 was the first collection by an American composer made up completely of
his own music. Five other collections followed; his pieces
became extremely popular, widely sung, and reprinted
in various later collections. A passionate patriot, his
friends numbered such men as Paul Revere, who did
some of his engraving. He wrote many of his own texts,
including those of some of the patriotic songs and anthems that helped stir up his fellow New Englanders
against the British.

**The Ecstatic
and the Didactic**

These two men, so different in personality and character, had quite different attitudes toward music, even though they lived at the same time. That is one of the points of this paper—that even though it is perfectly valid to divide the history of music into chronological and stylistic periods, valid to demonstrate that there are differences between music in the seventeenth century and the nineteenth and between music in Russia and the United States, it is equally valid and important to demonstrate that at a given time and place there may be musicians whose ideas about music are widely different, and whose music and musical activities may be just as variant. Law and Billings were Americans, living through and after the American Revolution and in the same part of the country. Yet music was something altogether different for Law and for Billings. And this difference shows up as clearly in what they had to say about music as in the music itself.

Law believed, first of all, that the present state of music was bad. He says in the introduction to his *Art of Singing* (1793): "A considerable part of American composition is in reality faulty. . . . To correct our taste, and give to our music the energy and variety it requires, we must begin at the root of the evil. The cause that gives currency to bad composition, and operates to destroy the efficacy of our psalmody must be removed."[8]

This is similar to the language of the Puritan reformers, who likewise thought that the then-current state of music was bad. Billings, to the contrary, thought that music was wonderful. One is struck, time and again, in reading the prefaces to his various collections, with what pleasure, excitement, passion, and even ecstasy he got from any involvement with music. The following typical passage, from the introduction to *Continental Harmony* (1794), was written by a man who—to use a term popular a few years ago—was "turned on" by music.

Scholar. Sir, I should be glad to know which key you think is best; the flat, or the sharp key?
Master. I believe your question would puzzle the greatest philosopher, or practitioner, upon earth; for there are so many excellent pieces on each key, that we are apt to fall in with a

certain man, who heard two very eminent law-
yers plead in opposition to each other; after
the first had done speaking, the man was so
charmed with his eloquence and oratory, that
he thought it would be an idle (as well as rash)
attempt for any one to gainsay, or contradict
him; but when he heard the second, he said,
that his reasons were so nervous and weighty,
he was about to give him the preference; upon
which the first made so forcible a reply, that
the man knew not what to say, at last he con-
cluded they were both best. Similar to this,
let us suppose ourselves to be auditors to a
company of musicians: how enraptured should
we be to hear the sharp key, express itself in
such lofty and majestic strains as these! *O
come let us sing unto the Lord, let us make a
joyful noise, to the rock of our salvation; let
us come before his presence with thanksgiving
and make a joyful noise unto him with psalms.
Sing unto the Lord all the earth, make a loud
noise, rejoice and sing praise!* Do I hear the
voice of men, or angels! Surely such angelic
sounds cannot proceed from the mouths of
sinful mortals: but while we are yet warm
with the thought, and ravished with the sound,
the musicians change their tone, and the flat
key utters itself in strains so moving, and pathet-
ic, that it seems at least to command our attention to such mournful sounds as these: *Hear
my prayer O Lord, give ear to my supplication,
hear me speedily: O Lord my spirit faileth,
hide not thy face from me; O my God, my
soul is cast down within me. Have pity upon
me, O ye my friends, for the hand of God hath
touched me.* O how these sounds thrill through
my soul! how agreeably they affect my nerves!
how soft, how sweet, how soothing! methinks
these sounds are more expressive than the
other, for they affect us both with pleasure and
pain, but the *pleasure* is so great it makes even
pain be pleasant, so that for the sake of the
pleasure, I could forever bear the pain. But
hark! what shout is that? It seems the sharp

**The Ecstatic
and the Didactic**

47

key is again upon the wing toward heaven;
jealous, perhaps, that we pay too much deference to his rival: he not only desires, but
commands us to join in such exalted strains as
these: *Rejoice in the Lord, and again I say, re-*
joice, O clap your hands all ye people, shout
unto God with the voice of triumph; God is
gone up with a shout, the Lord with the
sound of a trumpet; sing praises to God, sing
praises, sing praises unto our King, sing praises.
What an ecstasy of joy may we suppose the
Royal Author to be in when he composed this
Psalm of praise![9]

Law believed that the present state of music was bad because he was living in a period of moral and intellectual
decline. Music was poor because this moral climate was
poor; if music could be improved, perhaps morals would
be better. He obviously subscribed to the sentiments expressed in a letter he received in 1796 from Samuel Andrew Law, his nephew, who wrote, "There is thro all the
parts of the Country where I travel an universal languour
about music. I can discover little or no prospect of a revival of attention or correction of taste in our day. The
present period is in this country, the *triumph of quackery*
in *music.*"[10] But, nevertheless, he was determined to try
to improve the dismal situation. In a letter written in
1797 to the Reverend Ashbel Green, he says:

I have for several reasons thought it my duty
to give up the business of preaching and again
to attend the business of singing. I viewed the
Art of Psalmody as connected with the worship
of God. I considered also that the prevailing
taste in church music did not partake of that
chaste and sober, that sublime and solemn air
which becometh the house of God, or that is
calculated to excite the devout exercises of
the pious soul. I viewed a reformation in this
part of divine service as very important and
interesting to the cause of religion and virtue.
I viewed also the general character of singing
Masters as not favourable to religion.
These considerations have induced me to

believe I could do more for the promotion of
the glory of God and the interest of religion
in the singing business, than I could by preaching. I have, therefore, again entered into that
line of business with a full determination of
exerting myself to the uttermost of my ability
for the promotion of the glory of God and
the interest of Christ's Kingdom: by reform-
ing the taste in Music.[11]

**The Ecstatic
and the Didactic**

Given a situation in which the present state of music
seemed to Law to be bad, a solution seemed to be to
look to the past for guidance and models, since the past
had been better. This is exactly what he did in his teaching and writing about music and in the music contained
in his various collections. His later collections not only
contain fewer pieces by American musicians, but they
also have an increasingly large number of compositions
by older masters. Law wrote in the introduction to the
1800 edition of his *Art of Singing*:

It will, perhaps, not have escaped your observation that very much of the music in vogue is
miserable indeed. Hence the man of piety and
principle, of taste and discernment in Music,
and hence, indeed, all who entertain a sense
of decency and decorum in devotion are often-
times offended with that lifeless and insipid,
or that frivolous and frolicksome succession
and combination of sounds so frequently introduced into Churches, where all should be
serious, animated, and devout. And hence too,
the ever-varying vigor of Handell, of Madan,
and of others alike meritorious, are, in a great
measure suplanted by the pitiful productions
of numerous Composuists whom it would be
doing too much honor to name. Let any one
acquainted with the sublime and beautiful
Compositions of the great Masters of music
but look round within the circle of his own
acquaintance, and he will find abundant reason for these remarks.[12]

Billings thought otherwise. He was delighted with the

music of the present and printed nothing else in his collections. Though he must have known the same "sublime and beautiful Compositions of the great Masters" as did Law, since the two men learned their music from the same English collections that included some of this music, and though he taught himself the same elements of music theory by studying the same theoretical writings known to Law, Billings took quite a different attitude about the relationship of theory and history to creation. In the preface to his *New-England Psalm-Singer* (1770), he wrote:

Perhaps it may be expected by some, that I should say something concerning Rules for composition. To these I answer that *Nature is the best Dictator*, For all the hard, dry studied Rules that ever was prescribed, would not enable any Person to form an Air any more than the barren Knowledge of the four and twenty Letters, and strict Grammatical Rules will qualify a Scholar for composing a Piece of Poetry, or properly adjusting a Tragedy, without Genius. It must be Nature, Nature must lay the Foundation. Nature must inspire the Thought. . . . So, in fact, I think it is best for every *Composer* to be his own *Carver*. Therefore, upon this Consideration for me to dictate or pretend to prescribe Rules of this Nature for others, would not only be very unnecessary, but also a great Piece of Vanity.[13]

Another of Law's convictions was that there were certain absolute standards of taste and value in music, certain laws and principles that governed the art of composition and the critical judgment of music—and that these laws and principles could be understood and applied only by persons of superior intellect and morality. In a letter to his nephew Samuel concerning the proposed publication of his *Musical Magazine*, we read: ". . . I would have your judgement guided by one single point: the *'gooaness of the Music.'* . . . [The magazine] will never descend and be familiarized among the common herd of singers. They will ascend into a higher sphere and be conversant almost altogether with those whose taste and knowledge of music are of a rank more enlarged and refined. . . . I will carry the idea as far as this: that in the Magazine the Music may be actually reduced to the *true and genuine Standard of taste*."[14] And he writes in his *Essays on Music* in 1813: "[The musician must] feel the power of poetic numbers, and be able to unite these with those of music. . . . He must measure his time with mathematical skill; he must combine the sounds in harmony, with the knowledge of nature; he must regulate his proportions with the knowledge of architecture, and lastly, he must understand the great truths of christianity."[15]

Billings had no such exalted view of the art of composition. In a widely quoted passage in the introduction to his *Continental Harmony*, he has his say about this matter:

Musical composition is a sort of something,
which is much better felt than described, (at
least by me) for if I was to attempt it, I should
not know where to begin or where to leave off;
therefore considering myself so unable to perform it, I shall not undertake the task; . . . although I am not confined to rules prescribed
by others, yet I come as near as I possibly can
to a set of rules which I have carved out for
myself; but when fancy gets upon the wing,
she seems to despise all form, and scorns to be
confined or limited by any formal prescription
whatsoever.[16]

One final point concerning Law's beliefs: he felt that the responsibility for instruction in music, particularly instruction in aesthetic and moral matters, rested with one of the institutions of American life, the church. He wrote in the introduction to the 1800 edition of his *Art of Singing*: ". . . there are no descriptions of Citizens in community who have it in their power to do half as much as the Ministers of the Glad Tidings of Peace on Earth & good will to man, toward correcting and perfecting the prevailing taste in music."[17]

Billings, on the other hand, was sure that all aspects of music—composing, performing, instructing, perceiving, evaluating—were individual matters. Music was something different for each individual. Any "truth" in mu-

51

sic must come from within any given individual, not be imposed on him from without. This notion is offered in its most extreme form in the introduction to *Continental Harmony*:

Charles Hamm

For as our organs of sense, are differently constructed; so our notions of sensitive things are proportionably various, and this variety gave birth to a proverb which is common among us, viz "What is *one* man's *meat* is *another* man's *poison*." Therefore the *psalmodist* hears *music*, in a composition of *church music*: The *valiant soldier*, in the sound of the *fife* and *drum*, in the *roaring of cannon* and *whistling* of *bullets*: The *fearful soldier*, in the midnight cry of *"all is well:"* The *huntsman*, in the *sound* of the *horn* and *cry* of the *hounds*: The *stageplayer*, in the *clap* of *applause*: The *centinel*, in the *sound* of *"relief guard:"* The *merchant*, in the *sound* of *cent* per *cent*: The *usurer*, in the *sound* of *interest* upon *interest*: The *miser*, in the *sound* of his *double jo's, moidores* and *guineas*. To the two last mentioned, we may add another animal by far the noblest of the three, viz. the *horse*, who hears *music*, in the *sound* of his *provender, rattling* from the *pottle* to the *trough*. Therefore as music is nothing more than agreeable sounds, certainly that sound which is most pleasing is most musical.

A summary at this point might be useful. Law, in his writings about music and, more important, in his musical activities, offers the view that: 1. the present state of music is bad; 2. it is bad because the times are bad and immoral; 3. both music and people used to be better, so one should turn to the past for guidance; 4. by studying the past, one can formulate a set of rules and principles to use in improving the technique, taste, and morality of contemporary music; and 5. one of the institutions of the country should take the responsibility for instruction in these matters.

For Law, the essence of music is not so important as its purpose. Music should be didactic. It should be judged not by the pleasure it gives but by the instruction it gives. Nowhere in his writings is there a hint that he enjoys music or expects others to enjoy it. An entry in the diary of the Reverend William Bentley for May 23, 1796, describes an evening of music by students of Law: "Mr. Law had a Musical Exhibition this evening, & persons were introduced only as they had tickets to be delivered at the door. He aims to have his music very soft, & the treble is the leading part, not one note of tenour was heard through the Evening. The greatest good order prevailed, & the visiting Company was respectable. In their attempts to sing soft, many of the voices do not accent the notes so as to enable the ear to distinguish the strains from soft murmers."[18]

For Billings, on the other hand, music was first of all sensual. We have a description of his singing: "Billings had a stentorian voice, and when he [Dr. Pierce] stood by him to sing, he could not hear his own voice; and every one that ever heard Dr. Pierce sing . . . knows that his voice was not wanting in power."[19] Billings says in the introduction to his *Singing Master's Assistant* (1778): "In fugue in music you must be very distinct and emphatic, not only in the tune but in the pronunciation, for if there happens to be a number of greater voices at the concert than your own, they will swallow you up. Therefore, in such a case, I would recommend to you the resolution of a discarded actor who, after he had been twice hissed off the stage, mounted again, and with great assurance he thundered these words, 'I will be heard.' "[20]

Volume is not the main issue—it is merely one result of understanding music as a sensual, exciting, overwhelming, and joyous event. Billings's ecstatic, rapturous state when he is involved in music carries over even to his writings about it, as in this passage from the introduction to *Continental Harmony*:

It is an old maxim, and I think a very just one, viz. *that variety is always pleasing*, and it is well known that there is more variety in one piece of fuging music, than in twenty pieces of plain song, for while the tones do most sweetly coincide and agree, the words are seemingly engaged in a musical warfare; and excuse

53

the paradox if I further add, that each part
seems determined by dint of harmony and
strength of accent, to drown his competitor in
an ocean of harmony, and while each part is
thus mutually striving for mastery, and sweetly contending for victory, the audience are
most luxuriously entertained, and exceedingly
delighted; in the mean time, their minds are
surprizingly agitated, and extremely fluctuated;
sometimes declaring in favour of one part, and
sometimes another.—Now the solemn bass demands their attention, now the manly tenor,
now the lofty counter, now the volatile treble,
now here, now there, now here again—O in-
chanting! O ecstatic! Push on, push on ye sons
of harmony, and

Discharge your deep mouth'd canon, full
   fraught with Diapasons;
May you with Maestoso, rush on to Choro-
   Grando,
And then with Vigoroso, let fly your
   Diapentes
About our nervous system.

Law and Billings were contemporaries, products of a similar environment and the same culture. Yet music was
didactic for one, ecstatic for the other.

Several decades later a somewhat different type of music
was springing up in the South and West. Its origins were
in singing schools introduced in these regions by Yankee
singing masters bringing with them the music of Billings
and his contemporaries. In style, it moved in other directions, with melodies based on or similar to Anglo-Ameri-
can folk songs popular in these regions and a curious,
unique harmonic style making frequent use of such intervals as the second, fourth, and seventh as consonances.
It was disseminated in collections printed in shape notes;
at the height of its popularity, this music reached several
million Americans; it was ecstatic music, as anyone who
has heard shaped-note singing knows. Being ecstatic, it
was condemned and eventually "reformed" by people
who by nature and training were inclined to the didac-

tic. This is part of the pattern. Ecstatic musicians never bother to oppose didactic music; sometimes they even claim it for their own use. But didactic musicians were writing such things as:

Innumerable composuists, scarecely versed in the first principles of psalmody, sprung up on every side. The press groaned under the burden of their ponderous productions. . . . To copy the air of a march, or a song, in the middle of a tune to have one part fall in after another, and have four divisions of the choir repeating different forms of the words at the same time, and thus produce a Babel-confusion . . . was the grand design. The choir hurried with infinite volubility of note through the piece. The unconscious youth wondered at the charm, that refreshed in his remembrance in the sanctuary on the Sabbath the carouse and the festivity of the past week, and loved the music the more for these delightful associations. [The True Taste is to be found only in] the slow and solemn tunes of the great masters of old time —Luther, and Pleyel, and Handel, and Arne, and Arnold, and Boyce, and Madan, and Purcel.[21]

Music is never to be obtained without labor and care. It will never produce or regulate, or preserve itself. Its interests cannot safely be confided to those who are destitute of piety or deficient in general influence. If music, as a fine art, has its difficulties and its dangers, this is the very reason why the interests of song should be thoroughly taken in hand by those who have information, authority, and influence. Let the pulpit breathe the gentle language of instruction, persuasion, and encouragement, till the public mind is well enlightened; let singing-schools be religiously conducted. . . . Correct information should be widely diffused. Lectures and schools, the religious press and the pulpit, may furnish every facility which is needed.[22]

Charles Hamm

The names change but the rhetoric does not. Compressed into these two quotations are all five of the points making up the didactic view of music articulated by Andrew Law.

The purpose of this paper is not to run through the entire history of music in America, but rather to suggest that two contrasting, often conflicting views of the nature, purpose, and effect of music can be found at any given time.

Daniel Gregory Mason and Charles Edward Ives were contemporaries, from the same general region of the country, and had somewhat similar backgrounds. Mason was born in 1873, Ives in 1874. Both came from musical families. Mason graduated from Harvard, Ives from Yale. Both were rather prolific composers, writing symphonies, string quartets, choral works, and so forth. Here the similarity ends, however. Mason studied abroad, became a professor at Columbia University, lectured and wrote about the problems of music, enjoyed frequent performances and some favorable and even enthusiastic reviews of his compositions, and was an influential figure in the musical life of the country. Ives soon abandoned any thoughts of a professional career in music, became successful in the insurance business, wrote his music in virtual isolation from other musicians, and rarely heard one of his pieces performed. Their views of what music is and should be showed just as great a disparity.

Mason delivered a set of lectures at Northwestern University in 1925 that were revised and published by W. W. Norton and Company in 1927 as a book entitled *Artistic Ideals*. His ideals, as set forth in this book, place him squarely on the side of the didactics. Early in the book, on page 6, he quotes Gustave Flaubert, who wrote in 1865: "No one cares nowadays about art, for itself. We are being swamped in vulgarity at a terrifying rate, and I do not care to see the 20th century." From this point he develops the canon of the didactic musician, point by point, perhaps unaware that anyone had ever said these things before:

That the present world of industrial, political
and scientific achievement has not succeeded
in making us happy is in large measure due to
its having chosen or wandered into a direction

away from some of our most fundamental
human values, such as the quiet experience of
beauty. [P. 6]

In our own day, sincerity and moderation
seem hopelessly out of fashion in a world
given up to effects and sensations. [P. 178]

We see about us a fair array of promising
young men. . . . What they lack is not tal-
ent, but character. [P. 65]

There is a lack of breadth of vision, of the
sense of permanent values, of perspective and
proportion, and hence of power to deal greatly with the present. Is not this lack of the
sense of values due to a foolish contempt of
the past? . . . Most of our artists nowadays
are too vain to admire anything that is past;
and consequently their art remains for the
most part anemic, thin, inhumane, snobbish,
and ephemeral. . . . The votaries of every art
that has come to greatness have always wor-
shipped the past. They have claimed and re-
claimed the treasures and techniques that lie
buried in all the great works of the world.
[P. 175]

[Our composers] have plenty of ability, but
no staying power; they use no severity with
themselves; they have not cultivated the ideal
of workmanship. And so, whatever their native gifts, as artists they fail. [P. 65]

Whether it is beautiful is not your affair—
but perfect it must be. [P. 64]

Always and everywhere, agonizing toil is the
price. [P. 67]

In other words: the present state of affairs is bad; it is
bad because of a decline in moral values; the past was
better, and thus we should look to the past for guidance;
if that is done, some absolute values can be determined,

The Ecstatic
and the Didactic

57

the True Taste can be defined; and Mason's lifelong activities are a testament to his belief that the True Taste is best passed on through one of the institutions of the country—in this case, the schools.

For Ives, to the contrary, man and music are fundamentally good, music is an intensely personal, sensual, and ecstatic (his word was *extravagant*) experience, and man and music suffer only when unnatural restraints and restrictions are placed on them:

The instinctive and progressive interest of every man in art . . . will go on and on, ever fulfilling hopes, ever building new ones, ever opening new ones, until the day will come when every man while digging his potatoes will breathe his own epics, his own symphonies (operas, if he likes); and as he sits on an evening in his backyard and shirt sleeves smoking his pipe and watching his brave children in *their* fun of building *their* themes for their sonatas of *their* life, he will look up over the mountains and see his visions in their reality, will hear the transcendental strains of the day's symphony resounding in their many choirs, and in all their perfection, through the west wind and the tree tops![23]

Geniuses—and there are millions of them—differ as to *what* is beautiful and *what* is ugly, as to *what* is right and *what* is wrong—there are many interpretations of God—but they all agree that beauty is better than ugliness and right is better than wrong.[24]

Perhaps music is the art of speaking extravagantly. . . . some men, as for instance Mozart, are so peculiarly sensitive to emotion that music is to them but a continuation not only of the expression but of the actual emotion. . . . There is no doubt that in its nature music is predominately subjective and tends to subjective expression.[25]

But maybe music was not intended to satisfy

the curious definiteness of man. Maybe it is
better to hope that music may always be a
transcendental language in the most extravagant sense.[26]

This game could be continued with other pairs of musicians: Lowell Mason and Louis Moreau Gottschalk, Milton Babbitt and John Cage, William Henry Fry and William Walker. But the rhetoric would be the same. It *is*
the same, to the present. The following two quotations
refer to a new body of music, an ecstatic music. They
say the same things that have always been said about
ecstatic music, point by point, one through five:

You want to know what I think of that abomi-
nation, rock 'n' roll? I think it is a disgrace. Poison put to sound! When I hear it I feel very
sad not only for music but for the people who
are addicted to it. I am also very sorry for
America—that such a great country should
have nothing better to pour into the expec-
tant ear of mankind than this raucous distil-
lation of the ugliness of our times, performed
by juveniles for juveniles. . . . The French
have a word *abrutissant*, for anything that
brutalizes man and tends to turn him into a
beast. That's the word for this terrible, con-
vulsive sound. It is against art, against life. It
leads away from that exaltation and elevation
of spirit that should spring naturally from all
good music. . . . It's the parents who will have
to take action—not in forbidding children to
listen to rock 'n' roll but by educating them
to appreciate better music, by filling their
homes with it. Given the choice, man will
strive towards things of moral and cultural
value rather than the counterfeit.
    I sometimes enjoy watching television. I
never miss a Western if I can help it, because
you can be sure every story will have one
brave man, who stands for justice, acts
nobly, and wins out for the forces of good
in the end.[27]

Charles Hamm

Rock and roll is acoustical pollution. [In Boston I] came into conflict with the most violent and vicious rock and roll, apparently hour after hour jamming the airways. . . . Is this progress? We have lost our sense of values. . . . Without mass education we shall remain a voice crying in the wilderness—but unlike that voice, doomed to remain forever unheard until our nation sinks in swamps of mediocrity.

It is easier to describe symptoms than to prescribe a cure. One thing, however, seems clear, that our society with all its accomplishments in science and technology badly needs a resurgence of spiritual vitality and that we as individuals greatly need a rededication to those values which have permanent significance.[28]

Conclusions are unnecessary. The purpose of this paper has been to identify a situation, a pattern, that has existed in music in this country from the earliest days. We have always had didactic and ecstatic views of music. If all goes well, we will continue to have both.

Notes

1. John Eliot, *A Brief Discourse concerning Regular Singing* (Boston, 1725). I am indebted to David Stigberg—who was completing his master's thesis, "Congregational Psalmody in Eighteenth Century New England" (University of Illinois, 1970), when I was at work on this paper—for calling my attention to several descriptions of Puritan psalm singing.

2. Thomas Walter, *Grounds and Rules of Musick Explained* (Boston, 1721), pp. 4–5.

3. From a letter by "Jeoffrey Chanticleer," *New England Courant*, February 17–24, 1724.

4. Walter, *Musick Explained*, p. 3.

5. Cotton Mather, *The Accomplished Singer* (Boston, 1721),
    pp. 22–23.

6. Andrew Law quoted in Frank J. Metcalf, *American
    Writers and Compilers of Sacred Music* (New York:
    Abingdon Press, 1925), p. 79.

7. William Bentley, *The Diary of William Bentley, D.D.,
    Pastor of East Church, Salem, Massachusetts* (Salem:
    Essex Institute, 1905–1914), pp. 350–351.

8. Andrew Law quoted in Richard A. Crawford, *Andrew
    Law: American Psalmodist* (Evanston, Ill.: Northwestern
    University Press, 1968), p. 105.

9. William Billings, *Continental Harmony* (Boston,
    1794), pp. xxi–xxii.

10. Samuel Andrew Law to Andrew Law, December 5,
    1796, Cheshire, Connecticut.

11. Andrew Law quoted in Crawford, *Andrew Law*, p. 137.

12. Andrew Law, *Art of Singing* (Cheshire, Conn., 1800),
    pp. 11–12.

13. William Billings, *New-England Psalm-Singer* (Boston,
    1770), pp. 19–20.

14. Ibid., p. 118.

15. Andrew Law, *Essays on Music* (Philadelphia: R. & W.
    Carr, 1813), p. 6.

16. Billings, *Continental Harmony*, p. xxxi.

17. Law, *Art of Singing*, p. 9.

18. William Bentley quoted in Crawford, *Andrew Law*,
    p. 132.

19. Nathaniel D. Gould, *Church Music in America* (Boston:
    A. N. Johnson, 1853).

Charles Hamm

20. William Billings, *Singing Master's Assistant* (Boston, 1778), n.p.

21. Timothy Flint, preface to his *Columbian Harmonist* (Cincinnati, 1816).

22. Thomas Hastings, *Dissertation on Musical Taste* (New York: Mason Brothers, 1853), n.p.

23. Charles Ives, *Essays before a Sonata, and Other Writings* (New York: W. W. Norton and Co., 1961), pp. 128-129.

24. Ibid., p. 57.

25. Ibid., p. 53.

26. Ibid., p. 71.

27. Pablo Casals, "A Disgrace to Music," *Music Journal* 19 (January 1961): 18.

28. Howard Hanson, "Rock and Roll: Is This the Way?" *Clavier* 1, no. 5 (1961): 8.

Music and the Time Screen
Elliott Carter

Three

The sense of the above title was suggested to me by Professor Edward Lowinsky, the well-known musicologist, once when I was lecturing at the University of Chicago. He said something to the effect that "time is the canvas on which you consider music to be presented, just as the spatial canvas of a painting furnishes the surface on which a painting is presented." Such a provocative comparison reaches in so many directions that it is difficult to discuss it in some clear and intelligible way. Analogies between the structure and character of time and those of space tend to be superficial, if not pointless, because we experience these dimensions in such different although interconnected ways. Yet, if the "time screen" on which music in this statement is said to be projected is considered to be a stretch of the measurable time of practical life, while the music itself may be incorporating another kind of time but needs measurable time for its presentation, then it can, no doubt, be compared to the space screen of a flat, angular canvas on which the imaginings of the artist about space are projected, and there is some point to the comparison.

However, it becomes much more tenuous if we try to compare the connections a composer can make in a composition between "sooner and later," which, although existing in "clock time," can also gain many special meaningful relationships because they involve patterns related to the experience of time of both composer and listener, and the "up and down" or "right and left" of a picture, elements that, although also physically in the picture, also participate in the artist's and observer's common experience of weight, shape, color, and visual texture, which can only be applied to time metaphorically.

It is not my intention here to indulge in such comparisons but to describe how, out of a consideration for the special temporality of music, I have attempted to derive a way of composing that deals with its very nature. To start with, I must briefly deal with the formidable sub-

ject of time, a most confusing one because no common
vocabulary exists to help us—the "real time" of the
Bergson school is very far from that of electronic composers, and the various conceptions of "ontological time"
do not relate to each other, while the relationship of
"public time" (of Martin Heidegger) to "clock time" (for
some, synonymous with "mathematical time") and the
latter to such a notion as Pierre Suvchinsky's "chronometric time" is hard to establish. In an effort to isolate
the particular field under discussion, I would like to
start by quoting Charles Koechlin, who proposed four
aspects of time:

1. Pure duration, a fundamental of our deep-
est consciousness, and apparently independent
of the external world: life flows by. . . .
2. Psychological time. This is the impression
we have of (the above) duration according to
the events of our existence: minutes that seem
centuries, hours that go by too quickly. . . .
That is, duration relative to the circumstances
of life.
3. Time measured by mathematical means; all
of which depend on visual methods—sand
clocks, clocks, chronometers. . . .
4. Finally, I would like to talk of "musical
time." To us musicians this fact does not present itself as it does to scientists. Auditory time
is without a doubt the kind that comes closest
to pure duration. However, it appears to have
some connection with space in that it seems to
us measurable (by ear) and divisible. The divisions embodied in musical note values (whole
notes, half-notes, etc.) lead to a spatialization
of time very different from that (based on vision) which Bergson talks about. Besides, as
concerns the measure of this (musical) duration, the role of musical memory possesses an
importance that seems to escape many.[1]

To expand these aspects further: the first, "pure duration," is evidently the same as Bergson's "real" or "subjective time," *la durée réelle* which can be known only
by intuition, or, as Suzanne Langer, whose *Feeling and*

Form has been illuminating on these matters, comments:
". . . every conceptual form which is supposed to portray
time over-simplifies it to the point of leaving out the
most interesting aspects of it, namely the characteristic
appearances of passage."[2]

Koechlin's second aspect, "psychological time," would
be more or less clear from his definition if Heidegger had
not expounded a whole philosophy in *On Time and Being*,
which, as I understand it, combines the first and second
of the above aspects in an impressive demonstration that
every human (*Dasein*)[3] is experiencing duration according to his own life pattern, tinged as it inevitably is with
expectation, dread, and with the certainty of an end in
death, as well as with the sense that the experience of
living in time is a common human condition.

Of Koechlin's third aspect, "mathematically measured
time," Langer says it is "a special abstraction from temporal experience, namely time as pure sequence, symbol-
ized by a class of ideal events, indifferent in themselves,
but arranged in an infinite 'dense' series by the sole relation of succession. Conceived under this scheme, time is
a one-dimensional continuum."[4] Finally, of "musical
time" with its relation to "pure duration," Langer remarks: "The direct experience of passage, as it occurs in
each individual life is, of course, something actual, just
as actual as the progress of the clock or speedometer; and
like all actuality it is only in part perceived, and its fragmentary data are supplemented by practical knowledge
and ideas from other realms of thought altogether. Yet
it is the model for the virtual time created in music."[5]

The ambiguity of the term *time screen* becomes evident with the isolation of such aspects, for while it can
be said to be a mathematically measured stretch of time
(painfully evident at broadcasting or recording sessions),
still, the fact that music is intended for listeners creates
the impression that "musical" or "virtual" time is being
projected on a time screen of the listener's "pure (or
'subjective') duration," with all its added capabilities of
interpretation, memory, and shifts of focus of attention.
The relationship between these two aspects is made clear
in Langer's discussion of the experience of time, which
is based on contrasting it with "clock time," whose un-
derlying principle is change,

which is measured by contrasting two states of
an instrument, whether that instrument be the
sun in various positions, or the hand on a dial
at successive locations, or a parade of monot-
onous similar events like ticks or flashes,
"counted," i.e. differentiated, by being corre-
lated with a series of distinct numbers . . .
"change" is not itself something represented;
it is implicitly given through the contrast of different "states" themselves unchanging.

The time concept which emerges from such
mensuration is something far removed from
time as we know it in direct experience, which
is essentially *passage*, or the sense of transience.
. . . But the experience of time is anything but
simple. It involves more properties than "length,"
or interval between selected moments; for its
passages have also what I can only call, metaphorically, *volume*. Subjectively, a unit of time
may be great or small as well as long or short.
It is this voluminousness of the direct experience of passage, that makes it . . . indivisible.
But even its volume is not simple; for it is filled
with its own characteristic forms, as space is
filled with material forms, otherwise it could
not be observed and appreciated. . . . The primary image of music is the sonorous image of
passage, abstracted from actuality to become
free and plastic and entirely perceptible."[6]

Such ideas as these did not become important to me until around 1944; up to that time I had been concerned
with other matters and thought of "time" much as many
others did. I was familiar (but somewhat suspicious of)
the various proposals made to organize time according
to mechanical, constructivist patterns frequently discussed in the twenties and thirties. Like many other approaches to music of the time, this was primarily concerned with purely physical possibilities and their jug-
gling. Some applied numerical patterns to note values
derived from the tuning of the musical scales (as Henry
Cowell proposed in *New Musical Resources*);[7] others followed the schematic methods presented in *The Schillinger
System of Musical Composition*[8]—two points of view

taken up later and subjected to serial permutation by
Olivier Messiaen, Karlheinz Stockhausen, and others. As
the first phase of modernism began to die away with the
rise of Populist ideas during the late thirties and forties,
composers, for the most part, returned to the more or
less familiar ways of musical thought, and the matter
that began to interest me during that time found little
corroboration among most of my colleagues.

As one whose interest in music was aroused by hearing
the "advanced" music played in the twenties in the
United States and whose musical education took place
during the years of change to the Populist style, and who
then, out of political sympathy, wrote for a while in this
style, I still view with considerable perplexity the renewal of many of the so-called experiments of the earlier
avant-garde style, few of which led to interesting results
then and seem, even today, to be rather unproductive. In
any case, around 1945, as the Populist period was nearing
its end (as we now see in retrospect), I felt I had exhausted
my interest in that style and started a thoroughgoing re-
assessment of musical materials in the hope of finding a
way of expressing what seemed to be more important
matters—or at least more personal ones.

In retrospect, I can see that it took several years to
clarify intentions. During this time I wrote my 1945 Piano Sonata, my 1947 *Emblems*, and my 1948 Wind
Quintet and Cello Sonata, all of which foreshadow future
preoccupations. By 1948 and 1949 I had become very
concerned with the nature of musical ideas and started
writing music that sought to find out what the minimal
needs were for the kind of musical communication I felt
worthwhile. There were the Eight Etudes and a Fantasy
for Woodwind Quartet and six of the Eight Pieces for
Timpani. The seventh of the wind etudes, based on the
note G (which can be played on all 4 instruments), draws
out of the fifteen possible tone colors and their combinations and variants due to dynamic and attack differences,
a musical discourse entirely dependent on contrasting
various types of "entrances": sharp, incisive attacks as
opposed to soft entrances of other instruments. In the
third etude, the three notes of a soft D-major chord are
given different emphases by changes of tone color and
doublings. In the fourth etude, a unit of two eighth notes
rising a rapid semitone and resting, serves as the genera-

tor of an entire piece constructed after the fashion of measures sixteen to thirty-five (ex. 1), a mosaiclike technique I have used in many different ways.

At the same time, a whole complex of notions about rhythm, meter, and timing became a central preoccupation. In a sense, this was explored according to the principles of "clock," or in this case "metronomic," time, but its relationship to the jazz of the thirties and forties that combined free improvisation with strict time and with the music of early and non-Western music as well as that of Aleksandr Skryabin, Ives, and Conlon Nancarrow, made me always look toward ways that could incorporate into "musical time" the methods that interested me. The desire to remain within the realm of the performable and auditorily distinguishable divisions of time kept me from exploring the field of polyrhythms, for instance— as someone else might have done who was primarily concerned with mathematically measured time.

A few years previous to 1948, I had come across the ideas of Pierre Suvchinsky in his article in the May–June 1939 issue of *La Revue musicale*[9] and in Igor Stravinsky's long discussion of them in *La Poétique musicale*.[10] Here again, it was a question of the experience of time with an opposition between what the author calls "Khronos," which appears to be a version of "pure duration" ("real" time) and the many different "psychological" times—expectation, anxiety, sorrow, suffering, fear, contemplation, pleasure, all of which could not be grasped if there were not a primary sensation of "real," or "ontological," time. Different composers stress different combinations of "real" and "psychological" time—in Haydn, Mozart, and Stravinsky, the music is what Suvchinsky calls "chronometric," since the sense of time is equivalent to the musical process of the work. Musical time is equivalent to ontological time, while the music of the romantics, particularly that of Wagner, is "chrono-ametric," since it has an unstable relationship between the time of the music and the psychological time it evokes. Such

Example 1. Elliott Carter. Etude IV, mm. 16–35, from Eight Etudes and a Fantasy for Woodwind Quartet (1950), p. 8. (Copyright 1959 by Associated Music Publishers, Inc. Used by permission.)

Example 2. Elliott Carter. "Canaries," from Eight Pieces for Four Timpani, p. 19. (Copyright 1968 by Associated Music Publishers, Inc. Used by permission.)

thinking (which I am not sure I agree with) led me to the idea of the opening of the Cello Sonata of 1948, in which the piano, so to speak, presents "chronometric" time, while the cello simultaneously plays in "chrono-ametric" time.

With my Cello Sonata, a whole collection of rhythmic practices began to be developed. Ultimately these were to expand the basic divisions and groupings of regular pulses to include polyrhythmic patterns and rubato, shaped into several methods of continuous change. One, which first found its way into the Cello Sonata, has been called "metric modulation." The technique is illustrated in a passage from the "Canaries" (ex. 2), one of the pieces for timpani. To the listener, this passage should sound as if the left hand keeps up a steady beat throughout the passage, not participating in the modulations and playing the lower notes B and E at the slow speed of metronome (M.) 64, while the right hand part, made up of F-natural and C-sharp—goes through a series of metric modulations, increasing its speed a little at each change. Starting with the same speed as the left hand—64 to the dotted quarter—the right hand substitutes regular quarters (M. 96) for them in the next measure, and in the third measure these quarters are accented in pairs, and then triplets (M. 144) are substituted for the two previous quarters. The notation is then changed at the double bar so that the previous triplet quarter equals the new quarter, which then in its turn is accented in pairs for which, once again, triplets are substituted (these are now at M. 216). The whole process is then repeated on this new level, bringing the value of the quarters in the twelfth measure to M. 324—with the left hand still continuing its beat of M. 64, now notated in durations of eighty-one sixty-fourth notes. The maintaining of two layers of rhythm, in this case one retaining a steady beat while the other changes its speed step by step, is characteristic of many passages written since that time. Obviously, too, in music built, as this is, on four pitches, the matter of the formation of ideas with such minimal material was a constant preoccupation, as were the various ways of opposing as well as linking these ideas into phrases and larger shapes.

The preoccupation with reduction of musical ideas to their simplest terms became a general formal trend in some works. For instance, the Adagio of my First String Quartet, with its strong opposition between the soft, muted music of the two high violins and the loud, vigorous recitative of the viola and cello, is the presentation in their simplest terms of the oppositions of rhythm, theme, and character that are characteristic of the entire work, while the Allegro scorrevole is a reduction of the typically diversified texture to a stream of sixteenth notes with a seven-note theme, fragmented into diversified bits that form a constantly changing mosaic (ex. 3). This section itself has as one of its characteristics a tendency to be interrupted and then to return. One of the interruptions is formed by the relaxing break usually placed between two movements.

What preoccupied me through the fifties was a desire to find a new flow of musical thought and expression—a

Example 3. Elliott Carter. Allegro scorrevole, mm. 356–367, from String Quartet no. 1 (1951), pp. 34–35. (Copyright 1955–1956 by Associated Music Publishers, Inc. Used by permission.)

tendency to which the previous efforts seemed to be leading. This tendency was not a very pronounced one during the earlier part of the twentieth century, although Debussy expressed dissatisfaction with the conventional methods of "thematic development" of his time. This led him to explore static as opposed to sequential repetition and to reduce thematic material, especially in his last works, to elemental forms containing motives that formed the basis for a spinning out of coherent, ever-changing continuities, a procedure probably derived from the study of plainsong as taught at the Parisian Schola Cantorum in the 1890's. Stravinsky was to adopt this nonsequential development after 1913, as were many outside central Europe, as, for instance, Edgard Varèse. However, by the mid-1940's the excessive use of ostinatos and the rather limited uses of plainsong continuity began to seem outworn, especially since the serial technique seemed to provide other possibilities. There was, as is well known, at the end of the Second World War a sudden interest in Europe in all the forms of modernism previously banned, which once more brought back in music the earlier concern with special sounds, irregular divisions of time, and groupings of these according to the serialization of their physical parameters, with only a very elementary concern for their possible interpretation by the listener. This return to old-fashioned avant-gardism was, of course, stimulating, because it put so many things into question—but only peripherally, since it side-stepped the fundamental issues of music from the point of view I am describing here. In effect, none of this was really "experimental" or advanced, as intended, since its approach to "musical" or even "virtual" time was as routined as the regimes of the patients in Thomas Mann's *The Magic Mountain*.[11] It was, on the contrary, an effort to find a more significant temporal thought, such as Hans Castorp (who never had his broken watch repaired) sought in Mann's novel, that directed my own development in the fifties and sixties.[12]

It was with such an aim that the Second String Quartet and the Double Concerto (written at the same time in 1959–1960) were planned. The primary questions were: How are events presented, carried on, and accompanied? What kind of changes can previously presented events undergo while maintaining some element of identity?

and, How can all this be used to express compelling aspects of experience to the listener? In both works, the purely instrumental sound material—the four stringed instruments in the Quartet and the harpsichord and piano and their associated chamber orchestras in the Double Concerto, each with their unique expressive and sound capacities—was sufficient, and I saw no reason to extend beyond the usual methods of playing. In the Quartet, each of the four instruments has a repertory of musical characters of its own, while contributing to the total effect in many different capacities, sometimes following, sometimes opposing the leader, usually according to its own capabilities—that is, according to the repertory of expression, continuity, interval, and rhythmic patterns assigned to it. Each is treated as an "individual," usually making an effort to cooperate, especially when this seems helpful in carrying on the musical enterprise. The work begins and concludes (ex. 4) with each instrument contributing—sometimes the briefest fragments, each characterized in its own fashion—to a mosaic that joins these into one large, audible pattern, a concentrated version of the pattern of the entire work.

While the Second String Quartet deals with the separation of four instruments of more or less similar tone color, expressive qualities, dynamic capabilities, and performing techniques, the Double Concerto for Harpsichord and Piano and Two Chamber Orchestras uses soloists of such different capacities that an entirely different approach seemed necessary. The problem in the Quartet, given the kind of concept behind it, was to differentiate instruments of similar character, while the problem in the Double Concerto, as I saw it, was to join together instruments of very different basic characteristics. The harpsichord, as is obvious, is dynamically much softer than the piano when both are playing their loudest; its attack is much more incisive, however, while its response to the fingers is more mechanical. Dynamic shadings, which are the basis of a pianist's technique, are almost unobtainable by touch on the harpsichord, which has, to compensate, at least on some models, a vast number of possible mechanical-registrational color changes. The idea, therefore, of contrasting two worlds of musical expression and sound had to be carried out quite differently. It should be obvious that the idea of allowing four (as in the case

Example 4. Elliott Carter. Conclusion, mm. 599–607, from String Quartet no. 2 (1959), 2d. corr. ed., pp. 59–60. (Copyright 1961 by Associated Music Publishers, Inc. Used by permission.)

of the Quartet) or two (as in the Double Concerto) different streams of music to be heard together in any one of the possible uncoordinated ways that have been used either by Ives or by others in recent years will, from the point of view I am describing here, produce a form of entropy, a degrading of the possibilities of communication, which to me have ever to be revitalized and sharpened. Furthermore, while such works as mine do not always receive performances that present clearly all the materials, their relationships and expressive intentions, still, these are there in the score, and performers and listeners can gradually come to recognize them after successive performances. If they were to be played quite differently every time, as is the intention of most aleatory scores, there would be little possibility of learning to hear and interpret more and more of what is in the scores. So, to join the piano and harpsichord into one world of music that could have many inner contrasts, I chose two small orchestras, each with two percussion players, and, since this was to be an antiphonal piece, the two orchestras contained instruments that would underline the qualities of the soloist they were associated with and, in the case of the harpsichord, add dynamic volume to supplement its lack of dynamic range. It might be objected that the harpsichord could be amplified to make up for this, but I have always preferred to hear instruments, as well as people, present themselves in their own individual way without mechanical amplification, which gets in the way of direct contact, the whole point of a live concert. Under good acoustical and well-rehearsed conditions the harpsichord is perfectly audible and balanced in the way I consider effective for this piece. Because this work, as I got into it, took on the character of a percussion piece, with the soloists acting as mediators between unpitched percussion and pitched instruments, composing for percussion suggested certain ideas that do, indeed, have a rather "clock time" oriented attitude. This is especially true in the coda, which starts with a crash on the largest tam-tam and then is organized as a dying away over many measures of this crash, using the possible patterns of fading in and out of various partials in different phases as the sound shape of the music, with each different phase filled with various character patterns recalling ideas from the whole work. Indeed, this piece, even more than the Second String Quartet, depends for its material on the sound of intervals, combined with various tone colors. Any figurative material that exists is directly derived from the intervallic sounds associated with each group and each section of the piece.

These works, as well as those previously mentioned, depend on a special dimension of time, that of "multiple perspective" in which various contrasting characters are presented simultaneously—as was occasionally done in opera, for example, in the ballroom scene from *Don Giovanni*, or in the finale of *Aïda*. Double and some-times manifold character simultaneities, of course, pre-sent, as our human experience often does, certain emotion-ally charged events as seen in the context of others, pro-ducing often a kind of irony, which I am particularly interested in. In doing this so frequently, and by leading into and away from such moments in what seemed to me telling ways, I have, I think, been trying to make mo-ments of music as rich in reference as I could and to do something that can be done only in music and yet that has rarely been achieved except in opera.

The concept of the Second String Quartet and the Double Concerto had this dimension built into them, as does my Piano Concerto, which pits the "crowd" of the orchestra against the piano's "individual," mediated by a concertino of seven soloists. Here, the conflict was con-ceived as one of orchestral music that becomes more and more insistent and brutal as the work continues, while the piano makes more and more of a case for variety, sensitivity, and imagination. Over a very long stretch of time in the second of the two movements, the orchestral strings build up more and more dense, softly held chords, which form a kind of suffocating blanket of sound, while at the same time the rest of the orchestra plays patterns of strict, regular beats that increase in forcefulness and are layered into more and more different speeds. Against all this, the piano and instrumental soloists play much expressive, varied music, which near the end of the pas-sage finally becomes more insistent, with the piano crowded into repeating one note, the one note missing in the middle of an aggregate of eighty-one other notes (ex. 5).

Of course, in these works, all kinds of uses were made of metric modulation, both as a mode of proceeding

Example 5. Elliott Carter. Piano Concerto, Two-Piano Score, pp. 79–80; piano reduction by the composer. (Copyright 1967 by Associated Music Publishers, Inc. Used by permission.)

smoothly or abruptly from one speed to another and as a formal device to isolate one section from another. Generally, these work together, for very often a new section with a different speed and character starts while another layer continues in the same speed. In the course of exploring metric modulation, the idea of dealing with accelerandos and ritardandos intrigued me. The first notational solution of an accelerando, which speeds up regularly from beginning to end of a piece, occurred in the sixth variation of my Variations for Orchestra (1954), in which a scheme of six measures in 3/4 time speeds up during its course to three times its original pace, at which point there is a switch of notation, and a part previously playing quarter notes is written in triplets of eighths, while in other parts dotted quarters become eighths, dotted halves become quarters, and eighths become sextuplets of sixteenths. Yet, while each of these notational systems sounds as if it were continuing a regular acceleration, the beat has returned to the speed of that of the first beat of the six-measure scheme (ex. 6). The entire variation is projected onto this scheme, which repeats itself over and over. Its usefulness here proved to be that the canonic theme could be brought in at different places in the scheme, so that successive entrances, if brought in sooner (for example, as a dotted half note in measure 5), would sound slower, or, if brought in later, would sound faster. A whole pattern of total acceleration was thus achieved, for one of the final entrances occurs with the first note of the theme lasting the full six measures; the second note lasting the first three measures; the third note lasting the last three measures; the fourth to eighth notes lasting dotted halves; the next eighteen notes lasting quarters, and so forth. Similarly, the place at which the triplets of the theme are stopped comes later and later in the six-measure scheme, so that faster and faster notes are heard, until triplets finally invade the very last measure, sounding the fastest note values heard thus far. The matter of projecting regular beats against such a pattern interested me, too. In this variation, the harp gives the impression of playing in slow, regular time the notes of one of the ritornellos against the music just described. Sometimes, systems of accelerations, ritardations, and regular beating have been combined, as in the slow section of the Double Concerto (measures 314–466) and in many

Example 6. Elliott Carter. Variation 6, mm. 289–299, from Variations for Orchestra, p. 71. (Copyright 1957–1958 by Associated Music Publishers, Inc. Used by permission.)

(a)   (b)   (c)   (d)

(e) Rhythmic basis: groups of retarding phrases, each starting a little faster than the previous.

Movement II

(a)
8va sempre
                            (b)   (c)   (d)

8va sempre

(e) Rhythmic basis: starts very fast and gets slower throughout the entire work with each successive appearance.

Movement III

(a)   (b)   (c)   (d)

8 - ⌐

(e) Rhythmic basis: accelerating phrases, each starting at a slower point.

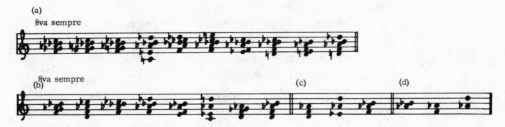

(e) Rhythmic basis: gets faster from beginning to end.

Example 7. Elliott Carter. Concerto for Orchestra (1969). Technical aspects: a. *five-note chords;* b. *four-note chords;* c. *three-note chords;* d. *two-note intervals; and* e. *general retarding or accelerating tendencies associated with each of the four movements.*

short stretches of the Piano Concerto.

The Concerto for Orchestra of 1969 carries out the idea of waves of sound, used briefly in the coda of the Double Concerto over a duration of more than twenty minutes. With this intention in mind, I started work, developing an overall dramatic and expressive plan and choosing the musical materials and form. After these had been clearly formulated, I came across the long poem, *Vents*, by the French poet who calls himself St. John Perse.[13] His Whitmanesque description of the United States swept by the winds of change seemed to revolve, as did the music I was writing, around four main ideas in the poem: (1) the drying up of autumn, suggesting the dryness and death of a previous time—men of straw in a year of straw; (2) the swiftness and freshness of the winds that blow away the old and bring in the new; (3) the exhortation of a shaman-poet calling for a rebirth and a destruction of worn-out things; and, finally, (4) the return of spring and life. These ideas are brought together in many different contexts, blended and mixed as the poet constantly stresses the motions of the wind. The music, too, has four main characters, and, while hints of all four are being referred to constantly, the concerto picks out one facet after another to dwell on at

83

some length, subordinating the others. Thus, while there can be said to be four movements, yet these are almost constantly heard in combination. The orchestra itself can be seated, when there is enough space, in such a way that the four strands of music are separated stereophonically as well as in timbre, material, and expression. The wind itself was thought of as being a composite of many elements, and the concerto treats the orchestra as groups of soloists, dividing each of the bodies of strings into five or more soloists that form the basis of each of the four sections: the celli, combined with harp, piano, wood percussion, and middle-register winds, are related to the autumnal rattling of pods and straw; the violins with flutes and metallic percussion, to the freshness of the wind; the basses, combined with tuba, timpani, and sometimes trombones, to the poet's invocations; and the violas, trumpets, upper-middle winds, and snare drums, to the reawakening.

Technically, the piece is constructed on a use of all the thirty-eight possible five-note chords (10 of which are symmetrical and 28 invertible) that are distributed among the four movements, as shown in spacings typical of their movements in example 7. Also shown is how the eleven two-note intervals, the twelve three-note chords, and the twenty-nine four-note chords, considered as components of the five-note chords, are distributed. (The inversions of the five-note chords and the seven-note chords, sometimes used, are omitted in the example.) Rhythmically, each movement has its general tendency: movement I is formed of groups of retarding phrases, each starting a little faster than the previous (see ex. 7); movement II starts very fast and gets slower throughout the entire work with each successive appearance; movement III is made up of accelerating phrases, each starting at a slower point (as in ex. 7); while movement IV gets faster from beginning to end.

The work starts with an introduction, "These were very great winds over all the faces of this world,"[14] in which a twelve-tone chord is presented in four groups (or chords) of three notes (ex. 8). Each of these groups forms the basis of one of the movements (as numbered), and "places" that movement in character in orchestration, tessitura, and general rhythmic behavior. Then, after a clamorous outburst, based still on a combination

Elliott Carter

84

I II III IV

Example 8. Elliott Carter. Concerto for Orchestra (1969). Compositional basis of each movement: three-note chords that together constitute the twelve-note chord.

of the four basic materials, the other three movements subside and allow the dry rattling of the first movement to predominate (measures 24–140). During this section, music from movement II makes several brief appearances, the most extended of which is at measures 42–47. The same is true of fragments of movement III, as at measures 117–120, and of IV, as at 79–80. After a brief tutti, movement II proper starts (141–285), which suggests the freshness of the wind. Here, too, are occasional incursions of bits of other movements. This leads to a four-layered tutti that subsides into the recitative of the third movement. Finally, the fourth movement occupies most of measures 420–532. This movement made its vestigial appearance in measure 30 at a slow speed that increased at each reappearance until its real emergence following measure 420, after which its speed continues to increase. The coda, from 532 to the end, is multilayered, alternating rapidly between the four sets of materials, which, at times, change their characteristic tessituras. The work finally dies away, sounding fewer and fewer notes of the characteristic chords of each movement.

The musical material of this is entirely built of similar and contrasting items of sound. Intervals and chords are the characterized immediacies, or "nows," out of which motions of constantly changing shapes flow. It is a work fundamentally organized to produce the "virtual image"

85

of "passage" discussed above. As such, it has to do, at least to me, with an image of internal time consciousness of which Edmund Hüsserl says:

Elliott Carter

> The sensible nucleus . . . is "now" and has just been and has been still earlier, and so on. In this now there is also retention of the past now of all levels of duration of which we are now conscious. . . . The stream of lived experience with its phases and intervals is itself a unity which is identifiable through reminiscence with a line of sight on what is flowing: impressions and retentions, sudden appearance and regular transformation, and disappearance and obscuration. This unity is originarily constituted through the fact of flux itself; that is, its true essence is not to be, in general, but to be a unity of lived experience. [15]

It should be obvious that the general approach to music rather fragmentarily presented here could be susceptible of exploration in many directions—that what I have done seems, even to me, like just a beginning both technically and artistically, although the works are meant to be considered primarily in themselves. It has cost considerable imaginative effort, since the artistic horizon of the American composer is not expanded by life in a society that is unable to furnish him with artistic and intellectual ideas and critiques of sufficient depth, clarity, and quality to be of much use. In fact, to have indulged in the foregoing explanations and to be faced with the prospect of their being used as a substitute for listening to the music itself and fed into the general hopper of American educational, artistic statements—later to be ground up and to come out as undifferentiated fodder to be forcibly fed to the young and permanently regurgitated at exams— is apparently the terrible fate of such efforts as these and the disheartening result of America's ambivalence toward the arts. Yet a composer cannot but be grateful for an opportunity to express verbally ideas important to him (for otherwise who would?) in the hope that they may be really helpful to a few others.

Perhaps the only consolation is that any such descriptive discussion as this has really consistently, although not intentionally, evaded the issues and visions most important and significant during the act of composing. For what is discussed here (as should be obvious, but never seems to be) is the outer shell, the wrapping of the music. The reason for writing it—for developing it in the way described, for weighing every note, chord, rhythm in the light of their expressive intention and their living, spontaneous interrelationships, and the judging of it all, almost unconsciously, against a private standard of what gives me genuine sensuous pleasure, of what seems fascinating, interesting, imaginative, moving, and of urgent importance—cannot be put into words. It is, I suppose, what is easily brushed off with words like *involvement* or *commitment* to music, as well as to what St. John Perse somewhat portentously calls "the horror . . . and honor of living."[16]

Notes

1. Charles Koechlin, "Le Temps et la musique," *La Revue musicale*, January 1926, pp. 45–62. My translation.

2. Suzanne Langer, *Feeling and Form* (New York: Scribner Library, 1953), p. 114.

3. I use this expression "human (*Dasein*)" exactly as it is used in Martin Heidegger, *On Time and Being*, trans. Joan Stambaugh (New York: Harper & Row, 1972), pp. 1–24. It refers not only to existence, or presence, but also to the cognitive activities associated with this.

4. Langer, *Feeling and Form*, p. 111.

5. Ibid., p. 113.

6. Ibid., p. 112.

7. Henry Cowell, *New Musical Resources* (New York: Knopf, 1930), pp. 45–108.

8. Joseph Schillinger, *The Schillinger System of Musical Composition* (New York: Carl Fischer, 1946), pp. 1–95.

9. Pierre Suvchinsky [Souvtchinsky], "La Notion du temps et la musique," *La Revue musicale*, May–June 1939, pp. 70–80.

10. Igor Stravinsky, *La Poétique musicale* (Cambridge, Mass.: Harvard University Press, 1942), pp. 19–24.

11. Thomas Mann, *The Magic Mountain*, trans. H. T. Lowe-Porter (New York: Modern Library, 1932). Contains many passages dealing with various aspects of time, especially the chapter "By the Ocean of Time," pp. 683–690.

12. Marcel Proust deals with the subject exhaustively in his *A la recherche du temps perdu*, 10th ed., 15 vols. (Paris: Gallimard, 1927). See especially the last pages of the last book, *Le Temps retrouvé*, 15: 249–261.

13. St. John Perse, *Vents (Winds)*, trans. Hugh Chisholm, Bollingen Series, no. 34 (New York: Pantheon Books, 1953).

14. Ibid., pp. 4–5.

15. Edmund Hüsserl, *The Phenomenology of Internal Time-Consciousness*, ed. Martin Heidegger, trans. James S. Churchill (Bloomington: Indiana University Press, 1966), pp. 149 and 157.

16. Perse, *Vents*, pp. 178–179.

Elliott Carter

Instruments and Voices in the Fifteenth-Century Chanson
Howard Mayer Brown

Chansons, polyphonic settings of elegant but highly formalized and stereotyped French poems, constituted the principal sort of secular music in western Europe during the fifteenth century. At least, they comprise the bulk of the secular manuscripts of the time and especially of the small, beautifully decorated anthologies that were prepared for the delight of various princes and noblemen in England, Spain, Italy, and Germany, as well as in France and Burgundy.[1] The texts that fifteenth-century composers chose to set, virelais, ballades, and especially rondeaux, express for the most part the dying ideals of chivalric love, in which the unworthy courtier pines for his unattainable lady. They reflect, in other words, the waning of the Middle Ages more obviously than they herald the intellectuals' claims of a new birth of arts and letters. Their music, on the other hand, often rises above the mediocre level of the poetry. An ornately beautiful, carefully wrought melody in the top voice is usually balanced by an equally fine but somewhat simpler melody in the tenor, and this contrapuntal framework is completed by a contratenor, which is mainly responsible for filling out the sonority and keeping the motion going forward at cadences. The history of the chanson from about 1430 to about 1500 involves a continuous process of refinement and change from Gilles Binchois and Guillaume Dufay, through Antoine Busnois, Johannes Ockeghem, and Alexander Agricola. Some of the later fifteenth-century composers began to control and manipulate their free-flowing melodic lines by means of a network of motives and by imitation among all the voices, but the basic stylistic conventions were not overthrown until the advent of the equal-voiced imitative chanson *a 4* by Josquin Des Près and his near contemporaries, Heinrich Isaac, Loyset Compère, and Pierre de La Rue.[2]

The quest to discover how these exquisite miniatures were actually performed, like all such inquiries, is complicated by the fact that no one simple formula can ever

Howard Mayer
Brown

be made to fit all cases. Fifteenth-century composers apparently conceived their music without regard for certain important elements that have since become an integral part of the compositional process. Thus, they left to the imagination of performers the tasks of fitting each syllable of poetry to the music, of adding accidentals, and of creating a specific sonority by selecting appropriate combinations of voice and instruments.[3] How the composer's intentions were realized in actual sound would have depended on the intelligence and musicality of the performers—on how well they understood the "meaning" of the music—to a much greater extent than today, and any one version of a piece would have varied according to the forces available and the acoustical environment in which the performance took place. Our task, then, is not to discover how any one individual chanson was performed on a specific occasion. Rather, we must attempt to uncover the basic principles and conventions that guided the fifteenth-century performers themselves in making their choices. We must, in other words, investigate the limits of freedom within which the earlier musicians operated. More specifically, I shall deal with only one of the most pressing problems faced by both fifteenth-century and modern performers of chansons: which combinations of voices and instruments are most appropriate to the genre.

The musical sources themselves offer few clues about performance practice, and those few are apt to be misleading. The presence of a complete text beneath the music, for example, indicates that the line can be sung but does not prove that it need always be sung, and the absence of a text does not necessarily signal an instrumental part.[4] We must, therefore, turn to other kinds of evidence to find the information we are seeking. But passing remarks about music in imaginative literature and notices of payments to musicians in various archives do not by themselves suffice, for they are apt to be too vague and general. And the rare descriptions of actual events in the fifteenth-century—the account of the Banquet of the Oath of the Pheasant given by Philip the Good, duke of Burgundy, in 1454 is the best known[5]—may be at least partially misleading, since they involve extraordinary events rather than the common practice in which we are interested.

Pictures, on the other hand, such as the depiction of musical ensembles in contemporary paintings, tapestries, manuscript illuminations, and so on, do supply the details we need, if we are careful in assessing their accuracy and if we can reconcile what they tell us with what we know from the musical manuscripts and literary documents. In using works of art as musicological evidence, we must first establish the artist's intentions, making certain that he did not include music for symbolic reasons or merely to illustrate a given text or to follow an outmoded and purely artistic convention.[6] In other words, our conclusions about the common practices of the fifteenth century ought to be based on pictures that show real people engaged in normal activities. Thus, angels, the largest category by far of the fifteenth-century musicians shown in works of art, must be excluded from our consideration, for there seems to be no objective way of differentiating those who appear in pictures for merely symbolic or conventional reasons from those who might actually reflect reality.[7] And, similarly, pictures of shepherds, grotesques, mythological figures, and groups of people like Muses and sibyls tell us nothing about the way chansons were performed. A certain number of art works from the time, though, do show well-born amateurs and professional musicians engaged in making music in a context suggesting that they are likely to be performing chansons. Some of these are scenes illustrating courtly life, like the tapestry showing the emperor Maximilian playing chess with Mary of Burgundy[8] or the painting of Philip the Good and his court gathered for breakfast before the hunt (pl. 1),[9] and these, it seems to me, can be accepted at face value; they are as instructive about the life of the times as photographs would be. But other pictures, too, seem to reflect reality, even though they illustrate such texts as romances or the Bible—the banquet for the prodigal son, for example, or Herod's feast;[10] or they elucidate some general concept, like the "garden of love" or the musical and other daily activities associated with one of the planets.[11] Pictures of the latter sort may not be as trustworthy as photographs, but they must perforce be used to construct plausible hypotheses about the life of the times, since they are the best evidence that has survived.

While the style and, especially, the texture, of fifteenth-

century chansons suggest that they were conceived for one or two solo voices accompanied by one or two instruments, the pictorial evidence proves that other kinds of combinations, too, performed them, including solo voices a cappella and purely instrumental ensembles. Using the painting done by a follower of Jan van Eyck about 1430 that shows the courtiers of Philip the Good, duke of Burgundy, gathered together outdoors before a hunt (pl. 1), as well other pictures, Heinrich Besseler has convincingly demonstrated that chansons were sung in the fifteenth century by unaccompanied voices, that women took part in such ensembles in contradistinction to the all-male groups of the preceding century, and that well-born amateurs joined with professional musicians for performances of secular music at court. Besseler suggests that the two ladies and two men, one of whom might be the composer himself, are singing Binchois's *Files a marier*, an unusual composition not only because it has four parts but also because it is based on a preexistent popular tune.[12] But other pictures show a cappella groups singing more conventional three-voiced chansons. The Fountain of Youth that decorates an astronomical manuscript prepared in northern Italy about 1470, for example, is surrounded by musicians, including three men singing from a sheet of illegible music headed *Mon seul plaisir* (pl. 2).[13] This miniature seems to depict the entire secular musical establishment of a small court of the time and should not be constructed as representing a single simultaneous performance. With typical artistic license the successive performances by four separate units are compressed into the one picture. Three of the four *hauts ménétriers* sound their loud music on shawms and a slide trumpet, another minstrel plays a tune on the three-holed pipe while accompanying himself on the tabor, a lutenist plucks his instrument with a plectrum while sitting at the base of the fountain, and, quite independently, the vocal trio sings *Mon seul plaisir*. The most widespread setting of the rondeau, *Mon seul plaisir, ma doulce joye*, for three voices, is attributed both to Guil-

Plate 1. *Follower of Jan van Eyck. Philip the Good and his court before the hunt. (Musée National du Château de Versailles.)*

Plate 2. Fountain of Youth. (MS lat. 209 (α.X.2.14), pl. 9; Libro "De sphaera" c. 10r; Biblioteca Estense, Modena.)

Example 1. Bedingham [or Dufay?]. Mon seul plaisir, *mm. 1–9, after Dufay,* Opera omnia, *piece 90, 6:108.*

laume Dufay and to Johannes Bedingham. Besseler publishes it among the *opera dubia* of Dufay and places the text beneath the superius only.[14] But the tenor can easily be made to accomodate the words, and in this case it is not very difficult to imagine how the contratenor, too, might have been sung. In example 1 the first line of the poem has been set to the first phrase of music in all three voices. Indeed, for most chansons composed during the fifteenth century, the tenor can as easily be sung as the superius. Problems arise when a poem is forced upon one of the rather fragmentary contratenors, filled with leaps and without clear phrase articulations. And yet, if the pictorial evidence is to be believed, these problems must have been overcome and chansons performed at least some of the time by unaccompanied voices.

Works of graphic art do not always make clear which

Howard Mayer
Brown

performers are meant to be singing while playing and which are merely playing instruments. Therefore, I shall discuss the possible combinations of voices with instruments according to the number of instruments involved, even though my remarks about mixed vocal and instrumental ensembles will then alternate with those about chansons arranged for instruments alone. A number of works of art from the fifteenth century show a single performer engaged in making music in middle-class or aristocratic surroundings. Since the soloists are undoubtedly intended to be playing secular music and chansons are so prominent a part of that repertoire, these musicians may well be performing intabulations of chansons. Israel van Meckenem's respectable burgher (pl. 3), for example, who operates his positive organ with the help of his wife in their solid and comfortable home, would very probably have included arrangements of chansons in his repertoire;[15] so might the slightly melancholy lady who sits outdoors pushing the double row of buttons on her portative organ in a drawing from about 1440 now in the Louvre (pl. 4).[16] In these two cases, the pictorial evidence merely confirms the purely musical evidence. Since the Faenza Codex and the Buxheim Organ Book have survived, as well as a number of smaller manuscripts containing keyboard music from the fifteenth century, we are well informed about this repertoire.[17] Along with dances, preludes, and settings of various sorts of cantus firmi, most of these sources also contain intabulations of vocal music, including chansons. Many of the arrangements in the Faenza Codex omit the contratenor or combine the two lowest voices into one and ornament the already ornate superius part to make a two-part texture consisting of a relatively slow-moving bottom line and an extraordinarily exuberant and highly decorated upper one. A comparison of a phrase from Dufay's chanson *Par le regard* with its arrangement in the Buxheim Organ Book (ex. 2) demonstrates the typical procedure of the fifteenth-century German intabulator.[18] He has literally duplicated the vocal model, taking both tenor and contratenor over into the keyboard version. The

Plate 3. Israel van Meckenem. An organist and his wife. (Cleveland Museum of Art.)

Plate 4. Fifteenth-century drawing. Lady playing a porta-tive organ. (Musée du Louvre.)

principal difference between the original and the key-board arrangement consists of the ornamentation applied liberally to the superius and rather more sparingly to the lower voices. Meckenem's burgher and the melancholy lady, then, might have performed chansons by Dufay, Binchois, Hayne van Ghizeghem, and others by playing all the original lines, or at the very least the tenor and superius, embellishing them according to their abilities.

The pictorial evidence, in this case, did not reveal any-

Example 2. Dufay. Par le regard, *mm. 1-6, after Dufay,*
Opera omnia, *piece 73, 6:88-89, and its intabulation in
the Buxheim Organ Book, after the edition by Wallner
in* Das Erbe deutscher Musik, *piece 30, 37:24-25.*

thing that we did not already know about the intabulation of chansons for the organ. What pictures do show us, though, are the other fifteenth-century instruments that were played unaccompanied and were capable of reproducing all the parts of a chanson. Without pictures we could not know that fifteenth-century musicians in all probability intabulated chansons for solo harp, solo lute, and perhaps even solo clavichord, for no musical sources survive that include such arrangements.[19] We can only guess that the elegant courtier standing with his lady in a garden, shown in a late fifteenth-century French tapestry now in the Philadelphia Museum of Art (pl. 5), is playing for her an intabulation of a chanson for solo harp,[20] but there can be no doubt about the composition that the lady harpist plays in an early fifteenth-century tapestry now in the Musée des Arts Decoratifs in Paris (pl. 6), for a gentleman holds up for her to read a roll of music headed *De ce que fol pense*, the incipit of a chanson written some years earlier by Pierre Des Molins.[21] She, it is true, may be singing to her own accompaniment, in which case she doubtless plays the two lowest voices on the harp while singing the superius. But whether she plays a harp solo or sings an accompanied song, none of the musical sources preserves such arrangements. They can, however, easily be imagined. Intabulations of chansons for solo harp or, for that matter, solo clavichord or virginals, must have resembled closely those for organ in the Buxheim Organ Book.[22] The instrumentalists duplicated all the voices of the original as closely as the technical limitations of their instruments permitted, and they embellished the top line according to their ability.

In theory, intabulations of chansons for solo lute should have followed the same principles, but that conclusion must be advanced with some reservations, since we know so little about the history of fifteenth-century lute technique. During much of the century the lute was played with a plectrum and hence was a monophonic in-

Howard Mayer
Brown

*Plate 5. Fifteenth-century French tapestry. A courtier and his lady. (*Scene of Courtly Life*; Philadelphia Museum of Art: Purchased: Subscription and Museum Funds '26-73-1. Photograph by A. J. Wyatt, staff photographer.)*

Plate 6. Fifteenth-century French tapestry. "Scene de roman: De ce que fol pense." (Collections du Musée des Arts Décoratifs, Paris.)

strument.[23] Virtuosity apparently consisted of the player's ability to improvise rapid embellishments—that, at least, seems to be what Johannes Tinctoris implies in his "De inventione et usu musicae" of about 1487.[24] At some point in the century, though, the technique of playing with the fingers was invented, and the instrument became capable of duplicating all the voices of a polyphonic complex. Tinctoris writes about this technique as though it were fairly new at the end of the 1480's, and he suggests that the Germans, by which he seems to mean Flemings, were especially good at it.[25] But finger technique on the lute may have been known almost as early in Italy. A fragmentary manuscript discovered some years ago in Bologna by Hans David contains an arrangement of Vincinet's *Fortune par ta cruaulté* for solo voice and lute, in which the lute plays the lowest two voices, as well as a purely instrumental composition in two parts.[26] The manuscript is bound with a mathematical treatise printed in 1484, and so the music may date from the last quarter of the fifteenth century.

It seems clear, then, that lutenists arranged chansons as solo intabulations late in the fifteenth century, although the technique was still so new then that it was probably restricted to comparatively few of the more adventurous virtuosi. Certainly, the plectrum continued to be used with the lute into the sixteenth century, as pictures make clear. Played with a plectrum, the lute was confined to a single line, and so it could scarcely be used as a solo instrument; but it could accompany a solo singer. For example, in the earliest known garden of love (pl. 7), an engraving made by the so-called Master of the Gardens of Love, a gentleman leans on a low fence in the foreground and sings from a sheet of music while his lady friend accompanies him on the lute.[27] Since her back is toward us, we cannot see whether or not she plays with a plectrum, but since the engraving was made about 1430, in all likelihood she does. Therefore, the man must be singing the superius while she plucks the tenor; the contratenor can easily be omitted from most fifteenth-century chansons without sacrificing anything essential to the musical meaning of the composition. Or else the lady sings the superius while plucking the contratenor, and the gentleman sings the tenor. The same two possibilities of performance are open to a musical couple depicted by Israel van Meckenem about 1500,[28] for even at that late date the lutenist still plays with a plectrum. On the other hand, in a similar engraving by Alart du Hameel made about the same time,[29] the lutenist must play both lower voices, contratenor as well as tenor, while his lady sings superius, for he clearly uses his fingers rather than a plectrum.

Three-voiced chansons could, then, be arranged for solo voice and lute in the fifteenth century, even though no such arrangements survive save for the single example in the Bolognese fragment. And songs could be sung to the harp—as we have seen from the tapestry depicting *De ce*

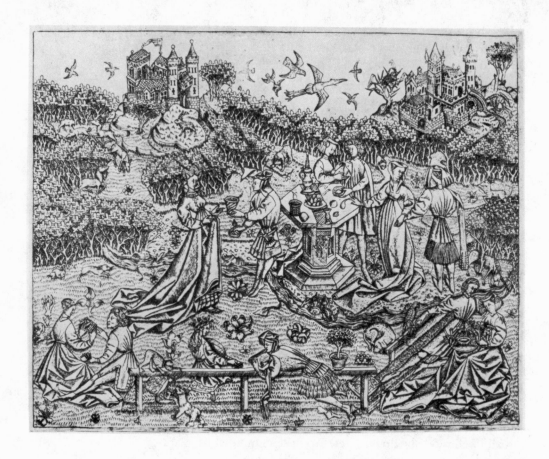

Plate 7. Master of the Gardens of Love. The large garden of love. (From Late Gothic Engravings of Germany and The Netherlands, *by Max Lehrs [New York: Dover Publications, 1969].)*

que fol pense—and perhaps to keyboard instruments as well. A single lute was also used on occasion to accompany two or more singers. The musical trio, two singers and a lutenist, portrayed in Hieronymus Bosch's *Haywain*,[30] probably performed a chanson, since they are meant to symbolize worldly pleasures. If so, the normal texture of the chanson would dictate that the woman sing superius and the man tenor, while the lutenist played the contratenor. A similar group of musicians furnished entertainment in a garden of love shown in one of the best-known miniatures from a late fifteenth-century manuscript of the Roman de la Rose,[31] save that here the two ladies probably sing superius and tenor, reading from their sheets of music, while the lutenist plays the contratenor and the fourth musician doubles either the lutenist or perhaps one of the women by singing in falsetto. In short, the pictorial evidence suggests that lutenists alone could support one or more singers by playing one or both of the lower voices of a chanson, using their fingers or a plectrum.

Sometimes a lutenist joined one other instrumentalist to play chansons. Many fifteenth-century works of art show two musicians in a context that clearly suggests they are performing secular music. Two lovers sit playing in a garden, for example, or a pair of minstrels entertain at a banquet or while their mistress bathes, or a gentleman and his friend serenade a lady who looks down at them from her window. In such cases, the combination of lute and harp is one of the most frequently seen.[32] For example, in the edition of *L'histoire du tresvaillant chevalier Paris et de la belle Vienne*, printed in Antwerp in 1487 by Gherard Leeu, a woodcut shows Paris, wearing a plumed hat, standing in a garden playing the lute, while his friend, Edward, sits on a nearby bench with his harp, and the beautiful Vienne watches them from her chamber (pl. 8).[33] Vienne was the daughter of the noble Godeffroy de Lanson, ruler of the Dauphiné and a relative of the French king. She was loved by Paris, son of a vassal; although his father was rich, Paris could not aspire to win in love a lady so far above him in social station. He kept his feelings secret, confessing them only to his friend Edward. Together they often went at night to serenade Vienne with chansons, for they both sang supremely well and could play melodious chansons on their instruments like men who were masters of the art.[34] After endless complications, needless to say, Paris marries Vienne, and they live happily ever after. Even though the romance dates from the fourteenth century, the fifteenth-century artist was most likely depicting contemporary reality, for the text he illustrated does not specify that the chevalier and his friend played their chansons on particular sorts of instruments, and, indeed, the combination of lute and harp succeeds admirably well in the performance of fifteenth-century chansons *a 3*. In the woodcut, Paris must be playing the principal melodic line, the superius, for he is the protagonist, and he can-

Plate 8. Serenade. (From L'histoire du tresvaillant chevalier Paris et de la belle Vienne fille du dauphin *[Antwerp: Gherard Leeu, 1487], fol. 3; Österreichische Nationalbibliothek, Handschriftensammlung, Vienna.)*

not manage more than one part, since he uses a plectrum. Thus, Edward must be responsible for supplying the two lowest lines, tenor and contratenor, on his harp.

In 1507 Francesco Spinacino published in his first book of tablature, the earliest such volume ever printed, a few pieces arranged for two lutes.[35] Like the other, similar pieces in this anthology, the anonymous chanson *Je ne fay plus* (ex. 3) has been divided unequally between the two instruments.[36] The second lute plays both the lowest lines simply, almost exactly as they appear in the vocal sources, while the first lute adds elaborate and rather directionless passage work to the superius. Probably Spinacino's arrangement closely resembles those used by Paris, Edward, and the many other fifteenth-cen-

tury musicians shown playing harp and lute. The chief
difference between the printed music and that played by
the fictional characters, the substitution of a harp part
for the second lute, changes the sonority relatively little.
Before the widespread use of fingers to pluck the lute, a
harp, an instrument capable of playing polyphonic music throughout the fifteenth century, as we have seen,
would have furnished a much more satisfactory accompaniment for the solo lutenist, eager to display his ability
to embellish. In supplying a few examples of music for
two lutes, Spinacino probably intended to counterfeit
an older convention, and he might even have approved
of performing these intabulations by combining the older
with the newer playing techniques; perhaps, then, the
first lutenist still used a plectrum, while his accompanist,
imitating a harp, plucked with his fingers.

According to the romance text, Paris and Edward
sang as well as played instruments beneath Vienne's window, and there is no reason to suppose that they and
their counterparts in fifteenth-century pictures could
not do both simultaneously. If one of the two musicians
sang, he would naturally have chosen one of the structural voices, tenor or superius. Sometimes the superius of a
chanson stays in a range low enough to be performed by
a high tenor, while at other times the fifteenth-century
soloist may have had to rely on his falsetto. Needless to
say, when a lady sang to harp and lute,[37] this problem
would not have arisen. But whatever the range of the superius, the tenor is often melodious enough, especially
in chansons from the second half of the century, to be
sung while the other parts are played. The remaining
structural voice, whether superius or tenor, would probably have been entrusted to the lute rather than the
harp, if my conjecture about their relative prominence is
correct, and so the harp was left with the contratenor.
On the other hand, if both Paris and Edward sang as well
as played, one part would have been doubled by an instrument, most likely the tenor—but possibly the superius.

Performances of chansons *a 3* by lute and harp, whether
in purely instrumental adaptations or using some combination of voices with instruments, emphasized the pre-
dominance of a single melodic line while relegating the
other lines to the role of polyphonic accompaniment.

Example 3. Busnois [or G. Mureau?]. Je ne fay plus, *after Florence, Biblioteca Nationale Centrale, MS Magl. XIX, 59 (Banco rari 229), fol. 54ᵛ, and its intabulation for two lutes by Francesco Spinacino in* Intabulatura de Lauto: Libro primo *(Venice: Ottaviano Petrucci, 1507), piece 11, fol. 21.*

In principle, then, one main voice ought to be performed either by a solo singer or by a monophonic instrument capable of sustaining an elaborate melody, and the remaining two voices, or only one of them if need be, can be entrusted to a less obtrusive accompanying instrument, invariably a plucked or struck string in the examples we have seen thus far. The pictorial evidence sustains this principle. Among the fifteenth-century works of art that seem to depict reality appear examples of secular music making—very probably involving chansons—in which instrumentalists play recorder and lute;[38] recorder and dulcimer;[39] rebec and lute;[40] cornet or recorder and harp;[41] and portative organ and harp.[42]

Two instruments can also accompany a solo singer, as we have seen. One such combination deserves special

comment, for it appears in a number of manuscript illuminations well into the sixteenth century. Books of Hours,
the small and elegantly decorated collections of office
hours and prayers assembled for the private devotion of
their noble owners, sometimes begin with a calendar.
Often each month of the calendar is illustrated with a
scene showing peasants engaged in a typically seasonal
occupation or courtiers and other well-born people passing time in an appropriate fashion. For the month of
May, Flemish artists occasionally depicted a boating
party in which a lady singer, reading her chanson from
a sheet of music, is accompanied by two friends playing
lute and recorder or transverse flute.[43] The version in
the Hennessy Hours, attributed to Simon Bening, dates
from about 1540.[44] Although it might be argued, then,
that such pictures ought not be associated with fifteenth-
century chansons, a similar illumination appears in the
recently recovered part book that belongs with the Tournai Chansonnier, dated 1511 (pl. 9).[45] Since that manuscript contains chansons by Hayne van Ghizeghem,
Johannes Ockeghem, Loyset Compère, Jacob Obrecht,
and Josquin Des Près, among others, there is good reason to suppose that the boatload of musicians is performing the sorts of pieces we have been discussing.

If the one lady sang the superius, leaving the recorder
player responsible for the tenor and the lutenist for the
contratenor—the obvious assumption—some care would
have had to be taken to ensure a properly musical result. Both the transverse flute and the recorder were
transposing instruments during the Renaissance—they
sounded an octave higher than their written pitch.[46]
Thus, in a composition in which the tenor crosses below the contratenor (see, for instance, ex. 1), the lowest written note would be inverted if it were played on a
recorder or flute, creating awkward and incorrect chord
spacings. But these barbarisms can be avoided in several
ways. The contratenor, too, might have been transposed
up an octave, although the lute would then play in an
uncomfortably high range, and the sonority of the ensemble might be unpleasingly shrill. A similarly unbal-
anced sound might result from transposing the entire
chanson to a higher pitch so that the recorder could
play in the proper octave. The musicians who favored
this combination of voice with instruments might have

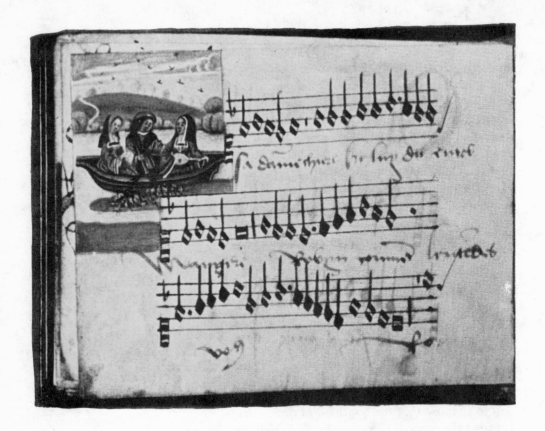

Plate 9. Boating party. (MS IV.90, fol. 11ᵛ; copyright Bibliothèque royale Albert Ier, Brussels.)

restricted their repertoire to the not inconsiderable number of chansons in which the contratenor stays below the tenor or goes above it for only one or two notes, which could easily be changed. The resulting inversion of tenor and superius parts would not be unpleasing, as long as the lowest written note retained its position. The best solution of all, though, would have been to assign the two lowest voices to the lutenist. He would then have preserved the proper contrapuntal relationship among the voices, whether they crossed each other or not, and the wind instrument would be free to double the tenor in its own characteristic octave. Perhaps, then, the combination of recorder, lute, and solo voice became commonplace for the performance of chansons only toward the end of the century, after a finger technique for the lute had become firmly established. With a few adjustments, this

sort of ensemble was equally capable of performing typical Parisian chansons *a 4*, composed in the 1530's, as the famous painting of three ladies by the Master of the Female Half Lengths makes clear.[47] Indeed, this combination of voice with instruments is one of the few conventional groupings that seems to have survived the stylistic change that took place around 1500. And musicians in Italy were as familiar with this sonority as northern musicians, if the evidence of Giorgione's famous *fête champêtre* is to be believed.[48]

When more than two instrumentalists performed chansons *a 3*, they did not adopt new principles but merely expanded slightly those we have been discussing. Thus, secular music in courtly surroundings could be furnished by recorder, presumably playing the superius, accompanied by harp and dulcimer (pl. 10),[49] or by pipe and tabor in place of the recorder—a surprising choice for an ensemble instrument—plus lute and harp.[50] One appropriate wind instrument—it could presumably as well be a solo voice, a portative organ, or even a lute with plec-

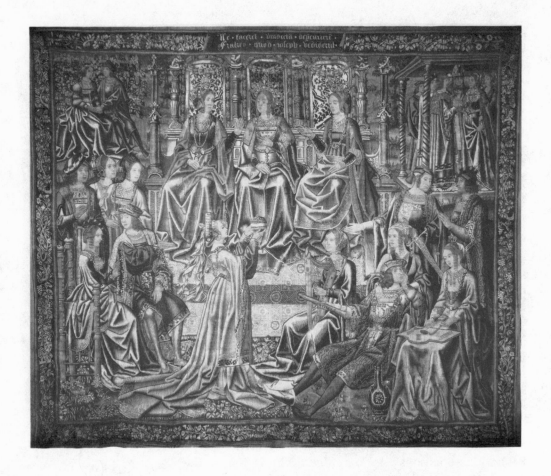

Plate 10. Sixteenth-century Flemish tapestry. The court of love. (Brussels, Musées Royaux d'Art et d'Histoire, Inv. m. Tx. 9864.)

trum—sustained the principal melodic line, and it was accompanied not by one but by two subsidiary instruments, that is, plucked or struck strings. If two instruments capable of sustaining their sounds were mixed with plucked or struck strings, they would doubtless have played the two structural voices, tenor and superius. Thus, in the well-known garden of love that forms a part of the series of early sixteenth-century French tapestries depicting scenes of courtly life,[51] the organist may play a superius part, while the fiddler bows the tenor and the lutenist plucks the contratenor, unless the organist has taken over all the voices of the composition as a solo intabulation and the others double whatever parts they fancy. The four instrumentalists who play in a late fifteenth-century Flemish garden of love found in a manuscript collection of sacred music (pl. 11)[52] probably joined forces in a similar way, with the recorder and fiddle playing superius and tenor and the lute and harp the two contratenors, if we can assume, as I think we can, that the presence of four players implies four-part music. Exactly the same combination of instruments accompanies the emperor Maximilian while he plays chess with Mary of Burgundy.[53] In both these scenes, as many singers as players seem to be taking part, offering evidence enough to support the notion that instrumentalists did sometimes double the singers during performances of fifteenth-century chansons.

The last three examples are the first we have seen in which a fiddle was used. It would be rash to generalize, though, on the basis of this incomplete sampling of fifteenth-century pictures, that fiddles rarely took part in the performance of chansons. Pictorial evidence will scarcely ever support such quantitative judgments—that a certain instrument was used more or less of the time than others in a specific context—since we cannot yet base our conclusions on an examination of every relevant fifteenth-century picture. And even if we could, there can be no assurance that a representative selection of art has survived the ravages of time or that works of art ever reflected reality in so precise a way, showing not only what took place but also how frequently. On the other hand, the rarity of fiddles in available depictions of secular music making should encourage us to make what conclusions we can from Tinctoris's discussion of the fiddle, or viola as he calls it, in *De inventione et usu musicae*. He cites as though it were unusual a performance by two Flemings, the brothers Charles and Jean Orbus, in which they played the superius and tenor parts of chansons on two fiddles. And then he goes on to say that "the viola and the rebec are . . . my chosen instruments, those that induce piety and stir my heart most ardently to the contemplation of heavenly joys. For these reasons I would rather reserve them solely for sacred music and the secret consolations of the soul, than have them sometimes used for profane occasions and public festivities."[54] The combination of the pictorial evidence and Tinctoris's enigmat-

117

Plate 11. Musicians in a Garden. (MS Chigi C. VIII.234, fols. 3ᵛ–4; La Biblioteca Apostolica Vaticana, Vatican City, Rome.)

Howard Mayer
Brown

ic remarks does, in fact, suggest that fiddles were not the most conventional instruments used to perform fifteenth-century chansons, but the full meaning of the theorist's statement cannot be appreciated until the problem of instrumental participation in liturgical services during the fifteenth century has been thoroughly investigated. And, similarly, an explanation for the scarcity of viola da gambas in fifteenth-century scenes of secular music making must wait until the early history of that instrument has been written, one of the pressing tasks of organology.

We have seen, though, that pictorial evidence can enlighten us about the common practice of an earlier time. It can help us to know what some of the conventional groupings of instruments were even if it does not show us all of them. The accuracy of the evidence must be tested partly by assessing the intention of the artist and partly by evaluating how well the evidence corresponds with what we know of the style of the music. Thus far, we have found that pictures that might be thought on purely art-historical grounds to reflect reality do in fact depict musicians playing instruments that can easily be made to fit the purely musical situations they are supposed to represent, and that correspondence is the best proof of the validity of using works of art as musicological evidence.

The question of the credibility of pictures arises surprisingly rarely. A case in point is the well-known early sixteenth-century tapestry probably made in Brussels about 1500 that seems to depict a group of courtiers entertaining themselves in the countryside (pl. 12).[55] Of the ten people shown, only seven hold musical instruments: three lutes, harp, dulcimer, rebec, and shawm. Four of them seem actually to be playing in a group of the sort we are now familiar with. I am fairly confident, in fact, that the rebec plays the superius, the lute tenor, and the harp and dulcimer the two contratenors. Nor do the remaining two lutes raise difficult issues, for their players may have used them in one of the various ways we have seen to be usual. But what of the shawm player? The shawm is not an instrument proper for a gentleman, nor would its raucous sound easily and obviously combine with any of the other instruments pictured. Perhaps the artist intended to represent all the ways of making a musical sound, by bowing, plucking, blowing, and strik-

Plate 12. Flemish tapestry, ca. 1500. Outdoor concert.
(Gew 813; Germanisches Nationalmuseum, Nürnberg.)

ing, and the picture ought to be interpreted as a purely symbolic combination.[56] And yet it seems to be a realistic portrayal of a scene from courtly life, much like the others. There can be no certainty, then, that a shawm did not occasionally mix its harsh voice with softer and gentler harps, lutes, and dulcimers.

More usually, of course, a treble shawm joined a tenor one and a trombone to form an ensemble for loud music—an *alta*, as Tinctoris call it.[57] A detailed discussion of this standard trio would lead us too far afield and would merely repeat the excellent studies by Besseler, Keith Polk, and others.[58] Polk's dissertation and his two articles constitute the most extensive treatment to date of the history of the Flemish wind band of the Renaissance, its composition, daily duties, and the manner in which its players learned to improvise over cantus firmi. But even Polk equivocates about the repertoire of the wind players over and above improvisations, even though he demonstrates convincingly that some minstrels at least could read mensural notation even in the fifteenth century and that printed or manuscript songbooks were used by wind bands in the sixteenth century.[59] His reluctance to admit that wind bands performed motets and chansons in addition to improvising *basses danses* over pre-existent tenors stems from the fact that the musicians are never shown in pictures playing from written music. But fifteenth-century works of art almost never depict instrumentalists of any sort reading from music books; it can scarcely be supposed, for example, that the courtiers and other well-born people shown playing chansons were all improvising, although they seldom play from music. Nor do later pictures include songbooks with wind bands, even though other evidence makes it abundantly clear that they were used.[60] In any case, the central issue does not involve the ability of the players to read mensural notation but rather whether or not they performed composed music as well as improvisations. Even musicians who are only semiliterate can absorb quite complicated compositions, as any honest teacher of opera singers today would probably admit. The accounts of the English wool merchant, George Cely, may well be revealing on this point.[61] During the two years he was in Calais, between 1473 and 1475, Cely paid a minstrel, Thomas Rede, to teach him both dancing and the harp. His record of payments is made according to the number of pieces he learned: for example, on October 22, 1474, he paid Rede seven shillings for having learned "to harpe xx daunsys," and on December 27 of the same year, Cely gave him five shillings "ffor myne fyngyryng and ffor myne tastying off the harpe and ffor myne hartys luste and offreschys fflour ii whayys." In the two years he studied with Rede, Cely learned forty dances, twenty-six on the harp and fourteen on the lute, as well as seven polyphonic chansons. His account books suggest that once he had mastered the elementary techniques of the instrument, he went to his teacher to learn pieces one by one, in order to build up a substantial repertoire. Once he had learned a piece, it would have mattered little whether or not he could read it. Perhaps that procedure was precisely the one followed by members of a wind band. Although Rede was a professional harpist, his own education would have been exactly like that of a shawm player; after apprenticeship to a master player, he was eventually admitted into the professional guild.[62] If Rede could teach a wool merchant how to play polyphonic chansons on the harp, presumably he was capable himself of playing them and other composed polyphonic compositions, whether or not he could read music. And if Rede played chansons on his harp, it is likely that such compositions were included, too, in the repertoires of wind bands, whether they were employed by a town, a prince, or some large organization like a guild or were formed into an independent unit that played whatever engagements the members could find. It seems likely, in short, that wind bands of the fifteenth century not only improvised over secular and sacred cantus firmi but also built up a repertoire of polyphonic compositions, motets, chansons, and perhaps even parts of Masses, which they could have used for concerts in the town square as well as at "banquets, nopces, et autres honnestes assemblées," as one of the commonest rubrics of the time reads.[63] Chansons, then, could have been transformed from soft and refined miniatures, played by lutes, harps, and recorders, into loud, boisterous pieces scored for a trio of wind instruments, the trombone playing the contratenor according to Tinctoris's description, and the two shawms playing the structural voices, superius and tenor.[64]

Played by loud wind bands, by soft chamber ensembles, or arranged for a solo instrumentalist, chansons thus could be adapted in a variety of ways to meet the needs of fifteenth-century musicians. Some combinations of instruments with or without voices seem to have become traditional—for example, lute and harp; lute and voice; lute, recorder, and voice; and two shawms and trombone. In a few cases, all the parts of a chanson were given equal weight in performance—when they were sung by voices a cappella, for example, or when they were played by a wind band. Most of these conventional groupings, however, were so arranged that one principal melody dominated the other parts, either because it was the only one sung, or because it was played by an instrument contrasting in timbre and method of tone production. Most often in the pictures the lowest lines were given to plucked or struck stringed instruments, while the superius was played by a wind. If the solo instrument did not differ markedly from its accompaniment, as in the pairing of lute and harp, attention was called to the principal melodic line by embellishing it profusely, if the fragmentary evidence can be trusted. Perhaps, then, the treble shawm player in a wind band also had this responsibility for enlivening his part.[65] Certainly, solo organists emphasized the superius by adding elaborate ornaments to it, as a number of musical sources demonstrate, and the intabulation technique of organists was presumably followed by solo harpists, and, late in the century, by solo lutenists playing without a plectrum. In these solo intabulations as well as in arrangements of chansons for two musicians, the contratenor could well be omitted without destroying anything essential to the composer's conception. And, finally, the pictures suggest that extensive doubling was by and large avoided, although we have seen several instances of instruments doubling solo voices and one traditional ensemble—of lute, voice, and recorder—in which one part would most probably have needed to be doubled in order to avoid an unmusical result. In short, even a brief survey of a relatively small number of pictures, used in conjunction with the fragmentary evidence supplied by the musical sources themselves, can be of valuable assistance in revealing the common practices of an age. These few examples doubtless do not exhaust the possibilities for combining voices with instruments in the performance of chansons, but they do bring us much closer to a precise notion of the limits of freedom available to a fifteenth-century musician.

Howard Mayer Brown

Notes

1. For lists of fifteenth- and early sixteenth-century *chansonniers*, see Eugénie Droz and Arthur Plaget, eds., *Le Jardin de plaisance et fleur de rhétorique*, 2 vols. (Paris: E. Champion, 1924), 2:105–109; Gustave Reese, *Music in the Renaissance*, 2d rev. ed. (New York: W. W. Norton and Co., 1954), pp. 97–101; and Howard Mayer Brown, *Music in the French Secular Theater: 1400–1550* (Cambridge, Mass.: Harvard University Press, 1963), pp. 285–293.

2. The classic general statement on the Burgundian chanson is still the introduction to Knud Jeppesen's edition of *Der Kopenhagener Chansonnier* (Copenhagen: Levin and Munksgaard, 1927), esp. pp. xxxvii–lxx. See also Martin Picker, ed., *The Chanson Albums of Marguerite of Austria* (Berkeley and Los Angeles: University of California Press, 1965), esp. pp. 58–97; and Howard Mayer Brown, "The Transformation of the Chanson at the End of the Fifteenth Century," in *Report of the Tenth Congress of the International Musicological Society, Ljubljana, 1967*, ed. Dragotin Cvetko (Kassel: Bärenreiter, 1970), pp. 78–94.

3. On text underlay, see Edward Lowinsky, "A Treatise on Text Underlay by a German Disciple of Francisco de Salinas," in *Festschrift Heinrich Besseler* (Leipzig: VEB Deutscher Verlag für Musik, 1961), pp. 231–251; idem, introduction to *Ottaviano Petrucci: Canti B numero ciquanta. Venice 1502*, ed. Helen Hewitt, Monuments of Renaissance Music, vol. 2 (Chicago and London: University of Chicago Press, 1967), pp. v–xvi; and Knud Jeppesen, "Die Textlegung in der Chansonmusik des späteren 15. Jahrhunderts," in *Beethovenzentenarfeir, Wien . . . Internationaler musikhistorischer Kongress* (Vienna: Universal Edition, 1927), pp. 155–157.

On musica ficta, see the various essays on the subject by Edward E. Lowinsky and especially his introduction to *Musica nova*, ed. H. Colin Slim, Monuments of Renaissance Music, vol. 1 (Chicago and London: University of Chicago Press, 1964), pp. v–xxi.

On instrumentation, see Curt Sachs, "Die Besetzung dreistimmiger Werke um das Jahr 1500," *Zeitschrift für Musikwissenschaft* 11 (1929): 386–389; Heinrich Besseler, "Die Besetzung der Chansons im 15. Jahrhundert," in *Report of the Fifth Congress of the International Society for Musical Research, Utrecht, 3–7 July 1952* (Amsterdam: G. Alsbach, 1953), pp. 65–78; Geneviève Thibault, "Le Concert instrumental au XVe siècle," in *La Musique instrumentale de la Renaissance*, ed. Jean Jacquot (Paris: Centre National de la Recherche Scientifique, 1955), pp. 23–33, and "Le Concert instrumental dans l'art flamand au XVe siècle et au début du XVIe," in *La Renaissance dans les provinces du nord*, ed. François Lesure (Paris: Centre National de la Recherche Scientifique, 1956), pp. 197–206. For a detailed discussion of somewhat later problems of instrumentation, see Howard Mayer Brown, *Sixteenth-Century Instrumentation: The Music for the Florentine Intermedii*, Musicological Studies and Documents (Rome: American Institute of Musicology, 1973).

4. On this point, see, for example, Jeppesen, *Der Kopenhagener Chansonnier*, pp. lxv–lxviii.

5. On the music at this banquet, see Jeanne Marix, *Histoire de la musique et des musiciens de la cour de Bourgogne sous le règne de Philippe le Bon (1420–1467)* (Strasbourg: Heitz and Co., 1939), pp. 37–43; and Edmund Bowles,

"Instruments at the Court of Burgundy (1363–1467),"
Galpin Society Journal 6 (1953): 41–51. The principal
source of their information is Mathieu d'Escouchy,
Chronique, ed. G. Du Fresne de Beaucourt, 3 vols. (Paris:
Société de l'histoire de France, 1863–1864), 1:346–355.

6. On this point, see Emanuel Winternitz, "The Visual Arts
as a Source for the Historian of Music" and "The Knowledge of Musical Instruments as an Aid to the Art Historian," in his *Musical Instruments and Their Symbolism
in Western Art* (New York: W. W. Norton and Co., 1967),
pp. 25–56; and Howard Mayer Brown and Joan Lascelle,
*Musical Iconography: A Manual for Cataloguing Musical
Subjects in Western Art before 1800* (Cambridge, Mass.:
Harvard University Press, 1972), pp. 1–12.

7. On musical angels, see especially Reinhold Hammerstein,
Die Musik der Engel (Bern and Munich: Francke Verlag,
1962), and Emanuel Winternitz, "On Angel Concerts in
the 15th Century: A Critical Approach to Realism and
Symbolism in Sacred Painting," *Musical Quarterly* 49
(1963): 450–463. See Sachs, "Die Besetzung," for an
uncritical treatment of angels.

8. Reproduced in Besseler, "Die Besetzung," pl. 8, and
"Umgangsmusik und Darbietungsmusik im 16. Jahrhundert," *Archiv für Musikwissenschaft* 16 (1959): pl. 2. I
shall normally cite a single readily available book as the
source for the works of art discussed in the following
pages.

9. Reproduced in Robert Wangermée, *La Musique flamande
dans la société des XVᵉ et XVIᵉ siècles* (Brussels: Editions
Arcade, 1965), pl. 40, and discussed in Besseler, "Die
Besetzung," pp. 68–69, and "Umgangsmusik," pp. 27–
28; and P. Post, "Ein verschollenes Jagdbild Jan van
Eycks," *Jahrbuch der preussischen Kunstsammlungen*
52 (1931): 120–132.

10. For instance, the painting of the prodigal son in the style
of the sixteenth-century Flemish painter, Ambrosius
Benson, reproduced in Georges Marlier, *Ambrosius Benson et la peinture à Bruges au temps de Charles-Quint*
(Damme: Musée van Maerlant, 1957), p. 64, catalogue

no. 167, seems to depict reality. It is related to a number of paintings by Benson and his followers, reproduced by Marlier, which show informal music making after meals.

For an example of Herod's feast with apparently realistic musical details, see the woodcut by Hans Sebald Beham, reproduced in George R. Kernodle, *From Art to Theatre* (Chicago and London: University of Chicago Press, 1944), fig. 41, p. 113.

11. Gardens of love are discussed below, n. 27. For examples of music associated with the planets and that seem to show reality, see the series of woodcuts by Barthel Beham or Hans Sebald Beham reproduced in Anna C. Hoyt, "The Woodcuts of the Planets Formerly Attributed to Hans Sebald Beham," *Bulletin of the Museum of Fine Arts, Boston* 52 (1954): 2-10.

12. Besseler, "Die Besetzung," pp. 68-70, and "Umgangsmusik," p. 28. Binchois's *Files a marier* is printed in *Die Chansons von Gilles Binchois (1400-1460)*, ed. Wolfgang Rehm, Musikalische Denkmäler, vol. 2 (Mainz: B. Schott's Söhne, 1957), piece 55, p. 52.

The instrumental equivalent of the a cappella ensemble was the unmixed consort. For evidence of the use of such consorts in the fifteenth century, see Keith Polk, "Municipal Wind Music in Flanders in the Late Middle Ages," *Brass and Woodwind Quarterly* 2 (1969): 3.

13. The Fountain of Youth appears in Modena, Biblioteca Estense, MS lat. 209 (α.X.2.14), fol. 9, which is a manuscript copy of Johannes da Sacrobosco, *De Sphaera*, illuminated by a painter of the Lombard school, possibly Cristoforo de Predis. It is reproduced in Wangermée, *Musique flamande*, pl. 84; François Lesure, *Musik und Gesellschaft im Bild* (Kassel: Bärenreiter, 1966), pl. 43, and *Music and Art in Society*, trans. Denis and Sheila Stevens (University Park and London: Pennsylvania State University Press, 1968), pl. 37; and S. Samek Ludovici, *Il "De Sphaera" Estense e l'iconografia astrologica* (Milan: Aldo Martello Editore, n.d.), pl. 11.

For another example of secular a cappella singing, see the sixteenth-century Flemish tapestry reproduced in Besseler, "Die Besetzung," pl. 10.

14. Guillaume Dufay, *Opera omnia*, ed. Heinrich Besseler, 6 vols. (Rome: American Institute of Musicology, 1947–1964), 6:108. As well as adding text to the lower voices, I have also slightly changed Besseler's texting of the superius.

15. Reproduced in Wangermée, *Musique flamande*, pl. 45.

16. Reproduced in ibid., pl. 74. It is, of course, not clear that the lady could play more than one voice at a time on her portative organ. Another solo organist likely to be playing intabulated chansons is shown in one panel of the Unicorn Tapestries, now in Paris, Musée de Cluny, reproduced in Paul Collaer and Albert Van der Linden, *Atlas historique de la musique* (n.p.: Editions Meddens, n.d.), no. 195.

17. On the Faenza Codex, see Dragan Plamenac, "Keyboard Music of the 14th Century in Codex Faenza 117," *Journal of the American Musicological Society* 4 (1951): 179–201, and "New Light on Codex Faenza 117," *Report of the Fifth Congress of the International Society for Musical Research, Utrecht, 3–7 July 1952* (Amsterdam: G. Alsbach, 1953), pp. 310–326. The manuscript is reproduced in facsimile in *An Early Fifteenth-Century Italian Source of Keyboard Music*, ed. Armen Carapetyan, Musicological Studies and Documents, vol. 10 (Rome: American Institute of Musicology, 1961).

The Buxheim Organ Book is reproduced in facsimile in *Das Buxheimer Orgelbuch*, ed. Bertha Antonia Wallner, Documenta Musicologica, Second Series, vol. 1 (Kassel: Bärenreiter, 1955), and in modern transcription in *Das Buxheimer Orgelbuch*, ed. Bertha Antonia Wallner, Das Erbe deutscher Musik, vols. 37–39 (Kassel: Barenreiter, 1958–1959). For a study of the manuscript, see Eileen Southern, *The Buxheim Organ Book* (Brooklyn: Institute of Medieval Music, 1963).

All the smaller German keyboard manuscripts of the fifteenth century have been published in modern editions in Willi Apel, ed., *Keyboard Music of the Fourteenth and Fifteenth Centuries*, Corpus of Early Keyboard Music, vol. 1 (Rome: American Institute of Musicology, 1963). See also Theodor Göllner, "Notationsfragmente aus einer Organistenwerkstatt des 15. Jahrhunderts," *Archiv für*

Musikwissenschaft 24 (1967): 170–177, which deals
with a fifteenth-century fragment that includes an intabulation of a Dufay chanson.

18. The chanson is printed in Dufay, *Opera omnia*, 6:88–89,
    and the intabulation in *Buxheimer Orgelbuch*, ed. Wallner,
    37:24–25. I have doubled the time values of Besseler's
    edition in order to facilitate comparison with the intabu-
    lation.
    Some of the arrangements in the Buxheim Organ Book
    are much less literal than this example and depart from
    the original structure for entire passages.

19. Arrangements of chansons for solo harp and for solo lute
    are discussed below. On fifteenth-century clavichords,
    see Edwin M. Ripin, "The Early Clavichord," *Musical
    Quarterly* 53 (1967): 518–538, which includes a list of
    representations of the instrument in works of art. Fif-
    teenth-century musicians may also have arranged chan-
    sons for solo harpsichord or virginals.

20. For another example of a solo harpist in a secular con-
    text, see the illustration from a manuscript copy of
    Boccaccio's *De claris mulieribus* now in the Spencer Col-
    lection of the New York Public Library, showing the
    poetess Sappho; it is reproduced in the pamphlet *The Li-
    brary and Museum of the Performing Arts at Lincoln
    Center* (New York: n.d.), p. 11.

21. The tapestry is reproduced in Wangermée, *Musique fla-
    mande*, pl. 38. Pierre Des Molin's *De ce que fol pense* is
    printed in Eugénie Droz and Geneviève Thibault, eds.,
    Poètes et musiciens du XVe siècle (Paris: G. Jeanbin,
    1924), pp. 21–24.

22. A setting of Binchois's *Je loe amours* in the Buxheim
    Organ Book (*Buxheimer Orgelbuch*, ed. Wallner, 37:14–
    15) is intended either for harp or organ, since it is marked
    "in cytaris vel etiam in organis." It is indistinguishable
    in style from the other intabulations. That *cythara* (and
    its variant spellings) means "harp" is suggested by the
    fact that Pierre Attaingnant's address in the rue de la
    Harpe, Paris, is given as "in vico cythare" on the Latin
    title page of Oronce Finé's *Epithoma musice instrumen-*

talis (Paris: Pierre Attaingnant, 1530); and that Ottomar Luscinius's Latin translation (*Musurgia seu praxis Musicae* [Strasbourg: Johannes Schottus, 1536]) of Sebastian Virdung's *Musica getutscht* (Basel, 1511) labels the harp (p. 12) a *cythara*.

23. On the technique of playing the lute in about 1500, see *Report of the Eighth Congress of the International Musicological Society, New York, 1961*, ed. Jan La Rue, 2 vols. (Kassel: Bärenreiter, 1962), 2:72–76, and especially Daniel Heartz's opening remarks (note, however, that Heartz considers the composition cited in n. 22 above to be for lute or organ).

24. See Karl Weinmann, *Johannes Tinctoris (1445–1511) und sein unbekannter Traktat "De inventione et usu musicae"* (Tutzing: Hans Schneider, 1961), p. 45; and Anthony Baines, "Fifteenth-Century Instruments in Tinctoris' 'De inventione et usu musicae,' " *Galpin Society Journal* 3 (1950): 24.

25. Weinmann, *Tinctoris*, p. 45, and Baines "Fifteenth-Century Instruments," p. 24.

26. This manuscript, bound together with a printed copy of Pietro Borgi's *Chi de arte matematiche ha piacere* (Venice, 1484), is mentioned briefly in Walter Rubsamen, "The Earliest French Lute Tablature," *Journal of the American Musicological Society* 21 (1968): 299, and in Brown, *Sixteenth-Century Instrumentation*, pp. 41–42. Miss Elinore L. Barber of the Riemenschneider Bach Institute, Berea, Ohio, informs me that she will publish a more detailed description of the manuscript in a volume of essays by Hans T. David, left unfinished at the time of his death, which she is now editing.

Further examples of fifteenth-century pictures showing solo lutenists in a context suggesting they might be playing chansons are reproduced in George Kinsky, *Album musical* (Paris: Librairie Delagrave, 1930), no. 1, p. 63; Lesure, *Musik und Gesellschaft*, pl. 7, and *Music and Art in Society*, pl. 7; and *Le Siècle d'or de la miniature flamande: Le Mecenat de Philippe le Bon* (Brussels: Palais des Beaux-arts; Amsterdam: Rijksmuseum, 1959), no. 34, pl. 17.

Further examples of fifteenth-century pictures showing apparent combinations of lute and voice are reproduced in Hermann Ruth-Sommer, *Alte Musikinstrumente*
(Berlin: Richard Carl Schmidt, 1916), pl. 117, p. 173;
Max Lehrs, ed., *Late Gothic Engravings of Germany and
the Netherlands* (New York: Dover, 1969), no. 534; and
Kernodle, *Art to Theatre*, pl. 41.

Besides keyboards, harps, and lutes, several other fifteenth-century instruments were capable of playing more
than one line, for example, the dulcimer or psaltery and
the *lira da braccio*. The dulcimer is discussed briefly below. The *lira da braccio* was so closely identified in the
fifteenth century with Italian court improvisers and the
recitation of epics and other Italian poetry that it very
likely was not used for chansons.

Several common instruments, capable of playing a melodic line and a drone, might, however, have sometimes
played chansons in primitive arrangements. See, for example, the fool who serenades his ladylove with a solo
bagpipe in Sebastian Brant's *Ship of Fools*, trans. Edwin
H. Zeydel (New York: Dover, 1944), p. 186 (also reproduced, among other places, in Alfons Ott, *Tausend Jahre
Musikleben, 800–1800* [Munich: Prestel Verlag, 1963],
p. 11); and the knight, Girart de Nevers, who plays an
organistrum (labeled in the manuscript, "vyole") at a
large banquet in an illuminated Flemish manuscript (Brussels, Bibliothèque royale, MS 9631) of about 1467, containing the Roman de Girart de Nevers, reproduced in
*Bruxelles. Bibliothèque royale de Belgique. Section des
manuscrits (Bibliothèque de Bourgogne). Miniatures
médiévales*, commentaries by L. M. J. Delaissé (Brussels:
Editions de la connaissance, n.d.), pl. 43.

27. Reproduced in Lehrs, *Gothic Engravings*, no. 102. The
    engraving and the tradition of gardens of love are dis-
    cussed in Gustav Glück, *Rubens, Van Dyk und ihr Kreis*
    (Vienna: Anton Schroll, 1933), pp. 82–90, and the
    print is reproduced there, p. 84.

28. Reproduced in Wangermée, *Musique flamande*, pl. 41.

29. Reproduced in Lehrs, *Gothic Engravings*, no. 493.

30. Reproduced in Max J. Friedländer, *From Van Eyck to Bruegel*, ed. F. Grossmann, vol. 1, *The Fifteenth Century* (London: Phaidon, 1956), pl. 152. For another example of one lute and several voices, see a woodcut by Michael Wolgemut and Wilhelm Pleydenwurff from Hartmann Schedel's *Weltchronik* (Nuremberg: Anton Koberger, 1493), reproduced in Sir Frank Crisp, *Mediaeval Gardens* (1924; reprint ed., New York, 1966), pl. 127.

31. This scene from London, British Museum, MS Harley 4425, fol. 12, is reproduced in Lesure, *Musik und Gesellschaft*, pl. 5, and *Music and Art in Society*, pl. 5; Wangermée, *Musique flamande*, pl. 44; and Hewitt, ed., *Ottaviano Petrucci*, pl. 7.

32. Further fifteenth-century examples of the combination of lute and harp in secular contexts may be found in Crisp, *Mediaeval Gardens*, pls. 110, 131, 191, and 208a; Kinsky, *Album*, no. 4, p. 62; *Musica 1969: Ein Kunstkalender für Musikfreunde* (Kassel: Bärenreiter, 1968), week of September 7; Richard Muther, *Die deutsche Bücherillustration der Gothik und Frührenaissance (1460–1530)*, 2 vols. (Munich and Leipzig: G. Hirth, 1884), vol. 1, pl. 34; János Végh, *Fifteenth-Century German and Bohemian Panel Paintings* (Budapest: Corvina Press, 1967), pls. 27–28; Fritz Saxl and Hans Meier, *Catalogue of Astrological and Mythological Illuminated Manuscripts of the Middle Ages*, vol. 3, *Manuscripts in English Libraries* (London, 1953), fig. 227; and in the Minneapolis Institute of Arts, no. 16.721 (a Flemish tapestry showing the Feast of Ahasuerus).

33. The scene is reproduced in Droz and Thibault, *Poètes et musiciens*, opposite p. 55, and Wangermée, *Musique flamande*, pl. 10. The same scene in a late fifteenth-century manuscript decorated by Jean Wavrin (Brussels, Bibliothèque royale, MS 9632–9633) is reproduced in Wangermée, *Musique flamande*, pl. 39, and Collaer and Van der Linden, *Atlas*, no. 185.

34. Robert Kaltenbach, "Der altfranzösische Roman Paris et Vienne," *Romanische Forschungen* 15 (1904): 397, reads: "Souventes foiz Paris et Edardo aloient de nuyt soubz la chanbre de Vienne, faisant aubades de leurs

Howard Mayer Brown

chanssons, quar ilz chantoient souveraynement bien, et puys jouoyent de leur instrumens chanssons mellodyoses, comme ceulx qui de celluy mestier estoient les maistres." Nowhere in the romance does the author mention specific instruments.

35. Francesco Spinacino, *Intabulatura de Lauto: Libro primo* (Venice: Ottaviano Petrucci, 1507). The volume is described and the contents listed in Howard Mayer Brown, *Instrumental Music Printed before 1600* (Cambridge, Mass.: Harvard University Press, 1965), pp. 12–13.

36. The intabulation appears in Spinacino, *Intabulatura*, no. 11, fol. 21. The edition of the vocal original is made from Florence, Biblioteca Nationale Centrale, MS Magl. XIX, 59 (Banco rari 229), fol. 54^V. A slightly different version appears in Helen Hewitt, ed., *Harmonice Musices Odhecaton A* (Cambridge, Mass.: Medieval Academy of America, 1942), no. 8.

37. See, for example, the illustration in Wangermée, *Musique flamande*, pl. 73.

38. For example, in the Flemish sixteenth-century tapestry called *The Bath* from the series illustrating scenes of courtly life, now in Paris, Musée de Cluny; the tapestry is reproduced in Dorothy G. Shepherd, "Three Tapestries from Chaumont," *Cleveland Museum of Art Bulletin* 48 (1961): fig. 6. The combination of lute and double recorder appears in an illustration in Alexander Buchner, *Musical Instruments through the Ages* (London: Batchworth Press, 1961), no. 137.

39. For example, in a French sixteenth-century tapestry now in Paris, Musée du Louvre, called *The Concert* and reproduced in *La Tapisserie française du moyen age à nos jours. Palais des Beaux-Arts. Bruxelles, janvier–fevrier 1947* (Brussels: Editions de la Connaissance, 1947), fig. 27. The fact that the dulcimer is played with two hammers suggests that it could play two voices of a polyphonic composition. In a late fifteenth-century French manuscript of Boccaccio's *Filostrato* (Paris, Bibliothèque nationale, MS fonds fr. 25528), one scene shows a group of ladies entertaining a knight in an effort to overcome

his melancholy (on fol. 85^V, reproduced in Lesure, *Musik und Gesellschaft*, pl. 60, and *Music in Art and Society*, pl. 53). Two of the ladies play dulcimer and harp, both instruments capable of playing more than one line. It is not clear, then, which would more naturally have taken the superius. If one or more of the ladies were singing, the two instruments would have played the lower lines.

40. For example, in the engraving by Lucas van Leyden reproduced in the *Cleveland Museum of Art Bulletin* 18 (1931): opposite p. 22.

41. For example, in the fifteenth-century German tapestry in Nuremberg, Germanisches Nationalmuseum, showing the feast of the prodigal son, illustrated in *Musica 1967: Ein Kunstkalender für Musikfreunde* (Kassel: Bärenreiter, 1966), week of January 1.

42. For example, in Baltimore, Walters Art Gallery, MS 219, fol. 86^V, reproduced in *Illustrated Books of the Middle Ages and Renaissance: An Exhibition Held at the Baltimore Museum of Art* (Baltimore: Walters Art Gallery, 1949), no. 87, pl. 38.

43. Besides the boating parties discussed in the following paragraph, see also the one shown in a Book of Hours of about 1515 (New York, Pierpont Morgan Library, MS 399 ["Da Costa Hours"], fol. 6^V), reproduced in *Treasures from the Pierpont Morgan Library: Fiftieth Anniversary Exhibition* (New York: Pierpont Morgan Library, 1957), no. 41, pl. 33; and the one shown in an early sixteenth-century hours, the so-called Golf Book (London, British Museum, MS Add. 24098, fol. 22^V), reproduced in *Miniatures and Borders from a Flemish Horae, British Museum Add. Ms. 24098, Early Sixteenth Century, Reproduced in Honour of Sir George Warner* (London, 1911), pl. 26 and color pl. II. Both miniatures show a combination of voice, lute, and recorder.

44. Brussels, Bibliothèque royale, MS II.158, fol. 5^V, reproduced in Wangermée, *Musique flamande*, pl. 46.

45. Brussels, Bibliothèque royale, MS IV.90, fol. 11^V, reproduced in Wangermée, *Musique flamande*, pl. 47. On the

Tournai Chansonnier, see Charles van den Borren, "Inventaire des manuscrits de musique polyphonique qui se trouvent en Belgique," *Acta musicologica* 6 (1934): 119–121; and Paul Faider and Abbé Pierre van Sint Jan, *Catalogue des manuscrits conservés à Tournai (Bibliothèques de la ville et du Séminaire)* (Gembloux: J. Duculot, 1950), p. 96.

46. See Michael Praetorius, *Syntagma Musicum*, vol. 2, *De organographia* (Wolfenbüttel: Elias Holwein, 1619; facsimile ed. Wilibald Gurlitt [Kassel: Bärenreiter, 1958]), p. 21; and the English translation of the section on instruments by Harold Blumenfeld (New York: Bärenreiter, 1962), p. 21. See also the brief discussion of the effects of this transposition in Brown, *Sixteenth-Century Instrumentation*, p. 66.

47. On this painting, see John A. Parkinson, "A Chanson by Claudin de Sermisy," *Music and Letters* 39 (1958): 118–122.

48. Among other places, Giorgione's *fête champêtre* is reproduced in Lesure, *Musik und Gesellschaft*, pl. 3, and *Music and Art in Society*, pl. 3. On the music in the painting as symbol, see Patricia Egan, "*Poesia* and the *Fête Champêtre*," *Art Bulletin* 41 (1959): 303–313.

49. The early sixteenth-century Flemish tapestry *The Court of Love*, reproduced as pl. 10, is in the Cleveland Museum of Art.

50. In a fifteenth-century tapestry, *Condamnacion de Banquet*, which once belonged to Charles the Bold of Burgundy. It is reproduced in Michel Louis Achille Jubinal, *Les Anciennes Tapisseries historiées, ou collection des monumens les plus remarquables de ce genre* (Paris, 1838), pl. 2. Three instruments—pipe and tabor, recorder, and harp—are shown in an early sixteenth-century manuscript edition of Petrarch (Paris, Bibliothèque nationale, MS fonds fr. 225), reproduced in Georges Ritter and Jean Lafond, eds., *Manuscrits à peintures de l'école de Rouen: Livres d'heures normand* (Paris, 1913), pl. 18. Aristocratic ladies hold two lutes and two recorders in the well-known fresco by Francesco Cossa in the Palazzo

Schifanoia in Ferrara that depicts the month of April and the triumph of Venus; it is reproduced in Besseler, "Umgangsmusik," pl. 5. And two men sing while three play instruments for an outdoor serenade in Brant, *Ship of Fools*, p. 206.

51. Reproduced, among other places, in André Chastel, *The Age of Humanism: Europe 1480-1530* (New York: McGraw-Hill, 1963), pl. 36.

52. Vatican City, Biblioteca Apostolica Vaticana, MS Chigi C.VIII.234, fols. 3^V-4, reproduced in Johannes Ockeghem, *Collected Works*, ed. Dragan Plamenac, vol. 2, *Masses and Mass Sections IX-XVI*, 2d corr. ed. (Rome: American Musicological Society, 1966), pl. 1.

53. For reproductions, see n. 8 above.

54. The translation is taken from Baines, "Fifteenth-Century Instruments," pp. 24-25; see also Weinmann, *Tinctoris*, pp. 45-46.

55. The tapestry is in Nuremberg, Germanisches Nationalmuseum. It is reproduced in Wangermée, *Musique flamande*, pl. 1, and Ott, *Tausend Jahre*, pls. 21-22.

56. From at least the time of Boethius, *musica instrumentalis* was often defined by theorists according to the ways sound is produced. See, for example, Boethius's and Cassiodorus's explanations of sounds produced by tension (as in strings), by blowing, and by percussion, in Oliver Strunk, *Source Readings in Music History* (New York: W. W. Norton and Co., 1950), pp. 85 and 89.

57. Weinmann, *Tinctoris*, p. 37, and Baines, "Fifteenth-Century Instruments," p. 21.

58. Heinrich Besseler, "Die Entstehung der Posaune," *Acta musicologica* 22 (1950): 8-35; Keith Polk, "Flemish Wind Bands in the Late Middle Ages: A Study of Improvisatory Instrumental Practices" (Ph.D. diss., University of California at Berkeley, 1968), "Wind Bands of Medieval Flemish Cities," *Brass and Woodwind Quarterly* 1 (1968): 93-113, and "Municipal Wind Music in Flanders

in the Late Middle Ages," *Brass and Woodwind Quarterly* 2 (1969): 1-15.

59. Polk, "Municipal Wind Music," pp. 13-15.

60. For sixteenth- and seventeenth-century pictures of instrumentalists playing without music, see, for example, Lesure, *Musik und Gesellschaft*, pls. 12, 14, 16, 19, 31, 41, 44, 45, 47, 65, 66, and 68, and *Music and Art in Society*, pls. 10, 12, 14, 17, 29, 36, 38, 39, 41, 58, and 60. In fact, throughout the fifteenth and sixteenth centuries instrumentalists are more often shown without music than are singers.

61. See Alison Hanam, "The Musical Studies of a Fifteenth-Century Wool Merchant," *Review of English Studies*, n.s. 8 (1957): 270-274.

62. On the guild system in France, see B. Bernhard, "Recherches sur l'histoire de la corporation des ménétriers ou joueurs d'instruments de la ville de Paris," *Bibliothèque de l'école des chartes*, 1st ser. 3 (1841-1842): 377-404; 4 (1842-1843): 525-548; 5 (1843): 254-284; and 5 (1844): 339-372; and François Lesure, "La Communauté des 'joueurs d'instruments' au XVIᵉ siècle," *Revue historique de droit français et étranger*, 4th ser. 31 (1953): 79-109.

63. For examples of this rubric, see Lesure, "Communauté," pp. 101 and 108; and Brown, *French Secular Theater*, p. 76.

64. See Baines, "Fifteenth-Century Instruments," p. 21, and Weinmann, *Tinctoris*, p. 37.

65. That was true in the late sixteenth century in Spain, according to a notice from Seville dated 1586, published in Robert Stevenson, *Spanish Cathedral Music* (Berkeley and Los Angeles: University of California Press, 1961), p. 167.

Nottebohm Revisited
Lewis Lockwood

Five

The reputation of Gustav Nottebohm (1817–1882) as a pioneer of nineteenth-century musicology rests fundamentally on his role as a Beethoven scholar.[1] More than any other figure in the early decades of serious musicological studies, Nottebohm is now regarded as a specialist in matters of text criticism and detail rather than those of broad historical sweep. He was a man devoted to editorial labors in the service of the complete editions of Bach, Beethoven, Mozart, and Mendelssohn, to the compilation of thematic catalogues (especially for Beethoven but also for Schubert and Mendelssohn), to close textual and historical studies of individual works by Beethoven, and, above all, to the decipherment of the Beethoven sketches. Because his Beethoven studies have clearly and deservedly attracted more attention than his other work, the commonly accepted portrait is too narrow to do justice to his breadth of interests or to the remarkable musical preparation that Nottebohm brought to his scholarly work. In an age in which specialization often seems to be regarded as not merely a necessary but a sufficient condition of scholarly achievement, a brief glance at Nottebohm's development may be of value.

Born in Westphalia (he remained a fervent North German patriot all his life), Nottebohm studied piano in Berlin with Ludwig Berger beginning in 1838 and had lessons in composition there with Siegfried Dehn.[2] From Berlin he went to Leipzig in the early 1840's, where his composing and performing ability attracted the favorable attentions of Mendelssohn and Schumann. In 1846 he transferred to Vienna, where he remained for the rest of his life, earning his living principally as a teacher of theory and of piano while achieving a growing reputation as a scholar. More formal activity was evidently uncongenial: in 1864 he was appointed librarian and archivist of the Gesellschaft der Musikfreunde, but a year later he gave up the position in favor of C. F. Pohl, the Haydn scholar. During the last twenty years of his life Nottebohm was on close personal terms with Brahms, who cordially admired him as both musician and scholar, recommended theory pupils to him, and helped to arrange for the publication of his essays in book form beginning in 1870. Brahms wrote to the publisher Rieter-Biedermann in October 1870, "I am no scholar, and I should not attach my recommendation to Nottebohm's work. . . . But you may be certain that it is the result of immense industry and will be of the highest interest to artists, connoisseurs, and amateurs."[3] Six years earlier, in a letter to Adolf Schubring dated January 17, 1864, Brahms had said of Nottebohm, "His seriousness, his thorough knowledge, and his quiet industry give me joyful recollections of North German friends and musicians."[4]

Nottebohm's role in musical circles in Vienna from the early 1860's until his death in 1882 was much more independent than that of many of the *Liebhaber* around Brahms who lacked serious intellectual purposes of their own. Although his compositions were evidently all written early in his career and are now largely lost to view, they ran to seventeen published works bearing opus numbers, besides others that were unpublished. Among them was a set of Variations on a Theme by Bach for piano four hands (his op. 17) that was admired by Clara Schumann and also by Brahms, who is said to have played them with Nottebohm in private musical sessions. In later years Nottebohm seems to have become increasingly misanthropic and irascible in the eyes of his Viennese contemporaries. If the anecdotes reported by Max Kalbeck are reliable, they would fit in with the impression created in Nottebohm's essays by the absence of virtually all reference to the exact location of his sources; Nottebohm rarely goes beyond a general indication of the library in which a source might be found and often omits even this.[5] It is only with full awareness of Nottebohm's reputation as a thorny and difficult personality that one can sense the irony in a letter from Joseph Joachim to Brahms of 1874, in which Joachim writes, "Grüsse unsern jovialen Beethoven-Freund herzlich von mir."[6]

Even putting aside the Beethoven essays, thematic catalogues, and *Gesamtausgabe* volumes, Nottebohm's other published writings show a broader range than is commonly realized. They include a historical essay entitled "Über die Suite,"[7] a valuable essay on Bach's *Art of the Fugue*[8] and several essays on Mozart, as well as the documentary collection issued as *Mozartiana* (Leipzig, 1880). Nottebohm also wrote the preface to the 1881 edition of volume four of August Wilhelm Ambros's *Geschichte der Musik*, first brought out in 1878 after Ambros's death.[9]

But the core of Nottebohm's work is clearly Beethoven, and the basic publications that call for renewed examination and for careful scrutiny are, of course, primarily his studies of the Beethoven sketches. To put these in chronological order is to come swiftly to the main problem that will be discussed in this paper—the publishing history of his collected essays on Beethoven and the discrepancies between their earlier and later published versions.

A list of the main writings is first. Still controversial is the traditional attribution to Nottebohm of the *Thematisches Verzeichnis der im Druck erschienenen Werke Ludwig van Beethovens*, brought out in 1851 by Breitkopf and Härtel without the name of its compiler.[10] This first attempt at a thematic catalogue was followed in 1865 by Alexander Thayer's attempt to establish not only the Beethoven canon but also its chronology in a single reference work, his *Chronologisches Verzeichnis* of 1865.[11] In turn, this was followed by Nottebohm's thematic catalogue of the published works, issued in 1868 by Breitkopf as *Zweite, vermehrte Auflage* ("second and enlarged edition"—in relation to the one of 1851 and now explicitly and unquestionably by Nottebohm). This monumental catalogue remained the standard reference work of its kind until the appearance of Georg Kinsky and Hans Halm's *Das Werk Beethovens* in 1955. In 1861, Nottebohm was engaged to take on an important collaborative role in the editorial work that would lead to the first and still standard edition of Beethoven's work—the Breitkopf and Härtel edition of *Beethovens Werke* that was produced in twenty-four series within the short span of 1862–1865 (to which was later added the single supplement volume of 1888).[12]

The period from 1865 to 1880 saw the steady production of his major essays on aspects of Beethoven:[13]

N 65   *Ein Skizzenbuch von Beethoven: Beschrie-*
1865   *ben und in Auszügen dargestellt.* Leipzig:
          Breitkopf and Härtel, 1865. 43 pp. A de-

scription of the "Kessler" sketchbook of 1801-1802, with selected passages in transcription.

AmZ
1869-1871
Essays in the *Allgemeine musikalische Zeitung*, vols. 4-6 (1869-1871), published under the title *Beethoveniana*. These were later published in N I (see below) in a different order, some of them in revised form. A complete list of these essays as published in the *AmZ* is given in table 1.

N I
1872
Beethoveniana: Aufsätze und Mittheilungen. Leipzig and Winterthur: J. Rieter-Biedermann, 1872. 203 pp.[14]

Studien
1873
Beethovens Studien. Erster Band. Beethovens Unterricht bei J. Haydn, Albrechtsberger und Salieri. Nach den Original-Manuscripten dargestellt von Gustav Nottebohm. Leipzig and Winterthur: J. Rieter-Biedermann, 1873. 232 pp. Although this volume is entitled *Erster Band*, a second, which would have dealt with Beethoven's teaching, never appeared.[15]

MW
1875-1879
Essays on Beethoven in the *Musikalisches Wochenblatt*, vols. 6-10 (1875-1879). These were incorporated into N II. A complete list of these essays is given in table 2.

N 80
1880
Ein Skizzenbuch aus dem Jahr 1803. Leipzig: Breitkopf and Härtel, 1880. 80 pp. A description of the "Eroica" sketchbook, (formerly Berlin Preussiche Staatsbibliothek, MS Landsberg 6; lost since 1945).

N II
1887
Zweite Beethoveniana: Nachgelassene Aufsätze von Gustav Nottebohm. Leipzig: J. Rieter-Biedermann, 1887. 590 pp. Prefatory note by Eusebius Mandyczewski.

To evaluate these publications, it is essential to realize that N II, which was the largest collection of his essays and included the majority of his articles dealing with the sketchbooks, was edited after Nottebohm's death by Eusebius Mandyczewski, who had been a theory pupil of Nottebohm's and in the year of publication, 1887, succeeded Pohl as archivist of the Gesellschaft der Musikfreunde.[16] It should be clearly understood, too, that the two monographs dealing with individual sketchbooks (N 65 and N 80) had not been previously serialized when they were issued as separate volumes. On the other hand, N I and N II were largely made up of previously published articles. The twenty-nine essays brought out in 1872 under the title *Beethoveniana* begin with a preface by Nottebohm explaining that all except one (item XXIII) had previously appeared in periodicals: essays I through XXII and XXIV–XXVII had been printed in the *AmZ* of 1869–1871; essay XVII in the "Presse" of February 13, 1868 (and also in *AmZ* 5); and essay XXIX in the *AmZ* of 1863–1864. It also mentions that they had been revised to some extent by Nottebohm himself for the 1872 volume.[17] The essays in N I are for the most part concise discussions of a variety of textual and historical problems in individual works; the first twenty are arranged in the volume in ascending order of opus number (essay I on op. 20, essay XX on op. 138), while nine articles on special subjects are grouped at the end in no apparent order.

The texts of several essays in N I differ somewhat from the versions published in the *AmZ* volumes four to six of 1869–1871 (and of 1863 for essay XXIX), but these discrepancies can presumably be attributed to Nottebohm's own hand. In many cases they consist only of minor changes in wording, but a few are more substantial and more drastic. For instance, in N I, essay VII is expanded, while XX is contracted and has some of its material transposed; in XXIV the text is rearranged. More important are certain revealing shifts of meaning or emphasis, even when only a single sentence is involved. Thus, in N I, essay XI (on a textual problem in the D-Major Violoncello Sonata op. 102, no. 2), the *AmZ* version evaluates the importance of the autograph for this passage in these words: "Es ist aber die Frage ob das Autograph massgebend sein kann" ("The question remains open whether the autograph version is authoritative here"), but in N I (p. 31) the sentence reads, "Ueberhaupt kann das Autograph im vorliegenden Falle nicht massgebend sein ("On the whole, the autograph in the present instance cannot be authoritative"). Evidently he had changed his mind between 1869 and 1872.

The music examples in N I contain a number of changes that show Nottebohm's reinterpretation of earlier transcriptions as well as the addition of more extensive examples in certain essays in the N I versions. Added examples are found in essays V, XXIII, XXIV, and XXV, and changes in particular readings in N I are shown in examples 1, 2, and 3. Striking in the last of these, from a sketch for Florestan's great second-act aria in *Fidelio*, is the removal of the parenthetical question mark that appears in the *AmZ* version.

But while few essays in N I deal with sketches, the much larger mass of material in N II is centrally concerned with description of sketchbooks and presentation of sketches as preliminary stages of well-known works. Its sixty-five essays are arranged in a much more complex pattern than those of N I, and even their ordering raises questions about the editorial role of Mandyczewski. While item I deals with six sketchbooklets of 1825–1826 and item II with sketches for the overture *Zur Namensfeier* op. 115, the next larger groups of articles follow fairly clear patterns: articles III–XXII deal with individual works (principally their sketches) in order of opus number from op. 1 to op. 125; articles XXIII–XXVI deal with lost or unfinished works; articles XXVII–XXXVI deal with selected sketchbooks in chronological order from 1800 to 1817 (Nottebohm's dates); articles XXXVII–XXXVIII deal with biographical matters; and articles XXXIX–LXV deal in random order with sketches for various works but not taken in any discernible order; these are interspersed by an essay on metronome markings (LII) and one on the draft of a letter of 1825 (LXIV).

It is as if articles III through XXXVI represent an established order that was abandoned for the last twenty-nine articles, even though it could have been used for the remainder of the volume. One likely reason for this is provided by the explicit correlation between the first part of N II and the antecedent versions in *MW*, 1875–1879. A tabulation shows that the first forty-one articles in N II are indeed derived from *MW* versions but that the remaining articles of N II had not been so derived. Mandyczewski himself states in his preface that the articles I–

Lewis Lockwood

XLII were previously published in *MW* (and that XLIII had appeared in the *AmZ* of 1873), but he says nothing about the rest; one must infer that they were simply a part of the unpublished *Nachlass*. Mandyczewski may well have found the earlier group of articles already arranged by Nottebohm for possible publication in collected form, but without the others; this inference is strengthened by Mandyczewski's remark that the articles previously published are now found in N II "in altered and extended form."[18] If Nottebohm himself had revised them, there was ample time for him to have done so between 1879, when the last item of his *MW* series appeared in print, and his death on October 29, 1882.

We are now in a position to evaluate the discrepancies in text and especially in music examples between N II and its corresponding articles in *MW* and thus to come to the really central point of this discussion. The basic changes are tabulated in table 2, but it will be of some value to single out the most notorious of them for special notice. In matters of text there are many slight changes that can be left to the reader who may have access to the *MW* versions. It can simply be noted here that the most drastic rearranging or restructuring of text occurs in N II, items VIII and IX (which divide the single essay *MW* 6:605–608), XII, XVI, XXII, XXIX, XXXI, and a few others.

Among the music examples, we can distinguish sharply between two groups. The first is made up of those in which the differences between earlier and later examples leave both readings at least potentially acceptable. A case in point is example 5. Both readings for this sketch (for the first subject of the opening fugue of op. 131) show the absence of the upbeat; the crucial question is whether the first bar is to be read A-B or B-sharp–C-sharp. Obviously, one's preference will profoundly affect one's interpretation of the "evolution" of this phrase and of the entire conception of bar one in relation to bar two. The N II version has, in fact, already been widely circulated: in Paul Mies's valuable book, *Die Bedeutung der Skizzen Beethovens zur Erkenntnis seines Stiles*, the A-B reading for op. 131 is given as an earlier stage of the subject with the comment, as translated by Doris Mackinnon, "In the last example, probably on account of the chromaticism, it was important to prepare the way for the apex more effectively than was done in the sketch."[19] Mies gives no sign of having consulted the *MW* version or any earlier readings, and his entire book is based on Nottebohm.

A similar problem emerges in example 12. The *MW* version, with its B implying B-flat in bars two and five, was apparently reconsidered in the N II version and read as A-natural; the latter is essentially identical to the final reading (Ninth Symphony, first movement, bars 19–20 and corresponding passages). Similar retouching of earlier transcriptions is seen in example 13, which illustrates a familiar problem in Beethoven sketches—the apparent indication in the sketches of a series of pitches that are one step higher than the pitch level at which musical sense indicates they should be read.

But a second group consists of those in which the reading in N II is patently inferior to that of the *MW* version; in some cases the N II version is defective when compared to both the *MW* version and the manifest content of the original source. Such a case is example 6. Here, bar five of *MW* 6:186 contains the familiar sixteenth-note pattern found in the final version (op. 14, no. 1, first movement, bar 5). In N II this bar is simply shown as blank, but in the British Museum Additional 29801 (the well-known Kafka papers, recently edited by Joseph Kerman), folio 121, the reading agrees with that of *MW*, not N II.[20] A parallel is example 8, an early sketch for a portion of the Finale of the Seventh Symphony. Here, the *MW* version agrees with N II through bar four, but we find that bar five of *MW* is lacking in N II (both must, of course, be read as if they had the signature of A-major). Despite Nottebohm's usual omission of reference to folio numbers, it is not difficult to find this passage in the "Petter" sketchbook, his explicit source for this essay, and when we do, on folio 32, we find that it, too, agrees with the *MW* version.[21] A related case is example 15, in which the *MW* version of the passage has the same question mark as in N II, but the latter fails to fill out the full 12/8 measure for this sketch for the slow movement of op. 127; while it is possible that the original is elliptical here, the *MW* version is rhythmically complete. In these instances we may either suppose that Mandyczewski found the examples used for the N II versions of the essays in defective condition and used them without comment or that errors crept into the preparation of the examples for N II from whatever their antecedents may have been (perhaps Nottebohm's own transcriptions). We must also assume that Mandyczewski's proofreading was far from adequate. His notes tell us nothing about the provenance of his material beyond a general reference to those essays that have earlier versions in *MW*; they neither refer to textual discrepancies nor give any indication of his awareness of them.[22] But further bits of evidence of haphazard proofreading show carelessness in the mere preparation of the published text, in such slips as the word *Adademie* for *Akademie* (N II, p. 12, top of page) or the upside-down flat sign in N II, page 280, fourth staff from the bottom.

While tables 1 and 2 make no claim to being exhaustive, they should nevertheless form a first substantial account of the differences between the earlier and later versions of the N I and N II essays. Further clarification of the many questions raised by the tables could come only from a serious investigation of Nottebohm's posthumous papers, a task no one has yet shown a disposition to undertake. In one sense this is only reasonable, since we are far more in need of Beethovenian than of Nottebohm scholarship—and yet the problem remains that Nottebohm's essays in their collected form continue to rank not only as a classic of nineteenth-century musicology but also as a standard work of reference in circles that up to now have had neither access to, nor awareness of, the textual problems that they present. Among later writers whose knowledge of Beethoven's sketches seems to be entirely or almost entirely derived from Nottebohm, we can count George Grove,[23] Heinrich Schenker,[24] and a host of other writers, not to mention popular literature of the program-note level, whose references to sketches have relied exclusively on Nottebohm. Even the accessibility of the Nottebohm essays in collected form is relatively recent. There seems never to have been a plan for translation into English, and by now it is probably too late for that; one may note, though, that both N I and N II were translated into Japanese in the early 1950's.[25] From the time of publication until the 1920's, both volumes were read by scholars, but they were not reprinted until 1925 (at the initiative of Paul Mies) and were recently reprinted again in 1970. Of course, only N I and N II were

Lewis Lockwood

reprinted, along with the monographs—the periodical versions lie buried in those more obscure corners of our libraries to which nineteenth-century periodicals of this type are normally relegated. Had they been reprinted long since, or if Mandyczewski's editing of N II had been more complete and thoroughgoing, or if subsequent work by scholars on the Beethoven sketches had already rendered the whole contribution of Nottebohm less essential than it still remains, this tabulation would not have been necessary nor would it still seem reasonable to suggest, as it does, that a reprint of the *AmZ* and *MW* volumes may still be of considerable value. Nothing would be more in keeping with Nottebohm's own fiercely independent, critical spirit than the abandonment of pious tributes in favor of serious approaches to those difficult problems—above all in the reading and interpretation of the sketches—whose true character and content he was the first to perceive and to set in perspective.[26]

Example 1. N I, p. 40, staff 4, bar 1
(AmZ 4:282)

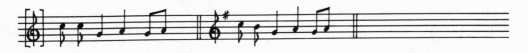

Example 2. N I, p. 74   (AmZ 5:18)

ein En - gel Le - o - no - re   ein En - gel Le - o - no - re

Example 3. N I, p. 76, staff 3, bar 4   (AmZ 5:19)

Example 4. N I, p. 76, staves 5-7

sich trö - stend   sich trö - stend zur Sei - te

En - gel   im ro - si - gen Licht sich trö - stend

(AmZ 5:19)

sich trö - stend   sich trö' - stend zur Sei - te   (?   )

En - gel   im ro - si - gen Licht sich trö - stend

Example 5. N II, p. 7, ex. 1, bars 1-4   (MW 6:427)

(?)

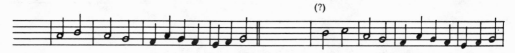

Example 6. N II, p. 48, ex. 2, bars 1-6

(MW 6:186)

Example 7. N II, p. 60, staff 3

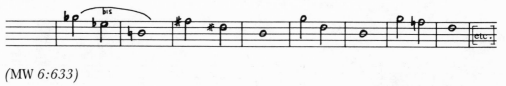

(MW 6:633)

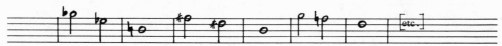

Example 8. N II, p. 110, ex. 3, bars 1–5

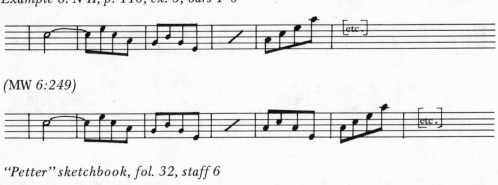

(MW 6:249)

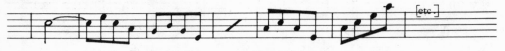

"Petter" sketchbook, fol. 32, staff 6

Example 9. N II, p. 119, staff 1, last bar (MW 7:721)

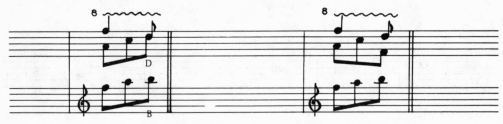

Example 10. N II, p. 132, system 2, last bar (MW 6:306)

Example 11. N II, p. 139, ex. 2, staff 1, bars 1–6

Du hast in dei - nes Er - mels Fal - ten

(MW 6:354, staff 1, bar 5)

Du hast in dei - nes Er - mels Fal - ten

Example 12. N II, p. 160, ex. 2, staff 1

(MW 7:170)

Example 13. N II, p. 166, 2d staff from bottom, bars 3– 4
                        (MW 7:186)

Example 14. N II, p. 174, system 4, bars 4–5

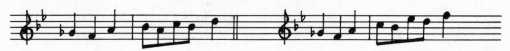

(MW 7:214)

Example 15. N II, p. 210, staff 1, bar 2   *(MW 7:561)*

Example 16. N II, p. 279, ex. 2, system 2, lower staff, bar 2
                        (MW 7:42)

TABLE 1
Variants in the Earlier and Later Versions of
Nottebohm's Articles in his *Beethoveniana* **N I** 1872

Lewis Lockwood

Beethoveniana article no.	Subject of article	Earlier place of publication
I	Op. 20; op. 49, no. 2	*AmZ* 4:289–290
II	Op. 29	*AmZ* 5:41–42
III	Op. 44	*AmZ* 6:86
IV	Op. 54	*AmZ* 5:149
V	Op. 58; op. 67	*AmZ* 6:101–104
VI	Op. 67	*AmZ* 5:148–149
VII	Op. 92	*AmZ* 4:340
VIII	Op. 93	*AmZ* 5:148
IX	Op. 93	*AmZ* 5:83
X	Op. 96	*AmZ* 5:83–85
XI	Op. 102, no. 2	*AmZ* 4:290
XII	Op. 102, no. 2	*AmZ* 4:290–291
XIII	Op. 109	*AmZ* 5:92
XIV	Op. 115	*AmZ* 4:281–283
XV	Op. 119, no. 12	*AmZ* 6:88–89
XVI	Op. 120	*AmZ* 5:92–93

Changes in text	Differences in music examples[27]	
Slight	None	**Nottebohm Revisited**
Slight	No music examples	
Slight	None	
Slight	No music examples	
Slight	Some music examples added in 1872 version	
Slight	Last measure of music example in N I, p. 17, is not found in *AmZ* version	
Expanded in 1872 version	No music examples	
Slight	None	
Slight	None	
Slight	Slur added in N I, p. 28, staff 3, last bar and in N I, p. 27, staff 6, last bar (no slur in *AmZ* 5:84)	
Slight	None	
Last sentence in N I version added	Last example in N I, p. 33 has beam for six 8th notes; beam and stems lacking in *AmZ* 4:290	
Slight	None	
Slight	In N I, p. 40, staff 4, bar 1, second note differs from *AmZ* 4:282 *(see ex. 1)* In N I, p. 42, heading over music ex. is "vielleicht so anfangen"; in *AmZ* 4:282, it reads: "vielleicht p anfangen"	
Unchanged	In N I, p. 45, staff 1, bar 3, the two 8th notes are separate; they are beamed in *AmZ* 6:88	
Footnote added in N I, p. 47	None	

	Beethoveniana article no.	Subject of article	Earlier place of publication
	XVII	Op. 121*b*	*AmZ* 6:87–88
Lewis Lockwood	XVIII	Op. 130	*AmZ* 5:93
	XIX	Op. 131	*AmZ* 5:26–28
	XX	Op. 138	*AmZ* 5:11–14, 17–19
	XXI	"Beethoven's last composition"	*AmZ* 5:93–94
	XXII	An unfinished opera	*AmZ* 4:321–322, 329–333
	XXIII	*Der Erlkönig*	*AmZ* 6:86
	XXIV	B.'s use of "cresc." marking	*AmZ* 4:291

Changes in text	Differences in music examples[27]	
Slight	Text below music example of N I, p. 51, bars 1–2, is not in *AmZ* version	
Slight	None	
None	In viola part of example labeled "Nr. 2," *AmZ* version has "später," while in N I, p. 56, this appears as "oder"	**Nottebohm Revisited**
Modifications in first paragraph; also N I, p. 66, after first music example, and N I, pp. 70, 71	In NI, p. 63, staff 3, the last two bars are added; N I, p. 74 differs from *AmZ* 5:18 *(see ex. 2)* In N I, p. 66, staff 3, final bar has bass clef instead of treble clef as in *AmZ* 5:13 In N I, p. 76, staff 3, bar 4 differs from *AmZ* 5:19 *(see ex. 3)* In N I, p. 76, staves 5–7 differ from *AmZ* 5:19 *(see ex. 4)* In N I, p. 67, staff 9 deletes erroneous treble clef in *AmZ* 5:13	
Slight	None	
Slight	None	
Text in *AmZ* longer, and it raises the question of the authenticity of the material; this point is not raised in N I version	Music ex. in *AmZ* consists of only first four bars of N I version	
Rearranged	Music ex. from op. 68 added in N I version; music examples shared by the two versions are unchanged	

	Beethoveniana article no.	Subject of article	Earlier place of publication
	XXV	"Punkte und Striche"	*AmZ* 4:337–340
Lewis Lockwood	XXVI	Metronome markings	*AmZ* 5:129–130, 138–140
	XXVII	A Beethoven *Stammbuch*	*AmZ* 6:65–68
	XXVIII	B. and Weissenbach	*AmZ* 5:33–35 (with note: "published in somewhat different form in the Vienna Presse of 13 Feb. 1868")
	XXIX	B.'s contrapuntal studies	*AmZ*, n. s. 1 (1863): 685–691, 701–708, 717–722, 749–754, 770–775, 784–789, 810–815, 825–829, 839–843 *AmZ*, n.s. 2 (1864): 153–158, 169–172

Changes in text	Differences in music examples[27]
Slight	Music examples partially re-arranged in N I version, in part new
Slight	No music examples
N I, p. 141: text under "VII" is substantially altered from *AmZ* version	No music examples
Slight	No music examples
Extensive revision (see N.'s preface to N I, p. v)	Revised

TABLE 2
Variants in the Earlier and Later Published Versions of
Nottebohm's Articles in his *Zweite Beethoveniana* **N II**
1887

N II, article no.	Subject of article	Earlier place of publication
Introduction (pp. vii–x)		*MW* 8:469–470
I	Six sketch-books of 1825–1826	*MW* 6:425–430
II	Op. 115	*MW* 7:1–3
III	Op. 1, nos. 2 and 3	*MW* 6:169–172

Changes in text	Differences in music examples
Slightly expanded in N II	None
None	In N II, p. 4, ex. 2, staff 3, bar 3, the second note is A♭ (= B♭ in *MW* 6:426)
	In N II, p. 6, ex. 2, bar 3, upper staff, the last two notes in bar are two 16th notes, E and F; in *MW* 6:427, this beat is a single quarter note, F. *AmZ* version also lacks trill in this bar
	In N II, p. 7, ex. 1, bar 1, the pitches are A and B; in *MW* 6:427, they are B (with question mark) and C *(see ex. 5)*
	In N II, p. 9, ex. 3, bar 5, the second quarter = D; in *MW* 6:429, the second quarter = E a half step higher
	In N II, p. 10, ex. 2, bar 12, the third quarter has natural sign; no accidental in *MW* 6:429
	In N II, p. 12, top, text from sketchbook includes word *Adademie*; in *MW* 6:429 correctly spelled as *Akademie*
	N II, p. 12, ex. 3 has "(dur)" in parentheses not found in *MW* 6:429
None	N II, p. 15, penultimate staff, penultimate bar has question mark not found in *MW* 7:2
	In N II, p. 16, last line of text reads "zuerst in C-dur"
Slight	N II, p. 24, staff 3 has question mark not found in *MW* 6:170

N II, article no.	Subject of article	Earlier place of publication
IV	Op. 10	*MW* 6:577–581
V	Op. 13	*MW* 7:29–30
VI	Op. 14, no. 1	*MW* 6:185–187, 197–200

Changes in text	Differences in music examples
Slight	In N II, p. 29, ex. 1 has signature of three flats; no signature in *MW* 6:577
	In N II, p. 30, ex. 2, lower staff corresponds to upper staff in *MW* 6:578; upper staff in N II differs from material given in *MW*
	In N II, p. 32, staff 6, last bar, last two notes are F-G; in *MW* 6:578, they are G-A
	N II, p. 32, last staff has question mark on penultimate 8th not found in *MW* 6:578. This example in N II, p. 32 lacks many accidentals found in *MW* 6:578
	N II, p. 34, ex. 2, staff 3, bar 5 has flat before last 8th; *MW* 6:579 has no accidental
	In N II, p. 37, ex. 2, staff 5, first three bars have two bars of minim rests with blank bar between; in *MW* 6:580, they are all blank
	N II, p. 38, ex. 1 has sharp only on first C in bar 1, not on C in bar 2; *MW* 6:580 has an explicit sharp on C in every bar of this example
Slight	None
Slight	In N II, pp. 45–46, example has signature only on first staff; *MW* 6:185–186 has signature of four sharps on all staves
	In N II, p. 46, system 3, bar 1, l.h., the last note is F♯; in *MW* 6:186, it is G♯
	In N II, p. 48, ex. 2, staff 1, bar 5 is blank; in *MW* 6:186, it contains the equivalent of the final version of the movement, bar 5, r.h. *(see ex. 6)*
	N II, p. 54, staff 3 from bottom uses figure "8" with wavy line following, to signify "an octave higher"; *MW*

N II, article no.	Subject of article	Earlier place of publication
continued VI		
VII	Op. 18, nos. 1 and 6	*MW* 6:633–634
VIII	Op. 15	*MW* 6:605–608
IX	Op. 19	*MW* 6:605–608
X	Op. 58	*MW* 10:361–363
XI	Op. 59	*MW* 6:649–652, 665–667

Changes in text	Differences in music examples
	6:199 gives notes an octave higher without sign
	In N II, p. 56, staff 6, bar 3, the first note is shown as tied back; no tie in *MW* 6:199
N II, p. 60: note referring to Petter not in *MW* version	In N II, p. 60, staff 3, bars 1 and 2 are marked "bis"; *MW* 6:633 has no indication whatever and omits bars 5–6 of the N II version *(see ex. 7)*
In N II the *MW* text is divided into two essays and is altered	No variants in those music examples that are in common
In N II the *MW* text is divided into two essays and is altered	No variants in those music examples that are in common
None	None
None	In N II, p. 79, staff 3, bars 2–3 have repetition signs; *MW* 6:650 has notes written out in both bars
	N II, p. 79, staff 3, bar 5 has flat before E not found in *MW* 6:650
	N II, p. 79, staff 4, bar 1 has flat before A not found in *MW* 6:650
	N II, p. 81, staff 6, bar 3 has notes written out; *MW* 6:650 has repetition sign
	N II, p. 84, ex. 1, staff 1, bar 4 has half rest with question mark; *MW* 6:651 has no half rest and no question mark
	N II, p. 84, ex. 1, systems 1 and 2 have "(oder)" not found in *MW* 6:651
	N II, p. 86, ex. 1, bar 1 lacks slur; *MW* 6:652 has slur over entire bar
	N II, p. 87, ex. 2, second staff from below, bar 4 has flat before B not found in *MW* 6:666

N II, article no.	Subject of article	Earlier place of publication
XII	Op. 74	*MW* 6:221–222
XIII	Op. 81*a*	*MW* 6:223
XIV	Op. 92 and 93	*MW* 6:245–249, 257–261

Changes in text	Differences in music examples
Text rearranged and expanded in N II, p. 93: footnote on difficulty of making exact pitch readings not found in *MW* version	In N II, p. 94, last staff, bar 1, third 8th beat = A♭ (= B♭ in *MW* 6:222)
Slight	N II, p. 98, staff 8, bar 4 has simultaneous F and D quarter notes on first beat; *MW* 6:223 has root B♭ below this pair N II, p. 99, last ex., staff 1, bar 2 lacks wedge-shaped accent mark on last note; *MW* 6:223 has accent on this note and on parallel last note of the next bar, but not in the bar corresponding to staff 2, bar 2 of this example
Slight; last part of *MW* essay not used in N II version but transferred to beginning of N II, article XXXI (pp. 288–290)	N II, p. 110, ex. 3 has ten bars while the same example in *MW* 6:249 has eleven; the *MW* version has as fifth bar the material shown in ex. 8, which is entirely lacking in N II *(see ex. 8)* The original reading, as found in the "Petter" sketchbook, fol. 32, staff 6, agrees with the *MW* version N II, p. 103, ex. 2 has no bar line before last two notes; *MW* 6:246 has bar line N II, p. 106, last ex., staff 1, final bar has quarter rest not found in *MW* 6:247 N II, p. 108, ex. 1, staff 2, bars 1-2, has bracket with "3 mal" over notes; *MW* 6:248 writes out the passage three times with no abbreviation N II, p. 108, staves 3 and 4, omits between bars 1 and 2 an extra measure found in *MW* 6:248 N II, p. 108, ex. 2 has whole example written with octave sign; *MW* 6:248

N II, article no.	Subject of article	Earlier place of publication
continued XIV		
XV	Op. 94	*MW* 7:721–722
XVI	Op. 106	*MW* 6:297–298, 305–306

Changes in text	Differences in music examples
	has example written an octave higher N II, p. 114, last staff has E♭ in bar 1, not in bars 2–4, then again in bar 5; *MW* 6:259 has explicit E♭ in each of these bars
None	In N II, p. 119, staff 1, last bar, first note is D; in *MW* 7:721, this note is E and is followed by 8th rest and 8th note E, both suppressed in N II *(see ex. 9)*
	In N II, p. 119, staff 4, bar 2, seventh note has sharp; *MW* 7:722 has no accidental
	In N II, p. 119, staff 6, bar 3, second note lacks sharp (though implied); *MW* 7:722 has sharp
	In N II, p. 119, last staff, notes 3–6 of the last bar are E-D-D-C♯; in *MW* 7:722, the same notes are D-C-B, with note 5 as a quarter instead of an 8th and note 6 deleted entirely
Text expanded and altered	Examples expanded in N II version In N II, p. 123, last bar, last four notes are D-B-F-D; in *MW* 10:53, they are C-B-E-D
	In N II, p. 124, first bar, note 5 is B; in *MW* 10:53, it is C
	In N II, p. 125, staff 6, bar 5, first note is G; in *MW* 10:54, it is F
	In N II, p. 125, last staves, repetitions are written out; *MW* 6:297 uses three repetition signs
	N II, p. 126, ex. 1, staff 2, last bar has quarter-note B lacking in *MW* 10:54
	N II, p. 130, ex. 1, staff 2, bar 4 has slur; *MW* 6:298, col. 2, ex. 1, staff 2, bar 4 has no slur
	N II, p. 132, system 2, last bar has different pitch content on last beat

N II, article no.	Subject of article	Earlier place of publication
continued XVI		
XVII	Op. 113	*MW* 6:353–355
XVIII	Op. 119	*MW* 10:161–162
XIX	Op. 123	*MW* 9:466–469

Changes in text	Differences in music examples
	from *MW* 6:306, last bar *(see ex. 10)* In N II, p. 133, system 2, bar 4 lacks figure 6 over bass as found in *MW* 10:78. In system 4, bars 4 and 5 lack dots after last two bass half notes; found in *MW* 10:78
	N II, p. 134, staff 1 has dotted half note lacking in *MW* 10:78
Slight. N II, pp. 144–145: last part expanded in N II version	Examples expanded in N II N II, p. 139, staff 1, bar 1 has natural sign before first note of second triplet; not found in *MW* 6:353
	MW 6:353, staff 2, bar 3 has question mark in parentheses above last notes; N II, p. 139, staff 2, bar 3 has no such indications
	MW 6:353, staff 4, bar 2, has question mark in parentheses over second note; N II, p. 139, staff 3, last bar, penultimate note, has no such indication
	In *MW* 6:353, example, N. observes that the two clefs in the example are added by him; in N II, p. 139, ex. 1, there is no such observation about clefs, and N. omits first clef but keeps the second (bass clef on staff 3)
	N II, p. 139, ex. 2, staff 1, bar 5 has five beats in the bar (half rest plus three quarter notes); in *MW* 6:354, staff 1, bar 5, the last two notes of the bar are 8th notes *(see ex. 11)*
Slight	None
None	None

N II, article no.	Subject of article	Earlier place of publication
XX	Op. 125	*MW* 7:169–171, 185–188, 213–215, 225–228, 241–244

Changes in text	Differences in music examples
None	N II, p. 159, system 1, upper staff, bar 2 has two readings superimposed; *MW* 7:170 has only the lower reading
	In N II, p. 160, ex. 2, staff 1, bars 2 and 5, the penultimate note is A; in *MW* 7:170, this note is B *(see ex. 12)*
	MW 7:170 has question marks; removed in N II, p. 161, ex. 1, bars 3 and 4, and one note added
	In N II, p. 161, ex. 1, bar 3, notes are C-B♭-A; in *MW* 7:171, they are D-C-B♭
	In N II, p. 161, second staff from bottom, bar 2, second note is D; in *MW* 7:171, it is E. In staff 3, bar 2, second note is B; in *MW* 7:171, it is A
	In N II, p. 162, last ex., staff 1, bar 4, first note is F; in *MW* 7:171, it is E
	MW 7:185 has parentheses around phrase "Herr Gott dich loben wir—alleluja"; no parentheses in N II, p. 163
	MW 7:186 has entirely different reading from N II, p. 166, second staff from bottom, bar 4 *(see ex. 13)*
	In N II, p. 171, staff 3, the last note of bar 4 and all of bar 5 replace a question mark in *MW* 7:188
	N II, p. 172, system 3, bar 4, lower staff has the complete three-note figure (dotted quarter, 8th, quarter), but *MW* 7:213 has only first beat as quarter-note A
	In N II, p. 173, final staff, the last two bars are an alternate version, while in *MW* 7:214 they are given as main reading without alternative
	N II, p. 174, system 4, bars 3–4 lack question mark in parentheses found in *MW* 7:214, col. 2, system 5
	In N II, p. 174, system 4, bar 5, the reading differs from *MW* 7:214 *(see ex. 14)*

N II, article no.	Subject of article	Earlier place of publication
continued XX		
XXI	Op. 126	*MW* 9:499–502, 515–517

Changes in text	Differences in music examples
	In N II, p. 175, staff 4 from bottom, the last note in bar 1 is E; in *MW* 7:215, it is F♯
	N II, p. 179 has small notes in systems 1, 2, and 3 not found in *MW* 7:226, where these bars are blank
	N II, p. 181, staff 1, bar 4 lacks question mark in parentheses found in *MW* 7:227
	In N II, p. 181, staff 2, bar 2, the last note is C; in *MW* 7:227, it is B
	In N II, p. 183, ex. 3, staff 1, bar 4 has fermata, which is lacking in *MW* 7:227
	In N II, p. 190, staff 4, bars 3 and 4, and staff 5, bar 1, each have one 16th note, which appears as an 8th note in *MW* 7:243
	N II, p. 191, staff 1: first five 8th notes are missing in *MW* 7:243
None	In N II, p. 202, last two systems on page, the B quarter and dotted half and the following F♯ quarter and dotted half are given without ties; but in *MW* 9:515, they are tied as pairs like the other notes in this passage
	N II, p. 203, ex. 2: system 1 and second staves of systems 2, 3, and 4 are lacking in *MW* 9:516
	N II, p. 205, ex. 2: staff 2 of system 1 does not appear in *MW* 9:516
	N II, p. 199, ex. 1, bar 1 has question mark not found in *MW* 9:501

N II, article no.	Subject of article	Earlier place of publication
XXII	Op. 127	*MW* 7:561–564, 577–579
XXIII	"Vergriffene Allemanden"	*MW* 10:493–494
XXIV	Unfinished pfte concerto (Hess no. 15)	*MW* 6:394
XXV	Sketches for *Macbeth*	*MW* 10:113–114
XXVI	An unfinished symphony	*MW* 7:17–18

Changes in text	Differences in music examples
MW 7:577 has a valuable paragraph on the sketchbook from which this material is drawn and on other material that it contains. This paragraph is omitted in N II	In N II, p. 210, staff 1, bar 2 lacks quarter-note G after 8th-note G, which is found in *MW* 7:561, staff 1, bar 2; N II reading thus gives bar with less than complete duration and is probably a misprint *(see ex. 15)*
	N II, p. 211, staff 3, bar 1: dot missing on first note; dot found in *MW* 7:562 version
	N II, p. 212, system 5, bar 2, lower staff: in *MW* 7:562, this entire bar has question mark in parentheses, which is lacking in N II
	N II, p. 213, system 1, bar 3 (upper staff): first and third notes are F♯; in *MW* 7:563, they are G
	N II, p. 214, system 1, bar 3 has no clef indications; *MW* 7:563 has bass clef at beginning of section marked "S. 13," two bars earlier, and suggested change to treble clef when upper voice enters at bar 3
	In *MW* 7:578, the first four bars are marked with question mark in parentheses; not found in N II, p. 218, system 5
	N II, pp. 218 and 219 have small notes, none of which appear in *MW* 7:578
	None
None	N II, p. 223, system 1, staff 2, bar 3 has slur not found in *MW* 6:394
Slight	Example in *MW* 10:114 not included in N II
Unchanged except for footnote on N II, p. 229	None

N II, article no.	Subject of article	Earlier place of publication
XXVII	Skbk. of year 1800	*MW* 8:469–472, 481–483, 493–495
XXVIII	Skbk. of year 1808	*MW* 9:429–430
XXIX	Skbk. of year 1809	*MW* 7:513–517, 529–530, 545–546; see also *MW* 10:397–399

Changes in text	Differences in music examples
	N II, p. 249, ex. 1, over staff 2 has "complimento prega (?)"; in *MW* 8:494, it reads: "complimento . . . parla"
	In N II, p. 233, staff 9, bar 2, note 1 has no accidental; in *MW* 8:471, same note has explicit flat
	In N II, p. 235, ex. 1, staff 6, the last five notes of bar 4 and all of staff 7, bar 3 have 8th notes a third below upper line, which are lacking in *MW* 8:472
	In N II, p. 247, ex. 1, staff 3, bar 2 has 8th rest followed by 8th note (E♭); in *MW* 8:494, the rest and note are reversed, with the 8th note on the first beat
	N II, p. 250, ex. 2, staff 2: final 16th note of bar 3 is omitted in *MW* 8:495. Staff 3, note 4 of bar 3 and notes of bar 4 are B♮-C-E; in *MW* 8:495, they are A♮-B-D
MW material is divided between N II articles XXVIII and XL	None
Some of text rearranged	Examples expanded in N II version
	In N II, p. 256, staff 3, the last note of bar 4 is G; in *MW* 10:398, it is F
	N II, p. 257, staff 3, bar 1 contains three lower notes not found in *MW* 10:398
	In N II, p. 262, ex. 2, staff 1, bar 2, first note is dotted quarter with bar through stem; *MW* 7:514 lacks bar through stem
	In N II, p. 265, ex. 2, system 1, staff 2, bar 4 has first 8th note as E; in *MW* 7:514, it is G. In system 2, staff 1, bar 1, the opening chord contains a G, which is lacking in *MW* 7:514
	In N II, p. 267, ex. 3, staff 1 lacks

N II, article no.	Subject of article	Earlier place of publication
continued XXIX		
XXX	Skbk. of year 1810	*MW* 7:41-43, 53-55

Changes in text	Differences in music examples
	quarter-note D, which appears directly before change to treble clef in *MW* 7:515
N II, p. 276: second paragraph on this page (on use of pencil outdoors) added in N II	N II, p. 279, ex. 2, system 2, lower staff, bar 2 lacks two 16th notes found in *MW* 7:42 *(see ex. 16)*
	N II, p. 280, ex. 1, bar 1 has two notes under the question mark not found in *MW* 7:42
	In N II, p. 280, fourth staff from bottom, the flat sign next to third note is upside down; correct in *MW* 7:43
	MW 7:43, bar 1 has question mark in parentheses over entire bar; omitted in N II, p. 280, second staff from bottom
	In N II, p. 281, ex. 2, bar 2, the first note is B ; in *MW* 7:53, it is C♭
	N II, p. 284, ex. 2, first complete bar has slur on third beat not found in *MW* 7:54
	In N II, p. 284, final staff, the first note of bar 4 is F; in *MW* 7:54, it is G
	In N II, p. 287, staff 1, bar 4, note 2 is 8th-note C; in *MW* 7:55, it is given as interval of C and A below
	In *MW* 7:55, last bar on page lacks "luftig," which is found in N II, p. 287, staff 1, last bar

N II, article no.	Subject of article	Earlier place of publication
XXXI	Skbk. of year 1812	*MW* 10:193–195, 205–206, 213–214, 229–230
XXXII	Skbk. of year 1814	*MW* 8:653–654, 669–671, 685–687
XXXIII	Another skbk. of the year 1814	*MW* 6:413–414
XXXIV	Skbk. of year 1815	*MW* 10:449–451
XXXV	Skbk. of years 1815 and 1816	*MW* 7:609–611, 625–627, 637–639, 653–655, 669–670
XXXVI	Skbk. of year 1817	*MW* 10:41–42, 53–54, 65–67, 77–78, 89–90

Changes in text	Differences in musical examples
MW text considerably longer, not only because the "Petter" skbk. is dealt with in another article, but because the *MW* version has an elaborate account of the skbk., its chronology, Thayer's dating, etc.	In N II, p. 291, staff 4, bar 2, last two notes are a dotted 8th and a 16th; in *MW* 10:230, both are 8th notes
	N II, p. 296, last staff, bar 1 has pitches C-G-E-C; *MW* 8:654 has pitches C-F-G-C
	N II, p. 299, ex. 2 has signature of four sharps; *MW* 8:670 has no signature
Slight	Examples expanded
	N II, p. 311, staff 4, bar 1 has two 16th notes, which appear as 8th notes in *MW* 6:414
Slight	
	N II, p. 330, last ex., system 1, staff 2, bar 3, lacks superimposed alternate reading found in *MW* 7:626
	In N II, p. 337, staff 4, bar 1, notes 2 and 3 are quarters; in *MW* 7:638, note 2 is a dotted quarter and note 3 is an 8th
	In N II, p. 338, staff 7, bar 2, the last note is G; in *MW* 7:634, it is B♭
Related to N II articles XXXVI, XVI, and XX	N II, p. 351, staff 1, bar 4 has sharps before C and F not found in *MW* 10:42
Music exx. in *MW* 10:53–54 appear in N II, pp. 123–127	In N II, p. 352, bar 3, third 8th beat has 16th rest and 16th note; *MW* 10:42 has dot on preceding 8th note and 16th (with no rest)

N II, article no.	Subject of article	Earlier place of publication
XXXVII	"Clavierspiel"	*MW* 7:65–68
XXXVIII	"Ein Spes-enbuch"	*MW* 6:394–395
XXXIX	Op. 90	*MW* 9:443–444
XL	Op. 68	*MW* 9:429–430
XLI	Op. 22	*MW* 7:705–707
XLII	WoO 77	Not previously published
XLIII	Op. 124	*AmZ* 8 (1873): 385–390, 405–408, 422–424, 436–440
XLIV, XLV, XLVI		Not previously published

182

Changes in text	Differences in musical examples
	Some music examples added N II, p. 363, staff 1, bar 1 has double turn instead of single turn in *MW* 7:66; staff 2, bar 2 has X (double sharp) before first upper note instead of ♯ in *MW* 7:66
Slight	No music examples
Unchanged	In N II, p. 367, system 1, staff 2, bar 1, notes 4 and 8 are E; in *MW* 9:443, both are C♯ In N II, p. 367, last staff, bar 1, the four 16ths in l.h. are not given in *MW* 9:443
MW material divided between N II articles XXVIII and XL	
Slight (especially at end)	Example from op. 22, Finale, given in *MW* 7:706; col. 2 not found in N II, pp. 380–381
	In N II, p. 404, ex. 2, bars 5–6 have pitches F-D-E; *AmZ* 8 (1873):438 has G-E-F; in N I, staff 4, bar 4, the last note is G, while in *AmZ* 8 (1873):438, it is F In N II, p. 406, staff 9, bar 1, the second note is B; in *AmZ* 8:438, it is C In N II, p. 407, system 1, staff 2, bar 2, the second note is A; in *AmZ* 8:440, it is G. The first note of system 1, staff 1, bar 3 is G; in *AmZ* 8:439, it is F N II, p. 408, staff 6, bar 4 omits two half notes found in *AmZ* 8:439

N II, article no.	Subject of article	Earlier place of publication
XLVII		*MW* 6:222–223 (in part)
XLIX, L, LI, LII, LIII, LIV, LV		Not previously published
LVI	Op. 67 (also 61 and 69)	*MW* 9:444–445
LVII, LVIII, LIX, LX, LXI, LXII, LXIII		Not previously published
LXIV	"Ein Brief-Concept"	*AmZ* 5 (1870):42–43
LXV		Not previously published

Changes in text	Differences in musical examples
MW deals with op. 67 only	Examples expanded

Notes

Lewis Lockwood

1. The lecture that I delivered at the University of Texas at Austin in March 1971 was a survey of the development of the study of the Beethoven sketches. With the kind permission of the editors of this volume, I am presenting this paper in place of the original lecture, in the belief that this elaboration of one part of the material delivered as a lecture may prove more useful to readers. I am indebted to professors John W. Grubbs and Leeman Perkins for their agreement to this proposal. For assistance in the checking of details for this article, I am indebted to Miss Katherine Rohrer. All translations are my own.

2. The earliest article on Nottebohm I know of is the one written by Carl Ferdinand Pohl for the first edition of *Grove's Dictionary of Music and Musicians*, ed. Sir George Grove, 4 vols. (London: Macmillan & Co., 1879–1899), 2:479; this came out in 1880, two years before Nottebohm's death, and concludes with an expression of regret that "no public institution has been inclined to offer a man of his great attainments a position commensurate with his services." The most important articles in the 1880's were those by J. S. Shedlock, "Gustav Nottebohm and the Beethoven Sketch-Books," *Monthly Musical Record* 8 (1883): 59-65, 81-84, 87, and 134; the highly informative obituary for Nottebohm, written by Karl Grün and originally published in the *Beilage zur Augsburger Allgemeinen Zeitung*, November 29, 1882, and reprinted in *Gustav Nottebohms Briefe an Robert Volkmann*, ed. Hans Clauss (Lüdenscheid: Kommissionsverlag Rudolf Beucker, 1967), pp. 50-59; and Pohl's excellent biographical article for the *Allgemeine deutsche Biographie* 24 (1887): 41-44 (including a substantial but not fully complete listing of his published works). Largely derived from Pohl but a useful survey nevertheless is Hans Joachim Moser, "Gustav Nottebohm," in *Westfälische Lebensbilder*, Main Series 6, Veröffentlichungen der historischen Kommission der Provinzialinstitut für Westfälische Landes- und Volkskunde, vol. 17 (Münster, 1957), pp. 135-146.

3. Johannes Brahms quoted in Moser, "Gustav Nottebohm," p. 140.

4. Brahms to Schubring, January 17, 1864, in Johannes Brahms, *Briefwechsel*, 16 vols. (Berlin: Deutsche Brahms Gesellschaft, 1906-1922), 8:201. Other Brahms correspondence containing more than passing references to Nottebohm includes: 1:8, 95, 96 (recommending him as a theory teacher); 3:163; 6:70, 105, 112, 118, 184-185; and 8:39.

5. Max Kalbeck, *Johannes Brahms*, 8 vols. (Berlin: Deutsche Brahms Gesellschaft, 1904-1914), 2:109-111. Kalbeck's view is that Brahms gladly endured Nottebohm's eccentricities not only because of his respect for Nottebohm as a musician and a scholar but also because he possessed many of the same qualities himself. Kalbeck portrays Nottebohm, presumably on the word of witnesses, as "the man who denounced a waiter because he accidentally overcharged him two *Kreuzer*; the man who had a postman fired because he left the mail with the landlord instead of climbing four steep flights to deliver it . . . this mean, stingy, and merciless defender of abstract moral concepts set the highest value not only on securing his own rights but also on aiding others to do so; for he saw his rights as being trampled upon by the deliberate malice, stupidity, or shortsightedness of others, or by the careless . . . routine of everyday life. He could not forgive Charlemagne—'improperly called the "Great" '—because more than a thousand years ago he had deprived Nottebohm's Saxon forebears of their freedom."

6. Joseph Joachim to Brahms, November 1874, in Brahms, *Briefwechsel*, 6:105. This may be translated as "Send my hearty greetings to our jovial Beethoven admirer."

7. Gustav Nottebohm, "Über die Suite," *Monatsschrift für Theater und Musik* (= *Recensionen und Mittheilungen über Theater und Musik*) 1 (1855): n.p., and 3 (1857): n.p.

8. Gustav Nottebohm, "Bach's Letzte Fuge," *Musik-Welt*, no. 20/21 (1881), n.p.

9. To the list of Nottebohm's writings given by Pohl (see n. 2) should be added these items: (1) "Die erste Aufführung des Prometheus," *Allgemeine musikalische Zeitung*

4 (1869): 289; and (2) "Zur Reinigung der Werke Beethoven's von Fehlern und fremden Zuthaten," *Allgemeine musikalische Zeitung* 11 (1876): 321–327, 337–343, 353–360, 369–373, 385–391, 401–407, 417–423, 465–471, 481–487, 497–501, and 513–516.

10. In the preface to Georg Kinsky and Hans Halm, *Das Werk Beethovens: Thematisch-bibliographisches Verzeichnis seiner sämtlichen vollendeten Kompositionen* (Munich-Duisburg: G. Henle, 1955), p. xiii, Halm reports that, in letters to him that were later destroyed during World War II, Kinsky had attributed the compilation of the 1851 catalogue to "a certain Geissler." After Kinsky's death in 1951, Halm was unable to confirm this attribution and leaves the question open.

11. Alexander Wheelock Thayer, ed., *Chronologisches Verzeichnis der Werke Ludwig van Beethovens* (Berlin: F. Schneider, 1865).

12. See O. von Hase, *Breitkopf und Härtel: Gedenkschrift und Arbeitsbericht*, 2 vols. (Leipzig: Breitkopf and Härtel, 1917), 2:327.

13. The abbreviations "N 65," "N I," "N II," and "N 80" are the now standard means of references to each of these volumes by Nottebohm, as introduced by Kinsky and Halm, *Das Werk Beethovens*, p. xxi.

14. The firm of Rieter-Biedermann was founded in Leipzig in 1862 as an offshoot of the company established earlier in Winterthur. In 1917 it was merged with C. F. Peters in Leipzig; this may explain why the copies of N I and N II used for the most recent modern reprint (by the Johnson Reprint Corporation, 1970) have as publisher "Leipzig, Verlag von C. F. Peters," while the original issues were imprinted "Leipzig und Winterthur, Verlag von J. Rieter-Biedermann." The Peters imprint was presumably added after 1917 to the original plates; what is crucial is that the reprint is made from the same plates as the original and has no differences in pagination or content. Important, too, is that the same firm of Rieter-Biedermann was the publisher of the *Allgemeine musikalische Zeitung* (= *Leipziger allgemeine musikalische Zeitung*) from 1866

to 1882, with Nottebohm as its Vienna correspondent. This doubtless facilitated the publication of N I and even the posthumous N II.

15. For more on this subject, see Alfred Mann, "Beethoven's Contrapuntal Studies with Haydn," *Musical Quarterly* 56 (1970): 711-726.

16. On Eusebius Mandyczewski, see Virginia Cysarz's article, "Mandyczewski, Eusebius," in *Die Musik in Geschichte und Gegenwart*, ed. Friedrich Blume, 14 vols. (Kassel and Basel: Bärenreiter, 1949-1968), 8:cols. 1575-1576, and, among other personal memoirs of the period, those of Artur Schnabel in his *My Life and Music* (New York: St. Martin's Press, 1963), pp. 15-17.

17. As Nottebohm puts it, "Sie erschienen mit einer Ausnahme . . . zuerst in Zeitungen . . . sind aber hier durchgesehen und zum Theil durchaus umgearbeitet worden" ("With one exception they appeared first in periodicals . . . but have here been reviewed and in part thoroughly revised") (N I, p. v).

18. Eusebius Mandyczewski's preface to N II, p. [iii].

19. Paul Mies, *Die Bedeutung der Skizzen Beethovens zur Erkenntnis seines Stiles* (Leipzig: Breitkopf and Härtel, 1925), p. 9; cf. the English translation by Doris L. Mackinnon, *Beethoven's Sketches: An Analysis of His Style Based on a Study of His Sketch-Books* (London: Oxford University Press, 1929; reprint ed., New York: Dover Publications, 1974), p. 9.

20. Joseph Kerman, ed. *Ludwig van Beethoven: Autograph Miscellany from circa 1786-1799; British Museum Additional Manuscript 29801, ff. 39-162 (the "Kafka Sketchbook")*, 2 vols. (London: Trustees of the British Museum with the cooperation of the Royal Musical Association, 1970), vol. 1 (facsimile), fol. 121; vol. 2 (transcription), p. 26.

21. Bonn, Beethoven-Archiv, Sammlung Bodmer, MS Mh 59 (= "Petter" sketchbook), fol. 32, staff 6 (as shown in example 8). On this sketchbook, see Max Unger, *Eine*

Schweizer Beethoven-Sammlung: Katalog (Zurich: Verlag der Corona, 1939), p. 164.

22. The only footnote I have found in N II that is explicitly added by Mandyczewski is the one on p. 35, marked "Anmerkung des Herausgebers."

23. George Grove, *Beethoven and His Nine Symphonies*, 3rd ed. (London: Novello, Ewer, and Co., 1898), pp. 57, 141-142, 177, 322-331. (There are many more references to Nottebohm's writings than are listed in the index.)

24. Heinrich Schenker, *Beethovens Neunte Sinfonie* (Vienna: Universal-Edition, 1912), and later appearing as *Beethoven: Neunte Sinfonie*, 2d ed. (Vienna: Universal-Edition, 1969); idem, *Beethoven: Fünfte Sinfonie*, in his *Der Tonwille*, 10 vols. (Vienna: Tonwille-Flugblätterverlag, 1921-1924), 1:27-37, 5:10-42, 6:9–35; idem, *Die Letzten Fünf Sonaten von Beethoven, Kritische Ausgabe mit Einführung und Erläuterung* (Vienna: Universal-Edition, 1913-1921), op. nos. 101, 109, 110, and 111, and later appearing as *Beethoven: Die letzten Sonaten*, ed. Oswald Jonas, 2d ed. (Vienna: Universal-Edition, 1971–1972); and idem, *Der Freie Satz* (Vienna: Universal-Edition, 1935), and later edited by Oswald Jonas, 2d ed. (Vienna: Universal-Edition, 1956).

25. See Keisei Sakka, "Beethoven-Literatur in japanischer Sprache von 1915 bis März 1956," *Beethoven-Jahrbuch* 2 (1956): 152.

26. This essay is intended as a partial realization of my remarks on the problem of tracing back Nottebohm's essays, made at the *Colloque de Saint-Germain-en-Laye* in September 1970, part of the panel discussion published under the title "Problèmes de création musicale au XIXe siècle," in *Acta Musicologica* 43 (1971): 196. Among recent articles on Beethoven sketchbooks, that of Douglas Johnson and Alan Tyson, "Reconstructing Beethoven's Sketchbooks," *Journal of the American Musicological Society* 25 (1972): 137-156, is unusual in systematically referring to several N II essays in their *MW* versions.

27. Tables 1 and 2 provide an extensive sampling of the differences in music examples found in the earlier and later versions of Nottebohm's essays. But they are not intended to list all the differences that entail the inclusion or omission of clefs, signatures, accidentals, octave indications, accent marks, slurs, and other elements of notation.

**Nottebohm
Revisited**

The Chanson in the Humanist Era
Daniel Heartz

Qu'on te prenne, beau Luth, pour la lyre d'Orphée.
Mellin de Saint-Gelais

Six

When the chanson composer Anthoine de Bertrand addressed his readers in a preface of 1576, he extolled the exemplary labors of his predecessors, saying that they left him little or nothing more to contribute. Such is my position with regard to the learned and engaging essays that have been devoted to the chanson during recent years.[1] Assaying a further contribution to the subject is done with hopes of conveying to younger scholars an enthusiasm for the age of the Renaissance and a sense of delight in some of its musical accomplishments. The past lives on through our imaginative attempts to meet it on its own terms. Were we to do any less, future ages would blame our negligence. Even a well-tended garden like the sixteenth-century chanson requires cultivation by each succeeding generation, for each will fashion an image relevant to its own tastes and experiences. What follows is a survey of a genre and a period through an examination of a few works by some of the leading poets and composers. Accompanying facsimiles from the original sources have been included in a few cases. All the pieces mentioned are of easy access; indeed, most are widely known and loved. The repertory is a vast one. Its great extent has worked to limit consideration mainly to what was connected with Paris. Even so, much of value and interest must be passed over or barely intimated.

The attempted reconquests of ancient music during the Renaissance period produced a series of innovations that were more or less fertile for the art, however mistaken they were historically—the culminating and most profitable mistakes of all being the birth of opera in Italy and of the Ballet de Cour in France. Musical humanism may be defined by its broad aims of reviving the "effects" reputedly achieved by the bards and musicians of ancient

Daniel Heartz

or legendary times. About the limitations of the term *humanist* and the neologism that is its substantive form, scholars have warned us sufficiently.[2] The danger lies in the inviting but erroneous extension of the word to embrace humanitarianism, a concept for which the eighteenth century must be given credit. At the time in question the issue was not primarily one of moral philosophy. A humanist was a scholar who taught the *studia humanitatis* and studied philology, mainly with an aim of restoring the ancient languages and literatures. Italy led the way along the path of reconquest during the fifteenth century. A sustained and widespread French reaction to the Italian advances awaited the sixteenth century. Recent studies have tended to emphasize the continual interchange between French and Italian intellectual life ever since the stay at Avignon of Petrarch.[3] No one has claimed an influence of Petrarchan lyric poetry on French poetry prior to 1500. And that is the crux of the matter, for the antique-inspired and Italian-led humanist movement had an impact on the chanson primarily through its verse, not its music.

Musicological practice in English understands the term *chanson* as referring solely or mainly to music. The French have always defined it in terms of text. They have a proverb that expresses the relationship in a characteristically pithy way: "L'air ne fait pas la chanson," roughly translated, "mistake not the music for the matter," or more allegorically, "clothes do not make the man." As understood by its practitioners, the chanson was a short verse, simple and sometimes even popular in character, capable of being sung or at least not precluding musical setting, the specification of which required further qualifying words, such as *chanson mise en musique*, or *chanson musicale*. The most admired poet of the chanson in the first half of the sixteenth century was Clément Marot. He, too, made the traditional distinction that separated text from tune when invoking a verse that had been set to music by Josquin:

La chanson est (sans en dire le son)
Alegez moy, doulce, plaisant brunette.[4]

Given a national habit of mind placing music second to text, it is not surprising that Plato's dictum on the subordination of melody to words found ready acceptance in France.

A case has been made for calling Jean Lemaire de Belges the earliest humanistic poet in France.[5] Born at Bavai in Hainaut (hence, "de Belges") about 1473, Lemaire became prominent as poet-chronicler to Margaret of Austria, regent of the Low Countries. In 1512 he left her service for that of Anne of Brittany, queen of France. Jean Frappier, in a more recent assessment of Lemaire, allows him no more than a few outer trappings of antique culture, gleaned from Italian or Latin texts and mixed in an incongruous fashion with the predominant strain, the late medieval heritage of the Grands Rhétoriqueurs.[6] Such a jumble prompts Frappier to compare his *Temple de Venus* with an elaborately ornate building in the late Gothic style, onto which a few antique details have been stuck—a fair description of what the typical princely *entrée* actually looked like around 1515. Not much of Lemaire's poetry attracted musical setting, as far as can be ascertained. An exception is found in his *Epître de l'amant vert*, a fanciful letter in verse lamenting the absence of Margaret of Austria, written by her favorite parrot. Published in 1510, it ends with the creature's epitaph:

Souz ce tumbel, qui est ung dur conclave,
Gist l'amant vert et le tres noble esclave,
Dont le franc cueur de vray amour pure yvre,
Ne peult souffrir perdre sa dame et vivre.[7]

Compared with most poetry of the rhetorical school, this language is simple and direct. Especially good is the last line, which tells the whole story. Two rhymed couplets (*a a b b*) suffice the poet. The decasyllabic line with caesura after the fourth syllable that he uses was much in favor with chanson composers, so it is not surprising to find an anonymous four-part setting in one of Margaret's music books.[8] The music, some seventy measures long in modern transcription, commences with Phrygian tones of lament and continues with them. There is nothing in it to suggest that this is a mock epitaph. Somber, long-winded, and diffuse in style, it requires many text repetitions, not all of which are clear from the beautiful manuscript that preserves the piece (see the superius part in pl. 1). The text could scarcely be understood in any case be-

Plate 1. A page of music from a chansonnier *that belonged to Margaret of Austria. (Copyright Bibliothèque royale Albert Ier, Brussels.)*

cause of the dense polyphonic writing and the overlapping caused by canons. Yet the composer takes some account of the poetic structure, by ordering the music *A A B C*. The last section is considerably extended and ends with an E pedal, around which triads wavering back and forth between A and E finally settle on the latter. As in the intertwinings of the Flemish-style initials adorning all the parts, or in Lemaire's phantasmagoric visions of a temple to Venus, there is much of the fifteenth century still present here. No perceptible glint of a radiance from antiquity can be discerned as yet.

The intricate rules and rhymes of the Grands Rhétoriqueurs persisted well into the sixteenth century. So did the traditional *genres à forme fixe* associated with them, such as the rondeau and the ballade. Clément Marot was the first French poet of consequence to give up the old models and look to those offered by Italian, Latin, and Neo-Latin verse. He and another court poet of Francis I, Mellin de Saint-Gelais, introduced the sonnet and the epigram into the French language during the 1530's. Marot owed some of his humanist leanings to the great Latin scholar, Etienne Dolet.[9] Saint-Gelais was an excellent Latinist himself. Even before Marot turned decisively to models other than those of French late-medieval tradition, he had achieved an ease of expression and simplicity that greatly appealed to composers. In creating new forms of diction and transforming the language, he never found it necessary to pose as a revolutionary and condemn his predecessors. It was to be a different matter with the Pléiade poets who followed him. Taking a line familiar in scholarly circles of all times, they found nothing in the generation before them worthy of being commended.

The first composer to set Marot's chansons was Claudin de Sermisy, who was also in the service of Francis I. Pierre Attaingnant began his music-publishing business by printing several of the results in *Chansons nouvelles en musique à quatre parties* (April 4, 1528). The book opened with "Secourez moy," followed by "Tant que vivray," then "Dont vient cela"—Marot poems all and printed for the first time here, under Claudin's music. These and other collaborative efforts in the initial book became great favorites with the public. They were reprinted over and over, arranged for various instruments, taken as models for all manner of paraphrases, and copied into many manuscripts. Most of the texts in the *chansonniers* that Attaingnant began turning out en masse are short and similar to Marot's verses. Very few can be ascribed to any poet. Some verses were provided by excerpting quatrains from the longer poems in the *formes fixes*. One example from Attaingnant's first collection shows a more complicated passage from the old poetry to the new. "Au pres de vous" was literally extracted from the first part of a rondeau, "La, non allieurs," as comparison shows:

La, non allieurs, *secretement demeure*
Mon povre cueur qui en peine labeure
Tout a part soy, *sans que nul le conforte*

197

Des grans *douleurs* qu'il soutient et *qu'l porte*
En attendant que pitié le sequeure.
Et se tiendra jusques a ce *qu'il meure*
En se propos, tousjours attendant l'heure
Que bon vouloir sa loyaulté raporte.
La, non allieurs, etc.[10]

Daniel Heartz

Au pres de vous secretement demeure
Mon povre cueur sans que nul le conforte
Et si languist pour la douleur qu'il porte
Puis que voulez qu'en ce tourment il meure.[11]

Attaingnant attributed the musical setting of "Au pres
de vous" to both Claudin and Jacotin, but the weight of
evidence points to the former as its composer.[12] Remarkable is the complete symmetry of the piece, the phrases
of which are parallel to the rhyme scheme *a b b a (rimes
embrassées)*. The first phrase returns intact for the last
line; the two middle phrases might be said to rhyme musically because of their identical length—which is half
that of the main phrase—and their nontonic cadences.
Making musical and poetic form mirror each other does
not, in this case, help convey the sense of the verse. The
full musical stop at the end of the first line undercuts the
need of the text to reach the subject of the sentence at
the beginning of line two. Musical formalism clearly
counted for more than declamatory effect. Yet there are
some subtly expressive details in the setting of individual
words, such as *secretement* and *demeure*. Typical of
Claudin's style, the piece is terse and wastes not a note.
No note could be changed, moreover, without damaging
the shape of the line, which is equally melodic in all four
parts. Claudin's sacred music has the same quality of com-
pression and artful simplicity, suggesting that Francis I
wished divine service to last no longer than necessary.[13]
A formal approach to the poem, concision, and an ineffable lyricism were Claudin's legacy in his chansons. His
heirs were many and were not limited to his direct pupils, such as Pierre Certon. Roland de Lassus, a great
eclectic, could copy the Claudinian miniature and lend
it new life with his expanded harmonic palette, as in his
setting of Pierre de Ronsard's "Bonjour mon coeur." The
tradition of English secular song (in contradistinction to
the madrigal) long maintained a formal approach to text

similar to Claudin's.[14]

But was it really the poem that inspired the perfect musical shape of "Au pres de vous"? Since the poem was but a compilation, is it not more likely that a prior conception of musical shape dictated the verbal garb? If so, we have here a real collaboration between music and poetry, although one that reverses the priorities dear to humanist theory. Quatrains of similar facture were called into existence by the hundreds at just this time. They must have been demanded by composers, perhaps under the influence of some singularly successful model. The da capo aria of the early eighteenth century offers a parallel situation in which poetry was constructed to make best advantage of a musical *fait accompli*. The parallel could be extended. Because the musical tradition of the early sixteenth-century chanson was strong, poetry was engendered to enhance music, just as the equally strong Italian-aria tradition inspired Metastasio to bend his muse accordingly.

The significance of Claudin's sure feeling for rounded ternary form can hardly be overstressed. Out of such tonally cogent, "abstract" musical shapes, the *canzona da sonare* and the sonata could grow. In fact, a historical continuity could probably be traced all the way to the aforementioned da capo aria, and beyond. The genesis of the *A B A* or *A B C A* chanson out of, or along with, the *a b b a* quatrain thus claims attention as a decisive moment in music history. There were a few models among the composers just prior to Claudin. His predecessor in the Royal Chapel, Jean Mouton, wrote such a chanson on the text "De tous regretz, ung tout seule me tourments."[15] It has the typical chordal beginning in slow dactyllic rhythm for the first four syllables, then imitative and more melismatic music after the caesura. The middle lines have different music, the second of the two cadencing on a nontonic degree, allowing the return of the whole first phrase for the final line. All the elements are here, but the piece is too long and diffuse. It could never be mistaken for Claudin's.[16] Harbinger though it may have been, it could not have been the hypothetical "singularly successful model" posited above. A more likely model, if model there was, is offered by a better known "regrets" chanson that was set by Josquin: "Mille regretz de vous abandonner." The melancholy la-

ment of the text is filled with the traditional expressions
of sadness and mourning:

Mille regretz de vous abandonner
Et deslongier vostre face amoureuse.
J'ay si grant deuil et peine douloureuse
Qu'on me verra de brief mes jours finir.[17]

There is nothing remarkable about the verse, unless it is
the laxity that allows *finir* to rhyme with *abandonner*.
The shapely phrases and subtle, motivic play of the music, on the other hand, are quite out of the ordinary. An
elegiac Phrygian strain opens the piece, using the characteristic opening rhythm. The "dying fall" of the superius
generates most of the subsequent melodic ideas. Music
for the second and third lines is less extended and cadences in the latter case on A. There is no literal reprise
for the fourth line as in Claudin. Rather, there is a brief
return to the original tonal region, then a kind of perora-
tion on the main motives introduced in the first phrase,
now heightened by expressive elaboration and repetition.
The very end recalls that of "Souz ce tumbel" in its wavering between the minor triads on E and A. But in its
cogency and motivic economy this piece bears little re-
semblance to the earlier one.

One of the mysteries about "Mille regretz" is the pau-
city of sources for it and their distance from Josquin.
The manuscripts that contain it are all late, and not one
names any composer. Tylman Susato's 1546 collection
devoted entirely to Josquin thus becomes the main
source, along with such intabulations as those in Hans
Gerle's *Tablatur auff die Laudten* of 1533 and the Narváez
tablature of 1538, where the piece inaugurates a section
of French chansons: "Comienzan las canciones frances-
cas y esta primera es una que llaman la *Canción del
Emperador*, del quarto tono de Josquin."[18] Helmuth
Osthoff suggests, plausibly, that the piece was among "au-
cuns chansons nouvelles" ("some new chansons") presented by Josquin to Charles V, for which the composer
was rewarded in 1520.[19] It is also plausible to suppose
that the person being lamented was the previous emper-
or, Maximilian, who died in 1519.

The enigmatic chanson has recently turned up in a
source from a time closer to Josquin. Attaingnant printed

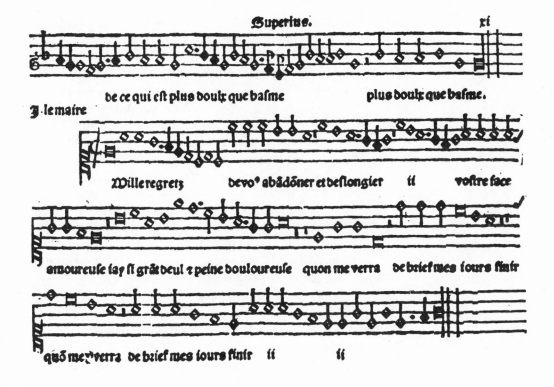

Plate 2. Josquin's "Mille regretz" printed by Attaingnant. (From Chansons musicales à quatre parties *[1533]; photograph Bibliothèque Nationale, Paris.)*

it in 1533 in his *Vingt et sept chansons musicales à quatres parties.* Only the superius survives, and it is reproduced in plate 2. This earliest printed source does not differ markedly from later sources. It shows Attaingnant being quite careful about the placement of the text, which leads him to abbreviate the spelling of many individual words. The surprise is to be seen just above and to the right of the beginning, where the printer places composers' names. Here we read "J. lemaire." No musician of this name is known. Attributing the piece to any one less than Josquin is out of the question. Quite extraordinarily, Attaingnant must have attached the name of the poet instead of the composer: Jean Lemaire. The "mistake" seems prophetic of more literary-minded times later in the century, when the poet's name often assumes importance along with that of the composer. Le-

201

maire is known to have provided Josquin with the text of another "regrets" chanson, "Plus nulz regretz," celebrating the Treaty of Calais in 1508.[20] If this is another instance of collaboration, as seems likely, the question of date must be raised anew. Lemaire did not outlive 1514–1515, at which time he was, like Josquin, in French royal service.[21] The lament, connected with both their names and taken up by a printer so close to the Chapel Royal as Attaingnant, may well have been intended originally for Queen Anne, who died early in 1514, or even King Louis, who died at the end of the same year. Josquin's primordial position with regard to the "new," or "Paris," chanson becomes even stronger, if our surmise is correct.

Claudin's relationship to a piece like "Mille regretz" may be gauged by comparing his "Allez souspirs," which shares the same elegiac mood.[22] The text has been fashioned by an anonymous poet into an *a b b a* quatrain derived from the beginning of Petrarch's famous sonnet "Ite caldi sospiri." Within its scant twenty-five measures the piece condenses an opening statement cadencing on A (minor), a second cadencing on C (major), a third on E (major, i.e., functioning as a dominant), leading to the reprise of the first phrase, which is literal. This chanson is another case in which the Claudinian manner, so formally perfect and purely lyrical, takes account of rhyme scheme and general tone but is otherwise neutral.[23]

More than Claudin, it was Clément Janequin who reconciled the popular and the courtly in his music—exactly what Marot did in his poetry. The lyrical miniature à la Claudin was at Janequin's command, along with several other manners, the best known of which was undoubtedly the "program" chanson, wherein battles, bird songs, street cries, and other phenomena of the real world came to life in sound. To these last Attaingnant devoted an entire volume in 1528 and again in 1537. Betweentimes he brought out, besides many individual pieces of the master, *Vingt et quatre chansons musicales à quatres parties composées par Clément Jennequin* (1533), a collection that allows a good idea of his range and variety. It opened with a pair of chansons describing the elderly rake's retirement to his bed and bonnet.[24] In the first, "Il me suffit du temps passé" ("I've had pastime enough"), Janequin begins by invoking the alternating 6/4 and 9/4 meters characteristic of an age-old country dance, the Branle de Poitou, a reference rich in suggestion to his audience, which probably extended the allusion to the rural bagpipe and the obscene connotations that went with it. Of a sudden the skipping, trochaic rhythms stop as all voices slowly entone the rake's request: "Ung lict mol, ung double bonnet" ("A soft bed, a warm bonnet"). In this anonymous text, as in many that Janequin selects, the point comes last, with epigrammatic effect: "Il n'y a plus d'encre au cornet" ("The ink horn is dry"), a sorry story the voices repeat over and over with unconcealed hilarity. Similar virtuosity in controlling rhythmic effects marks many of Janequin's chansons, along with an attention to the *sense* of the text, which is often conveyed in an ingenious and effectively witty way. His is an art of "badinage."

An anonymous engraving of the time, one of many revealing the naïve feeling of delight taken by urban society in contemplating simple rural pastimes, shows a group of shepherds and shepherdesses dancing the branle to the music of a bagpipe (see pl. 3). Their little speeches reveal such old country names as Robin, Margot, Alizon, and Gombault, the very characters with which Marot and Janequin liked to people their erotic tales. Interestingly enough, these country folk utter their pleasantries in terza rima, one stanza of which ends "Car bransler est tout mon desir" ("my sole desire is to dance the branle"). And it is typical, too, that the shepherd with his crook looking on from the side points up the moral by invoking the ancient deities Mars and Venus.

Whereas Claudin all but ceased composing chansons after the death of Marot in 1544, Janequin continued on, matching his wit and verve with the verses of the new generation of poets, particularly those of Pierre de Ronsard, chief of the Pléiade. The time was one of strivings to promote the vernacular and ensure its success in the task of reviving ancient eloquence. Joachim Du Bellay set the tone with his 1549 treatise defending French and rendering it "illustrious," a manifesto closely modeled upon a 1542 treatise by Sperone Speroni that attempted the same for Italian: "Sing me those odes," cried Du Bellay, "as yet unknown to the French muse, with a lute well tuned to the sound of the Greek and Roman lyre; let there be no verse without some vestige of rare and an-

Plate 3. Country folk dancing the branle, ca. 1530. (Photograph Bibliothèque Nationale, Paris.)

tique erudition."[25] The humanist movement was reaching its zenith. A scholar of Greek, Jean Dorat, was the principal mentor of the Pléiade poets. To be both lyric and learned at the same time proved no easy task for most of them, and all in all they were not very successful in their stated goals of attracting composers to their verses.

Ronsard was the exception. He wrote much in praise of music, although his knowledge of the real thing was scant. His claim of "measuring his verses to the lyre," that is, making them fit for musical setting, could not have been deemed novel by composers who had been setting Marot and Saint-Gelais with perfect ease for more than a generation. It passed for a revelation among the literary set, at any rate, as did the following pronouncement in the preface to his *Odes* (1551): "La lyre seule peut animer les vers et leur donner le juste poids de leur gravité," which probably should be interpreted as "the antique spirit that inspired poetry and music alike is the only one that can bring verses to life and give them their just weight of significance."[26] Or did Ronsard carry humanistic doctrine so far as to insist that poetry could not exist without musical accompaniment? Such an idea, as ridiculous as it seems and as inappropriate as it is to his own works for the most part, is elaborated in his *Abrégé de l'art poétique* (1565), in which his antithetical habit of mind pushes him to formulate an absurd corollary: "Poetry, without instruments, or without the grace of a solo voice or several voices, is not at all agreeable; nor are instruments, without being enlivened by the melody of a pleasing voice."[27] This, at a time when "pure" instrumental music was making spectacular strides and being printed in its own right! Some of the blindness (and deafness) of subsequent French aesthetic theory concerning instrumental music may be traced to Ronsard's dichotomy. His practical advice to poets in the *Abrégé* was confined to what any musician could have told them: Observe strophic regularity and some kind of alternation between masculine and feminine rhymes.

In 1552, as a supplement to the edition of Ronsard's *Amours*, Nicolas Du Chemin printed a small anthology of pieces by leading Parisian masters, such as Janequin, Certon, and Claude Goudimel. These were supposed to serve over 150 sonnets, a preposterous idea of which Lesure says "the procedure of 'blanket' musical covering for a whole series of poems, although customary in the case of those *chansons populaires* of which Ronsard disapproved, must have seemed to the music-loving audience of 1552 a challenge flung to the evolution of French music."[28] The final piece by Janequin was not a "cover-all" chanson but a carefully tailored raiment for the first part of one of Ronsard's most exquisite love lyrics:

Petite Nymphe folâtre,
Nymphette que j'idolâtre
Ma mignonne, dont les yeulx
Logent mon pis et mon mieulx;
Ma doucette, ma sucrée,
Ma grace, ma Cytherée,
Tu me dois, pour m'appaiser

Mille fois le jour baiser.[29]

Daniel Heartz

Following his usual custom, Janequin sets only this first
stanza; the other stanzas, although regular, could scarcely make such a good effect sung to the same music.[30] In
the general sense that the composer conjures an admirably light and airy music to match the exuberant endear-
ments of the poem, he might be said to have captured
and rendered its ethos and given life to the words. Has
his music rendered them their "just weight of significance"? Probably not, or not at least along the lines that
Ronsard imagined. The traditional opening formula of
the dactyl hardly does justice to *Pe-ti-te*, which is middle
accented in speech. And the individual word is not so
easily heard in performance, partly because the superius
lags behind the other three voices, reiterating in a delightful canon at the distance of two beats what the tenor
first sings. Such polyphonic ingenuity, a learning ever so
lightly worn, is of a different sort from the learning
sought by humanists in antiquity. Yet Janequin shows
great sensitivity to textual nuance. To mark the end of
the first quatrain, he achieves an effect of retardation by
broadening the harmonic rhythm. The fifth and sixth
lines are declaimed quite simply in new music that provides the needed tonal contrast (suggestion of a cadence
on what, to modern ears, is heard as the dominant). The
seventh line is declaimed more simply still, in strict homo-
rhythm, and once only, making clear to the Nymph what
she must do to appease her swain: "a thousand kisses a
day." This last line achieves its meaning with the prolif-
eration of the words in all the voices. True to the epigrammatic tendencies noted earlier, Janequin allows only the
fleeting appearance of the final word *baiser*—and in the
lower parts only. Thus, he can introduce it with forceful
effect as all the voices pronounce it together at the cadence. What inspired Janequin to organize the piece
around an initial canon? Perhaps his imagination is visual
to an extent even beyond the bare words. If one voice
(lover) pursues another through the first half of the piece,
there is no doubt that they catch up and combine in the
second. The piece is so well constructed that it could
stand as music without its words. In this respect Janequin
is still close to Josquin and Claudin. He differs from the
latter in the flexibility he is willing to bring in treating

every poem as a little world, unique unto itself.

For the generation of composers just coming to maturity at the middle of the century, Ronsard was the poet preferred above all others. One of the favorites for musical setting was his ode "Mignonne," a delicately sensuous invocation on a favorite Renaissance theme borrowed from the "Carpe diem" of Horace, probably by way of Italian imitations, such as those by Angiolo Poliziano and Lorenzo de' Medici.

Mignonne, allons voir si la rose
Qui ce matin avoit desclose
Sa robe de pourpre au soleil,
A point perdu ceste vesprée
Les plis de sa robe pourprée,   5
Et son teint au vostre pareil.

Las! voyez comme en peu d'espace,
Mignonne, elle a dessus la place
Las! las! ses beautez laissé cheoir!
O vrayment marastre nature   10
Puis qu'une telle fleur ne dure
Que du matin jusques au soir.

Donc, si vous me croyez, Mignonne,
Tandis que vostre âge fleuronne
En sa plus verde nouveauté,   15
Cueillez, cueillez vostre jeunesse:
Comme a ceste fleur la veillesse
Fera ternir vostre beauté.[31]

Guillaume Costeley, royal organist and a prolific composer of chansons, set the entire poem in a version first printed by Adrian le Roy and Robert Ballard in 1567.[32] The first stanza he assigned to the three high voices, the bass remaining silent. It begins with imitative entries, resulting in the repeated calls to "Mignonne" in the various parts. The continuation with more flowing motion is well suited to *allons voir* and the other verbs of motion that follow. An abrupt change calls a halt with the beginning of the second stanza, as all four voices join together in a declamatory rhythm well suited to the exclamations. The first *alas* is repeated after an expressive silence; two lines later the silence occurs before the word, throwing it into syncopation:

line 7: Las! ---- las!
line 9: --- Las! ---- las! las!

For the third stanza, Costeley recapitulates in abbreviated form his three-voiced polyphonic section, which nicely complements the poet's return to addressing "Mignonne" in the first line. He then concludes in his four-voiced homophonic style for the moral of the last three lines: "Gather ye rosebuds while ye may." The musical structure makes perfect sense by itself. At the same time, it is closely dependent on the thought structure of the poem. A more sensitive translation of Ronsard into the high polyphonic style of the time is hard to imagine. Yet Raymond Lebègue singles out this very poem when asserting that no part music was suitable to Ronsard's verses because it prevented understanding of the words and stifled their interior music.[33] His view is very far from that of the poet, who specifically mentioned several voices in the above-quoted passage from the *Abrégé*.

Presumably the littérateurs like Lebègue would be less offended by monophonic settings in the popular style, such as were accorded to some Ronsard lyrics. "Mignonne" was so favored within the poet's lifetime, having been included in Jean Chardavoine's collection of several score verses with the tunes to which they were commonly sung.[34] As a vaudeville (or Voix de Ville), "Mignonne" occupies only a page and a half in a book of very small format (see pl. 4). The economy of space is possible because the same little tune serves all three stanzas. Ronsard facilitated this by observing his own dicta about regularity in line length and rhyme scheme. The melody corresponds perfectly to the metric requirements of the verse. A falling second to mark the feminine ending, as at *ro-se*, must be one of the oldest features of French song. Lines four to six can use the same music as lines one to three except for the cadence, the difference being, as expressed in medieval parlance, *ouvert* and *clos* endings. There is nothing here that could have startled a musician of generations earlier. The tune is modal, syllabic, limited in range to just less than an octave, and fully "accorded" to the verse. Is this, then, what Ronsard and Du Bellay had in mind? Most assuredly it is not. No hint of erudi-

Daniel Heartz

Que du matin iufques au foir.
Donc, fi vous me croyez mignône,
Tandi que voftre aage fleuronne,
En fa plus verde nouueauté,
Cueillez, cueillez voftre ieuneffe,
Commé à cefte fleur la vieilleffe
Fera tenir voftre beauté.

Mignône allôs voir fi la rofe Qui ce ma-
tí auoit defclole fa robe depourp au foleil, Apoíct pdu cefte velpree, le lys de
fa robe pourpree, Et fon teinct au voftre pareil
    Las voyez comme en peu d'efpace,
Mignonne, elle a deffus la place.
    Helas les beautez laiffe choir,
Ha vrayment meraftre eft nature
Puis qu'vne telle fleur ne dure

Vt'é vas mamignône Tu ten vas
Ton bel œil m'abandône Et ie de
mon foucy, Helas ma chere vie Que
meure icy, Las ien'ay point déuie Ab-
ftace de moy, Lors eflongné de toy.
nt de toy m'amour,
De viure vn petit iour.
Comme quand la lumiere
Qu Du foleil s'obcurcit,

Plate 4. A setting of Ronsard's ode "Mignonne" from
Chardavoine's collection of vaudevilles. (From Recueil
des plus belles chansons en forme de voix de ville [1576];
photograph Bibliothèque Nationale, Paris.)

tion, antique or modern, informs such music, as charming
and well made as it is. It belonged to those Gallic traditions the poets denounced as *chansons vulgaires*. No one
would have believed it remotely approached that Platonic
ideal of tone united to word that enthralled men's souls
and accomplished all manner of wonders.

A kind of accompanied solo song was evolving during
Ronsard's time that satisfied humanist ideals more fully
than did either traditional polyphony or popular monophony. It was connected mostly with court festivals and

209

theater music. French humanists were particularly attracted to the fifteenth-century Italian scholar Marsilio Ficino, who claimed that ancient music had been revived in his day and laid stress upon the declaiming of verses to the accompaniment of the Orphic lyre.[35] Some kind of stylized recitation with supporting chords was required of the singer Baccio Ugolini, who played Orpheus in Poliziano's play of 1480.[36] In France the legend of Orpheus took a strong grip on poetic imaginations. Versifiers used it by preference when called upon to praise musicians or musical patrons. Nicolas Bourbon, a sought-after Neo-Latin poet of the earlier sixteenth century, did not hesitate to say of Attaingnant's polyphonic masses in folio, printed in 1532, that they breathed forth melodies similar to those by which "Orpheus, relying on his melodious lyre, moved tigers, rivers, mountain ashes and rocks, and softened the beastlike hearts of men"; another of Attaingnant's composers, Pierre de Manchicourt, was deemed superior to Orpheus, Arion, and Amphion in a liminary address.[37] Marot, somewhat more appropriately, praised the royal lutenist, Albert de Rippe, for his exquisite playing by saying it was even more prized than that of Orpheus.[38] In his "Enfer" of 1526, Marot had already laid claim to a special relationship between his Muse and Orphic inspiration.[39] He imagined in another poem that Venus came to Paris in her chariot, surrounded by the Graces, and spoke to him "in a voice more sweetly resonant than Orpheus singing to his harp."[40] By placing a harp, instead of a lyre or lute, in the hands of Orpheus, Marot shows the interchangeability of these instruments as supporters of antique monody. The Psalms of David, invariably associated with the harp, were regarded as another kind of ancient music, capable of producing "effects."[41] In this respect Marot's last enterprise, completing his French translation of fifty Psalms, may also be regarded as a labor of humanist inspiration.

The actual appearance of Orpheus and similar figures in court shows inevitably led to some kind of declamation supported by rudimentary musical accompaniment. King Henry II entered Lyons in 1548 to be greeted and praised by an "Apollo singing and reciting to the sound of his lyre several Tuscan rhymes in praise of the king."[42] One of the lesser Pléiade poets, Etienne Jodelle, had charge of the celebrations at Paris ten years later in honor

of the Duc de Guise; he placed Orpheus at the head of a
masquerade and specified that he sing while accompanying himself.[43] Some idea of what these antique recitals
to the lyre were like may be gained from a slightly later
occasion, for which some music has survived. Ronsard's
Intermède between the acts of a comedy given at Fon-
tainebleau in 1564 introduced the God of Love, who
vaunted his powers over all the other gods of antiquity:

Je suis Amour, le grand maistre des Dieux
Je suis celuy qui fait mouvoir les Cieux
Je suis celuy qui gouverne le monde,
Qui le premier hors de la masse esclos
Donnay lumiere et fendis le Chaos
Dont fut basti' cette machine ronde.[44]

Seven additional stanzas followed, all observing the same
decasyllabic line with caesura after the fourth syllable
and the same rhyme scheme—Ronsard knew this speech
had to be sung. One of the royal musicians, Nicolas de La
Grotte, made the setting.[45] He begins by distorting the
expected dactyl, with the first syllable lengthened to
three beats so that the next two are squeezed into the
fourth beat, an intimation of those affected whimsies so
characteristic of the Air de Cour with lute accompaniment, in which guise this piece also appeared. The lower
voices merely duplicate the rhythm of the soprano, which
chants monotonously on a few tones in a kind of psalmody, like a *falso bordone*. There are as many notes as syllables. The plainness and utter simplicity are belied to
some extent by the rhythmic sophistication of alternating triple and duple groups. One lyric effusion is all the
composer allows himself: he repeats the last line to a
phrase that takes the soprano up to high F, a melodic
peak reached only once before, in the first line. Thus
there is, in keeping with the chanson tradition, some feeling of rounded form. A point has been passed, nevertheless, in the history of the chanson. Take away the text
of Cupid's speech, and a viable piece of music does not
remain. The many repeated tones and lack of contrapuntal interest ensure the absolute priority of the words and
also their intelligibility, which is of primary importance
in a theatrical show. Here is music that Ronsard and his
generation could indeed believe had reached the desired

goal of uniting poetry and music, antique fashion. What Nicolas de La Grotte adumbrated was nothing less than accompanied monody.

A theorist on the restoration of ancient monody was not lacking among the members of the Pléiade. Pontus de Tyard's *Solitaire second ou discours de la musique*, first printed in 1552, gave the palm to the "Phonasce," an inventor of a single melody, over the "Symphonette," an inventor of several voice parts, because the former was more apt in conveying to the listener the poet's intention.[46] Tyard anticipated by many years similar arguments put forward by Vincenzo Galilei. His attempts to bring ancient lore to bear upon the music of his day led him to investigate the Greek modes and genera. He also recommended the imposition of quantity on French verse, after the model of Greek and Latin.

Costeley, encountered before in connection with his deft polyphonic setting of Ronsard's "Mignonne," was the first to introduce the quarter tones of the enharmonic genus in a chanson. His "Seigneur Dieu" of about 1558 prompted the monograph of Kenneth J. Levy, who calls it "the earliest practical monument of French humanistic chromaticism."[47] The Italianate nature of such an experiment is evident from Costeley's use of unusual accidentals and false relations to enhance certain expressive words in the text.

Anthoine de Bertrand has received less attention for his experimental pieces, which probably date from the 1560's, although they were not printed until 1576, when Le Roy and Ballard began bringing out a series of his settings devoted to Ronsard's *Amours*. Bertrand knew not only Tyard's *Discours* but also Nicola Vincentino's *L'antica musica ridotta alla moderna prattica* (Rome: Antonio Barre, 1555), which he cites in the preface to his first volume, mentioning the quarter-tone harpsichord. According to Alfred Einstein, Bertrand recalled more clearly than any other French composer the Italian madrigal style of the mid-century, meaning chromatic and harmonic boldnesses in the service of textual interpretation, as exemplified particularly by Cipriano de Rore.[48] Actually, Bertrand seems to reject the madrigalistic kind of text painting through chromaticism in his first preface: "Those people err," he says, "who believe that the chromatic genus consists of transposing diatonic music from one place to another and filling it with accidentals.''[49] He offers an alternative in his setting of "Ces liens d'Or," a sonnet in which the first eight lines betray no interval that does not belong to the chromatic genus. So that the listener would concentrate wholly on his intentions, he eschewed polyphonic or rhythmic complexity. The result is a study in the minor-second and minor-third intervals— those characteristic of the chromatic tetrachord (the perfect fourth and perfect fifth, which also occur in the piece, were considered neutral). When a few intervals become the cells of the composition, as here, the impression created is of a curiously modern, almost twentieth-century, linear intensity.[50] Bertrand's experiments with quarter tones were less felicitous, and he was obliged to tell his readers that they could be disregarded because they were too impractical for singers.[51]

Madrigalian chromaticism of the more conventional sort also abounds in Bertrand. Setting an Italian text, "Tutto lo giorno piango," in his *Troisieme livre de chansons* (1578), he used a descending chromatic tetrachord melodically for the cry of lament, "Haimé!"[52] The use of the descending diatonic tetrachord to express grief in the chanson is at least as old as Josquin's "Je me complains de mon amy."[53] Part of the expressive power of "Mille regretz" (see pl. 2) lay in the repeated descending tetrachords at the end. By raising the stakes from diatonic to chromatic descent, composers like Bertrand and Vicentino took a decisive step toward the ground basses for lament so prominent during the following century. Wherever the descending tetrachord comes into prominence, we may suspect some humanist intent, for it was the very symbol of the Greek tonal system, few other features of which were either understood or agreed upon. Even when Bertrand is at his most Italianate, he retains a sure feeling for clarity of form, based on the poetic structure. That is to say, his approach remains typically French.

No metamorphosis undergone by the chanson during the late sixteenth century has been more studied than that resulting from the application of quantity to French verse. Before Tyard, Du Bellay had recommended such a step, and both countered the argument that it was unnatural in a language without strong accents, like French, by saying that it was also unnatural to the ancient languages and had to be created.[54] Applying quantity to vernacular verse was an idea that had been around long before the Pléiade. Paul-Marie Masson has shown that Italian poets tried it repeatedly during the fifteenth century, and even in France the idea had been propounded as early as 1497 by Michel de Boteauville in *L'Art de metrifier*.[55] A little-known treatise by Jacques de La Taille, *La Manière de faire des Vers en Français comme en Grec et Latin*, was written in 1562 but not published until 1573.[56]

On the musical side, there were settings of Horatian odes in shorts and longs by Petrus Tritonius, Ludwig Senfl, and other German masters from the first part of the sixteenth century, but these may have been ignored in France, as was German music in general. Heinrich Glarean, the Swiss theorist, was well known and appreciated by Tyard and other savants at Paris. He described the German ode style at the end of the second book of his *Dodechachordon* (1547), saying that it originated in imitation of the Italian school of poet-improvisers. In 1555, Claude Goudimel, already famous for his settings of the Psalter, brought out a collection of Horatian odes with the printer Du Chemin, whom he served as editor. Not a single copy of these has been found to date, but presumably they were measured. By composing texts derived in turn from Latin and Hebrew antiquity, Goudimel affirmed their unitary powers of inspiration.

About 1567, Jean-Antoine Baïf, together with the composer-singer Thibaut de Courville, began laying the groundwork for a new poetry and music that would guarantee beyond doubt the revival of those "effects" achieved in ancient times. Their effort differed from other humanist experiments in the exalted status of its patrons. King and court were persuaded to treat the matter as if the welfare of the state depended on it—a conviction attributable to the reputed moral powers of ancient music. An official Académie de poesie et musique was founded in 1570 and ratified by Parliament the following year. Among its principal aims was the restoration of music to its ancient perfection, in which words would achieve their true force through melody and harmony.[57] Music was to be subordinate in the union with the result that the measured rhythm of the text (*vers mesurés à l'antique*) dictated that of the music as well. Lesure has painted a vivid picture of the behavior of the noble auditors and the carefully segregated musicians at the séances of the Académie: mandatory silence during the concert (which term now acquires its modern sense); no mingling between the two groups; and absolute prohibition against copying or divulging the works sung.[58] The will to be exclusive and esoteric was something new for the sixteenth-century chanson. What a distance has been traveled from the open and easy congress of Marot and his composers!

Little remains of Courville's music. The ban on circulating or printing *musique mesurée* was apparently effective in his case. One striking air with lute accompaniment, "Si je languis," on a text by Philippe Desportes, who was an initiate of the Académie, survives in a later source.[59] Its melody is very decorated and may indicate how Courville, as a singer, ornamented the spare melodic lines characteristic of measured music. If this is the case, much of the style's charm may have resided in the execution. Improvised diminutions would have helped greatly to lend variety when the same music had to be repeated for many strophes.

During the heyday of the Académie in the 1570's, its music remained, with few exceptions, the secret art it was intended to be. Increasing publication of the court pieces took place after this time. Twenty-three of Baïf's poems in the setting of Jacques Mauduit were brought out by Le Roy and Ballard in 1586 under the title *Chansonettes mesurées*; the very first piece, "Vous me tuez si doucement," was destined to become a great favorite. According to the poet, the shorts and longs were to fall as follows:

Vŏūs mĕ tŭēz sĭ dōūcĕmēnt
Ăvēcqŭe tōūrmāns tānt bĕnĭns
Qŭe nĕ scāy chōsĕ dĕ dōūceūr
Plūs dōūcĕ qu'ēst mă dōūcĕ mōrt
S'ĭl fāūt mŏurĭr, mŏurōn d'ămōūr.[60]

Baïf foregoes end rhymes. But his short, octosyllabic lines are filled with internal rhymes, for example, the *ou* sounds that accumulate from the initial *doucement*, to the double occurrence in the penultimate line, culminating with the three-fold occurrence in the lovely refrain

215

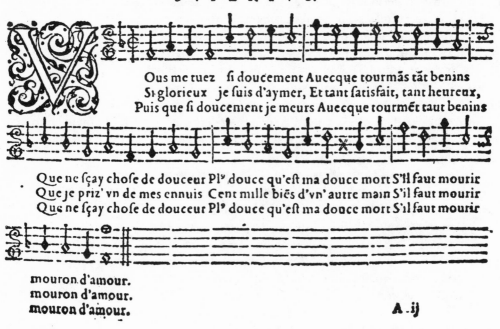

Plate 5. Mauduit's setting of Baïf's "Vous me tuez."
(*From* Chansonettes mesurées *[1586]; photograph Bibliothèque Nationale, Paris.*)

line, or *rechant*, to use Baïf's term. The number of liquid
consonants he succeeds in using is also remarkable. Baïf
offers the composer excellent material for music because
he is brief, direct, and very conscious of sonority. Mauduit's setting, the superius of which is shown in plate 5,
preserves the shorts and longs without deviation or elaboration (exception: *Plus*, line 4). The end of each textual
line is marked off by a bar line. No other "barring" would
be feasible because of the additive nature of the rhythm.
By beginning with a dactyl, Baïf is surely acting out of
deference to the musical practice. Mauduit chooses the
key, which is equivalent to F-major, the most frequent
choice for amorous ditties in chansons ever since Claudin
de Sermisy. The arrangement into shorts and longs follows more or less the accents of spoken French, however
fleeting and impossible these may be to define. Better
expressed, the shorts and longs do not flagrantly contra-

dict normal speech accent. In his melody, Mauduit subtly reduces the contrast between the two values by em-
phasizing the shorts, as, for example, at the end of the
first text line and the beginning of the second, with the
leap up to the C, then the succeeding peak notes E and
F—he is already preparing us for the stunning climax of
the last line. Metric irregularity intervenes with the two
longs for *tour-mans*, effectively breaking the pattern of
long-short since *tu-ez*, a pattern that might have been
heard as triple groupings. Why did Mauduit depart from
Baïf and set *Plus* at the beginning of line four as a short
instead of a long? Possibly he wanted to reinforce the
motivic reference to the beginning of line two.[61] We
might well ask also why Baïf assigned a long to *S'il* at the
beginning of the last line, when normal speech accent
might suggest a short. Perhaps he realized that a short
would result in a continuity of groupings that could be
interpreted as triple the length of the last two lines, with
an effect somewhat like a "vulgar" dance song, which
was the last thing desired. The charm of this style lies in
avoiding metric regularity. Given the limitations imposed
on him, Mauduit creates a little gem. His master stroke
was to make the short syllable on *Mou-rir* the melodic
climax of the piece. Without end rhymes to guide him,
he constructs a perfectly viable phrase sequence. Harmonic contrast and variety arrive with the D-major chord at
the end of the second phrase, which points to the arrival
of G-minor as the goal of the following phrase; it then
becomes logical and inevitable, by tonal analogy, that
the C-major of the fourth phrase points with the force
of a dominant to the tonic resolution of the final phrase.
The canvas is small, and the style must be terse. Mauduit
and Baïf may have ventured far from the "classical" chanson of Marot and Sermisy, yet how similar are the inti-
mate elegance and formal perfection of the result. The
old French traditions live on in *musique mesurée à l'antique*. It seems that no amount of humanist theorizing—
and the most outlandish amount of the century is at
work here—could destroy an innate sense of *le bon goût*.

Another, more prolific master, whose life and works
were rescued by Mauduit, deserves mention at the end
of any survey such as this. Claude Le Jeune, unlike most
of the composers that have been discussed, was from the
northern reaches of French-speaking territory, having

Daniel Heartz

been born at Valenciennes, not far from Mons, the native town of Lassus. His Franco-Flemish heritage, already a prediction of polyphonic elaboration, is borne out in several chansons published by Pieter Phalesius at Louvain in 1552. He was an early collaborator of Baïf's at Paris, but hardly any of his chansons appeared in print until after his death in 1600 or 1601. *Le Printemps*, brought out by the Ballard firm in 1603, united a few polyphonic chansons with a considerable number of homophonic *airs* in the measured style. An elaborate preface proclaimed Le Jeune the first to have wed ancient rhythms successfully with modern harmony.[62] In fact, he did bring a virtuosity exceeding other composers to the task of working within the narrow limits of the measured style. He expanded the rhythmic possibilities to include two ranges of short-long values, one in diminution, used mainly as a contrast for subsidiary sections. Mauduit also did this with great effect, as in his setting of Baïf's "Eau vive, source d'amour,"[63] but it was not characteristic of him. Unlike Mauduit, Le Jeune exploited contrasting textures, working sometimes with few, sometimes with many, voices to gain variety while traversing the many strophes of Baïf's poems. "Revecy venir du Printans," the second and surely best-known piece in the collection, contains four verses set to combinations increasing from two to five parts, always alternating with the refrain *a 5*.[64] As the texture thickens, the rhythms become less complex, that is to say, there is less subdivision of the basic units, so that a balance of interest is maintained between both aspects. A fine sense of climax is achieved as the final five-voiced verse reintroduces considerable rhythmic elaboration. Unity from one stanza to another emerges in subtle details, such as the repetition of certain melodic lines, but in a reordered way, or in inversion. A high degree of contrapuntal skill is evident but not flaunted. It works together with a delicately nuanced harmonic palette. However fervently the humanist mind, and composers themselves, for that matter, may have believed that music's purpose was merely to enhance the declamation of the text, the end result was often as truly musical and defensible on purely musical grounds as here. Le Jeune's range of creative responses under limiting conditions testifies to the unflagging vigor of the Renaissance chanson, of which he was one of the last and greatest masters.

The simile of the garden with which we began was neither haphazard nor unpremeditated. Order, neatness, and symmetry, the characteristics distinguishing French gardens since at least the sixteenth century, had their parallel in music. The chanson betrays them in all clarity. Its finest inflorescence happened to coincide with the humanist movement. It reflected humanist dreams, to be sure, because it was a mirror reflecting life in all its infinite variety, not excluding the crudest. The reflection still lingers, casting a peculiar and practical light upon the intellectual strivings of the humanist era.

Notes

1. See especially Frances A. Yates, *The French Academies of the Sixteenth Century* (London: Warburg Institute, University of London, 1947), chap. 3, "The Measured Poetry and Music"; Jean Jacquot, ed., *Musique et poésie au XVIe siècle* (Paris: Centre National de la Recherche Scientifique, 1954); François Lesure, *Musicians and Poets of the French Renaissance* (New York: Merlin Press, 1955); James Haar, ed., *Chanson and Madrigal: 1480–1530* (Cambridge, Mass.: Harvard University Press, 1964); and Howard Mayer Brown, *Music in the French Secular Theater: 1400–1550* (Cambridge, Mass.: Harvard University Press, 1963).

2. Marcel Françon, "Humanisme," *Renaissance Quarterly* 21 (1968): 300–303, points out that this term came into being as late as the nineteenth century. In his *Notes de Cours* (Cambridge, Mass.: Schoenhof's Foreign Books, 1960), p. 114, Françon calls attention to how imprecise and uncertain the modern sense of the term is, inasmuch as every specialist feels obliged to define it anew. His point is exemplified by the essays collected in *French Humanism: 1470–1600*, ed. Werner L. Gundersheimer (London: Macmillan & Co., 1969), where a variety of interpretations from the most rigorous to the most lax may be observed.

3. See Franco Simone, *The French Renaissance: Medieval Tradition and Italian Influence in Shaping the Renaissance in France*, trans. H. Gaston Hall (London: Macmillan & Co., 1969), especially chap. 5, "The Fortune of Petrarch in France."

219

4. *The song goes (saying nothing of the tune)*
   Relieve me, sweet, buxom brunette.
   Clément Marot, *Les Epigrammes*, ed. Claude Albert Mayer
   (London: Athlone Press, 1970), epigram 208, "Huictain,"
   pp. 267–268. This and all other translations are my own.
   The editor errs in referring to "Alegez moy" as an "incipit of a made-up chanson." He himself gives the entire
   text of the old chanson in a note accompanying Marot's
   earlier citation of it in chanson 18, "D'un nouveau dard
   je suis frappé," in Marot's *Oeuvres lyriques* (London:
   Athlone Press, 1964), p. 190. I extend the term *chanson*
   to include, besides verses so labeled, other secular verses
   in the vernacular that were set to music, of which a great
   quantity may be found among Marot's epigrams. It
   would be cumbersome to specify "chanson set to music"
   every time this concept is required; therefore, we shall
   understand the term to apply to music and text taken together.

5. Philip-August Becker, *Jean Lemaire: Der erste humanist-
   ische Dichter Frankreichs* (Strasbourg: K. J. Trübner,
   1893).

6. Jean Frappier, "L'Humanisme de Jean Lemaire de
   Belges," *Bibliothèque d'humanisme et renaissance* 25
   (1963): 289–306.

7. *Within this tomb, which is a cruel conclave,*
   Lies the green lover and very noble slave,
   Whose frank heart, drunk with pure love,
   Cannot suffer to lose his lady and live.
   From J. Stecher, ed., *Œuvres de Jean Lemaire de
   Belges*, 4 vols. (Louvain: Lefever, 1885–1891), 3:16.

8. Martin Picker, *The Chanson Albums of Marguerite of
   Austria* (Berkeley: University of California Press, 1965),
   p. 16, and transcription from Brussels, Bibliothèque
   royale, MS 228, no. 24, pp. 275–279.

9. Marot, *Les Epigrammes*, introductory chap., "Etude li-
   téraire," p. 9.

10. *There, nowhere else, secretly dwells*
    My poor heart, which in pain labors

Daniel Heartz

All by itself, with none to comfort it,
For the great pains it sustains and bears,
While waiting for pity to provide succor.
And it will hold, till it expires,
To this purpose, ever waiting the hour
When good will requites its loyalty.
There, nowhere else, etc.
From Marcel Françon, ed., *Poèmes de transition (XVe–XVIe siècles): Rondeaux du Ms. 402 de Lille*, 2 vols. (Cambridge, Mass.: Harvard University Press, 1938), vol. 2, poem 363 (italics added). In his commentary, Françon mentions another source for the poem (Paris, Bibliothèque nationale, MS fr. 19182), where it is called "Envoy du petit Martin de Housse."

11. *Near to you secretly dwells*
My poor heart, with none to comfort it,
And languishes for the pain it bears
Since you would have it expire in this torment.
The many sources of this chanson are discussed in Daniel Heartz, "*Au pres de vous*: Claudin's Chanson and the Commerce of Publishers' Arrangements," *Journal of the American Musicological Society* 24 (1971): 193–225. The article also contains a modern edition of the music.

12. Ibid., pp. 197–198. I am indebted to Lawrence Bernstein for kindly pointing out in a subsequent letter that Jacotin's name appears in the tenor part of the chanson in Pierre Attaingnant's *Trente et quatre chansons* (Paris, 1530–1531), fol. 2^v, as well as in his *Premier livre contenant xxxi. chansons musicales esleues* (Paris, 1536), fol. 18^v.

13. Claude Chappuys, in his rhymed *Discours de la court* of 1543, describes the king hearing Mass while listening to his "singers with voices of silver, intoning the divine praises, and reciting the Psalms of David, with motets of diverse fashions, made by Claudin, the father of musicians, or by Sandrin, equal to the ancients." For the original text, see Daniel Heartz, *Pierre Attaingnant: Royal Printer of Music* (Berkeley: University of California Press, 1969), p. 92.

14. Philip Brett, "Word-Setting in the Songs of William Byrd," *Proceedings of the Royal Musical Association* 98 (1971–1972): 47–64.

15. Modern edition of Jean Mouton's chanson in Hans Albrecht, ed., *Zwölf französische Lieder aus Jacques Moderne: Le Parangon des Chansons (1538)*, Das Chorwerk, vol. 61 (Wolfenbüttel: Möseler Verlag, 1956), piece 9, pp. 24–27.

16. See Howard Mayer Brown, "The Genesis of a Style: The Parisian Chanson, 1500–1530," in *Chanson and Madrigal*, ed. Haar, pp. 27–28. It is somewhat misleading to describe the form as "*A B C A* with the last section repeated to the same text." Both first and last lines must be repeated at least once to cover the big initial and final sections. Brown's "section" means the final subsection of *A*.

17. *A thousand regrets upon leaving you*
    And forsaking your lovely face:
    Such great grief and sorrowful pain are mine,
    That my days will soon be seen to end.
    From Josquin Des Prés [Desprez], *Werken*, ed. Albert Smijers (Amsterdam: G. Alsbach, 1925), vol. 1, chanson 24, p. 63. The piece is also edited by Friedrich Blume in *Josquin des Prés und andere Meister: Weltliche Lieder*, Das Chorwerk, vol. 3 (Wolfenbüttel: Möseler Verlag, n.d.), piece 1, pp. 4–5, and by Brown in *Chanson and Madrigal*, ed. Haar, ex. 2, pp. 143–146. I suggest two emendations in all these editions: (1) repetition of the word *abandonner* to cover the music in measures 7–9, where the first big section properly ends, and (2) sharping both F and G in the superius, measure 9, as does Narváez in his intabulation (see n. 18); Narváez also raises the second G of the tenor in measure 4 and the penultimate F of the superius (but *not* the ultimate G).

18. "Here begin the French chansons, and the first one is called *The Emperor's Chanson*, which is in the fourth mode and composed by Josquin." Luys de Narváez, *Los seys libros del Delphin de música* (Valladolid: Diego Hernández de Córdova, 1538); see also the modern edition, ed. Emilio Pujol, Monumentos de la Música Es-

Daniel Heartz

pañola, vol. 3 (Barcelona: Instituto Español de Musi-
cologia, 1945), pp. 37–38.

19. Helmuth Osthoff, "Josquin Desprez," *Die Musik in
    Geschichte und Gegenwart*, 14 vols. (Kassel and Basel:
    Bärenreiter, 1949–1968), vol. 7, col. 197.

20. Picker, *Chanson Albums*, p. 16.

21. Jean Lemaire de Belges, *La Concorde des deux langages*,
    ed. Jean Frappier (Paris: Droz, 1947), introduction, pp.
    xx–xxi.

22. Modern edition of Claudin's "Allez souspirs" in *Chanson
    and Madrigal*, ed. Haar, ex. 35, pp. 243–244.

23. For a discussion of the piece and its text, see Daniel
    Heartz, "Les Goûts Réunis, or the Worlds of the Madri-
    gal and the Chanson Confronted," in ibid., pp. 107–108.

24. See the modern edition of *Vingt et quatre chansons mu-
    sicales à quatres parties composées par Clément Jenne-
    quin* in Clément Janequin, *Chansons polyphoniques*, ed.
    A. Tillman Merritt and François Lesure, 6 vols. (Monaco:
    Editions de l'Oiseau Lyre, 1965–1971), pieces 18 and
    19, 2:1–7.

25. Joachim Du Bellay, *La Deffence et illustration de la
    langue françoyse*, ed. Henri Chamard (Paris: M. Didier,
    1948), pp. 112–113. Some reactions to Du Bellay's pre-
    tentions were negative; see Daniel Heartz, "Voix de
    ville: Between Humanist Ideals and Musical Realities,"
    in *Words and Music: The Scholar's View. A Medley of
    Problems and Solutions Compiled in Honor of A. Tillman
    Merritt*, ed. Laurence Berman (Cambridge, Mass.: Harvard
    University, Department of Music, 1972), pp. 115–135.

26. Pierre de Ronsard, *Odes: Les quatres premiers livres des
    Odes de Pierre de Ronsard Vandomois* (Paris: Guillaume
    Cavellart, 1550), preface (unpaginated).

27. Cited by Raymond Lebègue, "Ronsard et la musique,"
    in *Musique et poésie*, ed. Jacquot, p. 109.

28. Lesure, *Musicians and Poets*, p. 61.

29. *Wanton little nymph,*
    Whom I idolize,
    Nymphet, whose eyes
    Lodge my worst and my best,
    My darling, my sweetheart,
    My grace, my Venus,
    To calm me, thou must
    Kiss me a thousand times a day.
    From Pierre de Ronsard, *Les Amours de P. de Ronsard Vandomoys* (Paris: Veufue Maurice de la porte, 1552), fol. Diiii^v.

30. Modern edition of the music in *Ronsard et la Musique de son temps*, ed. Julien Tiersot (Leipzig and New York: Breitkopf and Härtel, 1903); *La Fleur des musiciens de P. de Ronsard*, ed. Henry Expert (Paris: A l'Enseigne de la Cité des Livres, 1923); and Janequin, *Chansons polyphoniques*, ed. Merritt and Lesure, piece 219, 5:196–198, where the initial canon is obscured by a misprint.

31. *Let us go, my dear, and see if the rose*
    Which this morning disclosed
    Its crimson dress to the sun
    Has not lost this afternoon
    The folds of its crimson robe
    And its complexion equal to yours.

    Alas! See how in such a short space,
    My dear, it has let fall to the ground—
    Alas! Alas!—its beauties.
    What a cruel stepmother is nature,
    When such a flower can endure
    Only from morning till evening.

    Thus, believe me, my dear,
    As long as your years flower,
    In their most verdant prime,
    Gather up your youth:
    For, like this flower, age
    Will tarnish your beauty.
    First printed in Pierre de Ronsard, *Le Premier Livre des Odes de P. de Ronsard gentilhomme Vandomois* (Paris: Guillaume Cavellart, 1550), ode 17.

32. Modern edition of Pierre de Ronsard's "Mignonne," in *Les Maîtres musiciens de la Renaissance française*, ed. Henry Expert, 23 vols. (Paris: A. Leduc, 1894–1908), piece 18, 4:75–81.

33. Raymond Lebègue, "Ronsard et la musique," in *Musique et poésie*, ed. Jacquot, p. 114. One is tempted to reproach Lebègue by quoting Ronsard's strictures about the man inimical to music: "Comment se pourroit on accorder avec un homme qui de son naturel hait les accords? Celui n'est digne de voir la douce lumière du soleil, qui ne fait honneur à la Musique" ("How can one be in harmony with a man whose nature it is to dislike harmony? He who does not honor music is unworthy to see the light of day"; preface to Ronsard's *Méllanges* [Paris: Le Roy and Ballard, 1560 and 1572]).

34. Jehan Chardavoine, *Le Recueil des plus belles et excellentes chansons en forme de voix de ville tirées de divers autheurs et Poëtes François, tant anciens que modernes ausquelles a esté nouvellement adapté la Musique de leur chant commun, à fin que chacun les puisse chanter en tout endroit qu'il se trouvera, tant de voix que sur les instruments* (Paris: C. Micard, 1576; rev. ed., 1588).

35. Yates, *French Academies*, p. 41.

36. See Nino Pirrotta, *Li Due Orfei: Da Poliziano a Monteverdi* (Turin: RAI, 1969), chap. 1, "L'Orfeo degli Strambotti." Musical ex. 5, pp. 45–46, a recitativelike *strambotto* setting that may be by Ugolini, is particularly suggestive of how a stage Orpheus may have sung and accompanied himself on his lyre.

37. Heartz, *Pierre Attaingnant*, pp. 176–181.

38. Marot, *Les Epigrammes*, epigram 121, "D'Albert Joueur de Luc du Roy," p. 192.

39. Claude Albert Mayer, ed., *Oeuvres satiriques* (London: Athlone Press, 1962), p. 67.

40. Clément Marot, "Le Second Chant d'amour fugitif," in ibid., p. 87.

41. Yates, *French Academies*, p. 44, quotes a poem of La Boderie that makes this explicit.

42. *La Magnificence de la superbe et triumphante entrée de la noble & antique Cité de Lyon faicte au Treschrestien Roy de France Henry deuxiesme de ce nom* (Lyons: Guillaume Rouille, 1549), p. 70. Modern edition, with supporting documents, edited by Georges Guigue (Lyons: Société des Bibliophiles Lyonnais, 1927). The Italian version, *La Magnifica et triumphale entrata* (Lyons: Rouille, 1549), p. 94, specifies: "Apollo suavemente sonando canto le seguenti stanze: 'Phebo son io per cui s'alluma il giorno' " ("Apollo, sweetly playing, sang the following verses: 'Phoebus am I, by whom day is illuminated' ").

43. Etienne [Estienne] Jodelle, *La Recueil des inscriptions, figures, devises et masquerades ordonnées en l'hostel de ville à Paris le jeudi 17 de février* (Paris: André Wechel, 1558), fol. 15^v: "Davantage scachant que la beauté d'une masquerade est la musique, je voulois qu'Orphée, qui estoit jadis l'un des Argonautes, marchant devant eus, sonant et chantant une petite chanson en la louange du Roy" ("Knowing, moreover, that music is the embellishment of a masquerade, I wished Orpheus, who was one of the Argonauts, to march ahead of them, while sounding and singing a little chanson in praise of the king"). The spectacle, for which the banquet hall was transformed *à l'antique*, was a failure because of the great confusion, insufficient preparation of the actors, and malfunction of the theatrical machines; see Etienne [Estienne] Jodelle, *Oeuvres complètes*, ed. Enea Balmas, 3 vols. (Paris: Gallimard, 1965), 1:42–43. See also Etienne [Estienne] Jodelle, *La Recueil des inscriptions 1558: A Literary and Iconographical Exegesis*, ed. Victor E. Graham and W. McAllister Johnson (Toronto: University of Toronto Press, 1972), p. 103.

44. *I am Cupid, the master of the Gods,*
    It is I who makes the skies move,
    Who governs the world,
    Who, the first-born of matter,
    Gave light and dissipated chaos,
    From which this round frame was made.
    From Pierre de Ronsard, *Elegies, Masacarades, et Bergerie*

par P. de Ronsard Gentilhomme Vandomois (Paris: G. Buon, 1565), p. 32.

45. Modern edition of musical setting for Ronsard's *Intermède* by Nicolas de La Grotte in *La Fleur des musiciens*, ed. Expert, pp. 62–64. For sixteenth-century sources, further discussion, and a different transcription of the soprano, see Daniel Heartz, "A Spanish 'Masque of Cupid,' " *Musical Quarterly* 49 (1963): 64–66.

46. I quote from the collected edition of Pontus de Tyard's prose works, *Les Discours philosophiques* (Paris: A. L'Angelier, 1587), fols. 113^V–114: ". . . car si l'intention de Musique semble estre de donner tel air à la parole, que tout escoutant se sent passioné, et se laisse tirer à l'affection du Poëte: celuy qui scet proprement accomoder une voix seule, me semble mieux atteindre à sa fin aspirée: vù que la Musique figurée le plus souvent ne rapporte aux oreilles autre chose qu'un grand bruit, duquel vous ne sentez aucune vive efficace: Mais la simple et unique voix, coulée doucement, et continuée selon le devoir de sa Mode choisie pour le merite des vers, vous ravit la part qu'elle veut. Aussi consistoit en ce seul moyen la plus ravissante energie des anciens Poëtes lyriques, qui mariant la Musique à la Poësie (comme ils estoient nez à l'une et à l'autre) chantoient leurs vers" (". . . music's purpose seems to be that of setting the word in such a fashion that anyone listening to it will become impassioned and carried away by the mood of the poet. The musician who knows how to deploy the solo voice to this end best attains his goal, in my opinion. Contrapuntal music most often brings to the ears only a lot of noise, from which you feel no vivid effect. But the simple voice alone, gracefully produced and consistently employed according to the mode required by the character of the verse, will carry you wherever it wishes. In this sole means was to be found the most ravishing energy of the ancient lyric poets, who married music to poetry [inasmuch as they were born for one another] when singing their verses"). He goes on to call part music a *vulgaire usage*.

47. Kenneth J. Levy, "Costeley's Chromatic Chanson," *Annales Musicologiques* 3 (1955):213–263.

48. Alfred Einstein, *The Italian Madrigal*, 3 vols. (Princeton: Princeton University Press, 1949), 1:404. Changes of tempo for expressive purposes are a debt owed the Italian madrigal by Bertrand, "who recalls Rore and his successors in his harmonic boldness also."

49. Facsimile of Anthoine de Bertrand's preface to *Premier Livre des Amours* (Paris: Le Roy and Ballard, 1576) and complete modern edition in *Monuments de la Musique française au temps de la Renaissance*, ed. Henry Expert, 10 vols. (Paris: M. Senart, 1924-1929), 4:[vi-vii].

50. Ibid., 4:8-9. Expert errs in supplying an accidental in the tenor that would render the music more conventional, to be sure, but would introduce a major second—the characteristic interval of the diatonic genus that would dilute the otherwise "pure" chromatic study in minor seconds. Bertrand, besides, was precise about his accidentals. He specifically warned in his first preface that they apply once only to the note before which they stand. Musica ficta is thus inapplicable.

51. For a summary of French experiments with the genera, see Levy, "Costeley's Chromatic Chanson," p. 248, n. 2.

52. I am indebted to my former student, Judith Tick Steinberg, for pointing out that Bertrand probably borrowed here from Vicentino's "Poi ch'el mio largo pianto," in *Madrigali a cinque voci* (Milan: Appresso Paolo Gottardo Pontio, 1572). Modern edition in Nicola Vicentino, *Opera Omnia*, ed. Henry W. Kaufman, Corpus mensurabilis musicae, vol. 26 (Rome: American Institute of Musicology, 1963), p. 82.

53. Alan Curtis, "Josquin and 'La belle Tricotée,'" in *Essays in Honor of Dragan Plamenac*, ed. Gustave Reese and Robert Snow (Pittsburgh: University of Pittsburgh Press, 1969), p. 1.

54. Du Bellay, *La Deffence et illustration*, pp. 144-145, chap. beginning "Quand auz piedz et aux nombres." Tyard discusses quantity on fols. 42^V and 51 and in his closing summation, fol. 128^V (see n. 46).

55. Paul-Marie Masson, "L'Humanisme musical en France au XVIe siècle," *La Mercure musicale* 3 (1907): 333–366.

56. Ibid., p. 341.

57. See Yates, *French Academies*, p. 320: ". . . remettre en usage la Musique selon sa perfection, qui est de representer la parole en chant accomply de son harmonie et mélodie" (". . . to restore music to its perfect state, which is to represent the word in song, completed by its harmony and melody").

58. Lesure, *Musicians and Poets*, pp. 94–97.

59. Modern edition of Thibaut de Courville's music for "Si je languis," with facsimile of the original, in André Verchaly, *Airs de cour pour voix et luth (1603–1643)*, Publications de la Société française de musicologie, First Series, vol. 16 (Paris, 1961), piece 32, pp. 72–77. Another transcription, with different rhythmic interpretation, may be studied in Carol MacClintock, ed., *The Solo Song: 1580–1730* (New York: W. W. Norton and Co., 1973), piece 50, pp. 176–178.

60. *You are killing me so gently*
    With such benign torments,
    That I know no sweetness
    More sweet than my sweet death.
    If one must die, let's die of love.
    The poem is taken from the modern edition of the music in *Les Maîtres musiciens*, ed. Expert, piece 1, 1:2–5. The prefatory facsimiles include one showing the poem with indication of shorts and longs; Baïf's unsuccessful attempt to make French spelling phonetic is evident here also.

61. Another composer, Fabrice Marin Caietain, did not diverge from the poet's rhythm at this spot when setting "Vous me tuez." See D. P. Walker, "Some Aspects and Problems of Musique mesurée à l'antique: The Rhythm and Notation of Musique mesurée," *Musica Disciplina* 4 (1950): 163–186 (ex. 1, p. 183). The musical examples are plagued with errors.

62. Yates, *French Academies*, pp. 56–57, translates this interesting preface at length; it does not forego mentioning
the Orpheus fable.

63. Jacques Mauduit's musical setting of Jean-Antoine Baïf's
"Eau vive, source d'amour," edited in Verchaly, *Airs de
cour*, piece 14, pp. 28–29, and in MacClintock, *The Solo
Song*, piece 47, pp. 170–171, with ascription to Gabriel
Bataille, in one of whose collections it occurs anonymous-
ly as an air for lute. D. P. Walker attributes the air to
Mauduit in "Some Aspects and Problems of Musique
mesurée," p. 164 (see n. 61). Verchaly, finding additional evidence for the attribution in Marin Mersenne, be-
lieves it entirely plausible. In his commentary on p.
xxxvii, Verchaly prints another version of this air showing several disagreements as to which syllables were to
be short and which long.

64. Modern edition of Claude Le Jeune's "Revecy venir du
Printans" in *Les Maîtres musiciens*, ed. Expert, piece 2,
12:11–27. I am indebted to another student, Douglas
Johnson, for a penetrating seminar paper devoted mainly to Mauduit and Le Jeune.

Daniel Heartz

Musicology, History, and Anthropology:
Current Thoughts
Gilbert Chase

Any good history book . . . is saturated with anthropology.
Claude Lévi-Strauss

Seven

Among the definitions of *current* (adj.) in *The Shorter
Oxford English Dictionary* are (1) running, flowing; (2)
running in time, in progress; (3) generally reported or
known, in general circulation; and (4) generally accepted,
in vogue. The thoughts that I shall discuss here have been
flowing in the intellectual stream of our time for several
decades, and among the more alert disciplines dealing
with the works of man, such as anthropology, sociology,
and linguistics, they are "generally reported or known,
in general circulation." Among certain branches or trib-
utaries of these disciplines—I like to think of them as
constituting "The Sciences of Man"—these flowing
thoughts have become "generally accepted, in vogue."
This is not the case with musicology as a whole, even
though current thought in ethnomusicology has been
running in this direction for some time. It is my conviction that the total field of musicology would benefit by
assimilating some of the current thought pertaining to
history and anthropology, particularly in the perspective
of cultural anthropology as formulated by Claude Lévi-
Strauss.[1]

But we cannot speak intelligently about "the total
field of musicology" without further clarification of the
latter term. We have not yet—unfortunately—reached
that point in time at which the term *musicology* is generally accepted as signifying the *total* study of music in human culture, in the same way that the term *anthropology* is generally taken to mean the total study of man and
his works. Anthropology has, of course, many branches,
each directed toward the study of a particular aspect of
man's behavior. Musicology, on the contrary, has tended
in recent years toward a polarization represented by its
historical and ethnological branches. Thus, one may hear

231

a young musical scholar say, "My approach is as an ethnomusicologist, not a musicologist." This would be the equivalent of saying, "My approach is as an ethnologist, not an anthropologist." An ethnologist is, of course, an anthropologist, just as an ethnomusicologist is a musicologist. If the distinction were made solely with regard to a particular approach or emphasis within a total field of study, then it would be quite legitimate—as in the distinction between physical and cultural anthropology. But in musical studies there is a semantic problem and a resulting conceptual confusion, because the term *musicology*, without any qualifier, has been tacitly appropriated by the historical branch of that discipline. The scope of the American Musicological Society, for example, cannot be deduced by analogy from the scope of the American Anthropological Association. The former is narrowly circumscribed both in subject matter and methodology, while the latter is multifaceted, all-inclusive, and mobile in its methodology. The one is static, the other dynamic.

Confining our attention to the semantic problem for the moment, the unilateral use of the term *musicology* seems all the more anomalous because of the weight of authority that goes against it. Let me illustrate by referring to a very important book published in 1963 and titled simply *Musicology*.[2] This is a volume in the Princeton Studies in Humanistic Scholarship in America, co-authored by Frank Ll. Harrison, Mantle Hood, and Claude V. Palisca. One would hope that this book has received the attention—and exerted the influence—that it merits. Yet one is discouraged to note that the most conspicuous and significant part of its message has apparently been ignored—or, if noticed, has not been made widely effective.

To decode this message, one simply has to interpret its meaning with relation to the conceptual content of the work. The longest essay, "Music, the Unknown," is by Mantle Hood, who in the current terminology is known as an *ethnomusicologist*. The opening essay, "American Musicology and the European Tradition," by Frank Ll. Harrison, is strongly slanted toward a sociocultural, anthropological view of the scope of musicology.

In spite of this obvious bias, the book is not titled *Musicology and Ethnomusicology*, or *Musicology and Re-*

lated Disciplines, but simply *Musicology*. Clearly, the message that we are meant to receive is that the term *musicology* signifies *all* aspects of the scholarly study of music and its role in human culture and society. Moreover, the circumstance that the volume appeared in a series on "humanistic scholarship" indicates that the general editor saw no fundamental conflict between the humanistic approach and that of the cultural-anthropological approach. How then, does it happen that the historical musicologists have chosen, by and large, to ignore the basic message of the Princeton volume by continuing to use the term *musicology* in a restricted rather than a global sense?

The clue to an answer may be found in the central essay of the Princeton volume, "American Scholarship in Western Music," wherein Professor Palisca states that "the musicologist is first and foremost a historian. . . ." (p. 119; I apologize for taking this statement out of context in order to make a point that I believe calls for further discussion in the framework of my present topic.) The view that history is the essential core of musicology, to which all other disciplines are marginal, represents a regression from the wider, more inclusive concept of musicology formulated by Guido Adler in 1885, which included not only historical, systematic, and comparative branches, but also musical theory, pedagogy, didactics, aesthetics, and psychology of music. This multifaceted view was also taken by Glen Haydon in his influential *Introduction to Musicology* (1941), wherein he includes anthropology among "the various auxiliary sciences which contribute to our knowledge and understanding of music."[3]

It is not my purpose to trace in detail the process whereby the historical approach became dominant in American musicology. I only wish to remark that this overriding emphasis led inevitably to the schism and consequent polarization represented by the formation of the Society for Ethnomusicology and its remarkable growth in importance and influence. Musical sociology and anthropology, which Professor Palisca dismisses as "pseudo-sciences," proved to be not only valuable but also indispensable for the comprehensive study of the musics of mankind. Hence, it was inevitable that a movement should develop, and an organization take shape, that

Musicology, History, and Anthropology

233

would fill the vacuum created by the rejection (speaking *grosso modo*) of the social sciences by the historical branch of musicology. It is, of course, possible to take the view that the separation of historical and ethnic musicology was not undesirable—that, on the contrary, it gave independence and freedom of action to each branch. But an increasing number of scholars (among whom I count myself) do not share that view; and in this lecture I should like to present the case for a synthesis of the historical and anthropological approaches in musicology.

The preemption of the term *musicology* by the historical branch of that discpline may be seen as a corollary of the historicism of the nineteenth century—the historico-centric view of culture and society that acquired such power and prestige in academic circles and that has only recently been challenged on various fronts, including that of the progressive historians in the second half of the present century. Linked to this view of history are the notions of causality, continuity, and chronology—which in turn are identified with the idea of temporal-linear progress as embodied in Western civilization. This view assumes that history enjoys a uniquely privileged position in man's quest for knowledge about himself and that it is indissolubly linked to the progress of mankind from savagery to civilization. The humanistic view likewise sees art as participating in this temporal-linear progress and insists on looking for continuity in this chain of development. The musicologist wishes to be regarded first and foremost as a historian, because he feels that this places him in the mainstream of a tradition that arose in the Renaissance and that he has been conditioned to regard as the supreme carrier of cherished aesthetic values. The social sciences are seen as a threat to these values. One might, however, regard them as a challenge rather than a threat.

Such a challenge to the humanistic view of history has been strikingly formulated by Professor Lévi-Strauss in the concluding chapter of his book *La Pensée sauvage* (deflowered into English as *The Savage Mind*).[4] This chapter, titled "History and Dialectic," is largely a polemic against his archrival Sartre, but in the process he makes a telling critique of the pretensions of history, particularly with regard to the irrationality of dates as used in historical chronology, as the following passage illustrates:

It is not only fallacious but contradictory to
conceive of the historical process as a continuous development, beginning with prehistory
coded in tens or hundreds of millenia, then
adopting the scale of millenia when it gets to
the 4th or 3rd millenium, and continuing as history in centuries interlarded, at the pleasure of
each author, with slices of annual history within the century, day to day history within the
year, or even hourly history within a day. All
these dates do not form a series: they are of
different species. . . . Or more precisely: the
dates appropriate to each class are irrational
in relation to those of other classes.[5]

Hence: "Given that the general code consists not in dates
which can be ordered as a linear series but in classes of
dates furnishing an autonomous system of reference, the
discontinuous and classificatory nature of historical
knowledge emerges clearly."[6]

Lévi-Strauss does not wish to "demolish" history, but
rather to cut it down to size. In his words: "The anthropologist respects history, but he does not accord it a special value. He conceives it as a study complementary to
his own: one of them unfurls the range of human societies in time, the other in space. And the difference is
even less great than it might seem, since the historian
strives to reconstruct the picture of vanished societies as
they were at the points which for them corresponded to
the present, while the ethnologist does his best to reconstruct the historical stages which temporally preceded
their existing form."[7]

Thus, Lévi-Strauss postulates a "symmetry" of method
and an equivalency of value between history and anthropology. The acceptance of this view would appear to be
the first step toward a unifying principle for musicology.
This implies, to begin with, the abolition of "special priv-
ilege" on both sides. Neither history nor anthropology
should be regarded as "first and foremost" in guiding us
to a knowledge of "man as music maker and music user"
(to borrow a memorable phrase from Charles Seeger),[8]
but each should be viewed as complementary and neces-

sary to the other.

In seeking such a "reconciliation," it is enlightening to turn to the introductory chapter on "History and Anthropology" in Lévi-Strauss's *Structural Anthropology*. Here, in measured and judicious terms, removed from the polemics of his dispute with Sartre, he sets forth the necessity for a rapprochement between these two great multidisciplines in the study of man. As he writes:

Gilbert Chase

Both history and ethnography are concerned with societies *other* than the one in which we live. Whether this *otherness* is due to remoteness in time (however slight), or to remoteness in space, or even to cultural heterogeneity, is of secondary importance compared to the basic similarity of perspective. . . . All that the historian or ethnographer can do, and all that we can expect of either of them, is to enlarge a specific experience to the dimensions of a more general one, which thereby becomes accessible *as experience* to men of another country or another epoch. And in order to succeed, both historian and ethnographer must have the same qualities: skill, precision, a sympathetic approach, and objectivity.[9]

The key word in the foregoing quotation, it seems to me, is *experience*. The Spanish philosopher José Ortega y Gasset once defined history as "the system of human experiences." And we know that no human society is without musical experiences of one kind or another. Therefore, we can say that both anthropology and history are needed for the full knowledge and understanding of music as human experience in time and space. As Lévi-Strauss says, "It is the solidarity of the two disciplines that makes it possible to keep the whole road in sight."

Anthropology in recent years has greatly enlarged its scope to include many aspects of modern, highly developed societies. A glance at the current literature will reveal that there are anthropological studies dealing with such fields as economics, politics, religion, literature, philosophy, and art—all of which involve a historical perspective. What part does music have in this general expansion of the scope of anthropology? It has a very large part indeed, and this is what we must now examine.

A year after the publication of the Princeton volume on musicology, there appeared a book titled *The Anthropology of Music*, written by Alan P. Merriam, chairman of the Department of Anthropology at Indiana University and one of the founders of the Society for Ethnomusicology. Merriam, who calls himself an "anthropologist-ethnomusicologist," represents the cultural-anthropological approach to musicology. The essence of this approach is expressed in the following quotation: "Music is a product of man and has structure, but its structure cannot have an existence of its own divorced from the behavior which produces it. In order to understand why a music structure exists as it does, we must understand how and why the behavior which produces it is as it is, and how and why the concepts which underlie that behavior are ordered in such a way as to produce the particularly desired form of organized sound."[10]

Very important for the kind of synthesis that we are seeking is Merriam's view that ethnomusicologists have "the responsibility to indicate the relationship between the study of ethnomusicology and studies in the humanities and social sciences in general" (p. 15). Moreover: "The functions and uses of music are as important as those of any other aspect of culture for understanding the workings of society" (p. 15). Thus, while musicology per se, through its analytical methods, can tell us much about the structure of musical works as individual objects of study, it needs to draw on "the anthropology of music" in order to understand and to describe "the functions and uses" of music in the society of a given time and place. Any supposed dichotomy between the "humanistic" approach of traditional musicology and the "scientific" approach of ethnomusicology becomes less and less meaningful when we keep in mind the vastness of the task to be accomplished. As Merriam writes: "The ethnomusicologist shares both with the social sciences and the humanities the search for an understanding of why men behave as they do" (p. 16).

Merriam has much to say about the humanities in his book. He sees a distinction but not a dichotomy: "The social sciences deal with man as a social animal and the ways in which he solves his biosocial problems in daily living, while the humanities take man beyond his social

237

living into his own distillations of his life experiences. The social sciences, then, are truly social; the humanities are primarily individual and psychological" (p. 24). He concludes that "what the ethnomusicologist seeks to create is his own bridge between the social sciences and the humanities." But why not regard this as a cooperative enterprise? If the ethnomusicologist is building a bridge between the social sciences and the humanities, why can not the historical musicologist, starting from the humanities, build his half of the bridge toward the social sciences? When the two spans meet, the bridge will be complete and passable in either direction. And, if they cross the bridge often enough, perhaps both groups will agree that they are both "musicologists"—though each may take a different approach for at least part of the way toward the understanding of music as human experience. All they really need to agree on is that "the sounds of music are shaped by the culture of which they are a part" (p. 27).

I would like to see the day when no candidate for a doctorate in musicology could pass the examination without demonstrating a thorough knowledge of *The Anthropology of Music*. Pending that Utopian era, I recommend immediate perusal of at least the following chapters: 12, "Music as Symbolic Behavior"; 13, "Aesthetics and the Interrelationship of the Arts"; and 14, "Music and Culture History" (which is not exactly the same as what humanists generally understand by "cultural history"—the distinction will prove illuminating).

In further search of elements for a bridge between the humanities and the social sciences—and specifically in terms of musicology and anthropology (by which we understand cultural and social anthropology in particular)—let us turn again to the Princeton volume, *Musicology*. Professor Harrison, in his discussion of "Musicology in America," argues for "a widening of the range of musicological interest," including the field of musical history itself: "If the subject of musical history is the history of musical man in society, then its province must include the musician and the audience at all levels of the social scale."[11] Developing this idea, he writes:

A more significant corollary of a further social object for musicology is the need to consider

Gilbert Chase

the relation between all the circumstances of
music making and the styles and forms of musical composition, rather than to regard musical forms as autonomous growths that come
and go according to the inclination of composers and the tastes of audiences. It becomes no
less essential to re-create as far as possible the
function, social meaning, and manner of performance of every type of musical work than
to establish the notes of the musical texts that
make the re-creation possible. With the further
emphasis on the history of music as an aspect
of the history of man in society, the traditional enterprises of musicology can no longer be
pursued *in vacuo*. For their ultimate meaning and value rest on their contribution to restoring silent music to the state of being once
more a medium of human communication. Re-
creation in any full sense cannot be divorced
from the original function of the music, any
more than a musical work from another society can be fully understood apart from its social context. Looked at in this way, *it is the
function of all musicology to be in fact ethnomusicology*, that is, to take its range of research
to include material that is termed 'sociological.'[12]

If all musicology were in fact to become ethnomusicology, the result would be neither musicology nor ethnomusicology as now understood, but a new, multifaceted
discipline, comparable to sociology, anthropology, or
linguistics, that could legitimately be called Musicology—
with a capital "M"—and with as many designated subdivisions or branches as might be necessary to accomplish
its immense, many-sided task of knowing and explaining
not only the history but also the mystery "of musical
man in society." When I speak of "mystery" I have in
mind the words of Lévi-Strauss in the extraordinary
"Overture" to his book on mythology, *The Raw and the
Cooked*, in which he calls music "the supreme mystery
of human knowledge"—adding that it holds the key to
progress in all the "human sciences." If a professor of social anthropology (albeit a professed music lover of high
degree) takes such a transcendent view of the importance

239

of music in human knowledge, how can musicologists acquiesce in the present reluctance of their discipline to meet such a great challenge? If we are willing to accept Professor Harrison's thesis that "every aspect of music as human experience and as part of human history is a responsibility of the musicologist,"[13] then we must live up to that responsibility—and seek the means to do so, wherever and whatever they may be.

Actually, what Professor Harrison proposes as a model for musicology simply spells out in detail what Professor Palisca proposed in his essay for the Princeton volume: "The musicologist is concerned with music that exists, whether as an oral or a written tradition, *and with everything that can shed light on its human context*."[14] My main proviso with regard to this statement is that it expresses what historical musicologists *should* be concerned with, rather than what they *are* concerned with in actual practice. But we can readily accept it as a desideratum rather than as a model of present reality. Its main virtue is that it reveals a community of thought (in this aspect at least) between Professor Palisca, who represents historical musicology, and Professor Harrison, who represents ethnomusicology. The significance of this rapprochement should not be underestimated: it is another link in the bridge we want to build. Unfortunately, however, I find internal inconsistencies in Professor Palisca's essay with respect to his statement that the musicologist is (or should be) concerned with "everything that can shed light on [the] human context" of music. Frankly, I do not see how this can be done without recourse to "the anthropology of music"—or to the social sciences in general, including sociology, economics, linguistics, and psychology.

The inconsistency to which I refer is summarized in the following passage from Professor Palisca's essay: "My purpose has been to show that there is a unity in the fields that belong in musicology. This unity bears the characteristics of humanistic scholarship *and excludes the fields that have rather a community of methods with the sciences*."[15] Unity purchased at the price of exclusion is too dearly bought. To exclude "the fields that have . . . a community of methods with the sciences" is to exclude ethnomusicology, whose main thrust is precisely the endeavor to make musicology more scientific by drawing on the methodology of the social sciences. But I do not wish to continue in a polemical tone. Having pointed out this inconsistency, I prefer to emphasize the positive aspect of Professor Palisca's contribution, when he asserts that musicology is concerned with everything that can shed light on the human context of music: this path leads directly to the social sciences via the bridge between historical and anthropological musicology.

Here I would like to quote from Mantle Hood's essay, "Music, the Unknown," in the Princeton volume: "Music history and criticism have remained insular in their promulgation of Western theories and tradition. Any kind of insularity is hardly compatible with the demands of the last half of the twentieth century."[16] That statement I fully endorse, with emphasis on *any kind of insularity*. That includes not only geocultural insularity—such as historical musicology has practiced for most of the twentieth century—but also the insularity of theory and method, which has become progressively more acute, particularly in American musicology, since this discipline was accorded full academic status some decades ago. Any discipline turned in upon itself becomes a routine or a ritual, a cult of scholarship rather than a search for knowledge.

The famous French social anthropologist Marcel Maus held that "anthropology is an original mode of knowing rather than a source of particular types of knowledge." No matter what particular type of knowledge one is concerned with, various "modes of knowing" can always be profitably explored as a means of avoiding insularity. For example, the distinguished French musicologist François Lesure, writing in the first issue (1970) of the *International Review of Aesthetics and Sociology of Music*, had some interesting observations on the function of sociology as "un moteur pour la musicologie." In his opinion, the sociology of music should endeavor by all possible means "to create a dialogue between historical musicology and ethnomusicology."[17] He also urges musicologists to be more audacious in breaking away from "the routine of historicizing methods" (p. 91).

All methodology consists of routine to a certain extent. That is why the continual generation of theory, the formulation of hypotheses to be tested empirically, is necessary for the renewal of all scholarly and scientific dis-

Musicology, History, and Anthropology

241

ciplines. But progress cannot be achieved in isolation. Social anthropology made a great leap forward when it developed a new methodology derived from the structural linguistics of Ferdinand de Saussure and the phonetics of the "Prague Circle"—particularly the work of Roman Jakobson and of N. S. Trubetzkoy.[18] European musicologists, such as François-Bernard Mâche, J. J. Nattiez, and Nicolas Ruwet, have taken the initiative in applying the principles of structural linguistics to musical analysis.[19] It is true that these scholars are trained in both linguistics and musicology; but that simply reinforces the argument in favor of an interdisciplinary approach.

It is pertinent here to refer to a paper titled "Pour une sociologie historique des faits musicaux," presented by François Lesure at the Eighth Congress of the International Musicological Society (New York, 1961), in which he deplored the intellectual isolation of historical musicology: "For example, the renewal of certain methods in linguistics, and the considerable developments in sociology and ethnology have left musicology virtually untouched."[20]

Those words were written more than a decade ago, and it may be asked whether there have not been changes since then with regard to the traditional position of historical musicology. The answer, I believe, is that there has been no fundamental change but that there are signs of impending change. The session on "Urban Popular Music" at the joint annual meeting of the American Musicological Society and the Society for Ethnomusicology in 1971 may have signalled a turning point toward moving away from cultural insularity. But, on the whole, the traditional paradigms prevail, and it may require a revolutionary breakthrough in order to change them.[21] There is evidence that the present decade—the 1970's—may bring about a conceptual revolution in musicology. If so, it will be primarily a *scientific* revolution with a global base, receiving its impetus from the mainstreams of contemporary thought. It will involve the destruction of accepted paradigms and a concerted interdisciplinary effort to penetrate the "mystery" of music as a universal human experience.

One development in this direction might well be, as I have suggested, the recognition of a multifaceted, global musicology, representing the interests of both humanists and social scientists in an interdisciplinary context characterized by the interrelationship of various methods, approaches, and emphases. The beginnings of such a development might be tentatively represented by the following model:

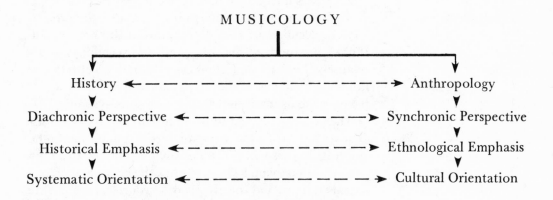

The bidirectional broken lines indicate interrelationships that give the model its essentially mobile and global character. They also signify complementarity rather than dichotomy. The terms *diachronic* and *synchronic* were taken over by anthropology from the structural linguistics of Saussure. The diachronic perspective focuses on the temporal order of social structures; the synchronic perspective is directed toward those elements of a social structure that are regarded as constant and therefore in a sense (though not literally) "outside" of time. Lévi-Strauss repeatedly insists on the complementarity of these two approaches, upon which hinges the "solidarity" of history and anthropology.

Charles Seeger has defined the systematic orientation as an "intrinsic view of music as known by the musician in music space-time."[22] The latter he describes as an "aesthetic-semantic discontinuum." There is a question as to whether this view is compatible with the anthropological approach. This is a point that requires further discussion. But at present the systematic orientation represents common ground for both the historical and ethnological emphases, insofar as they concentrate on the analysis of individual musical works or styles. It is imperative, however, to explain the concept of the "cultural orientation" in order to understand fully the significance of the proposed model.

This orientation refers to the method of "cultural analysis" formulated by Dr. John Blacking, professor of social anthropology at the Queen's University at Belfast, in his book *Venda Children's Songs*[23] and in several more recent writings. As he explains it: "The purpose of the technique is not simply to describe the cultural background of the music as human behavior, *and then* to analyze peculiarities of style in terms of rhythm, tonality, timbre, instrumentation, frequency of ascending and descending intervals, and other essentially musical terminology, but to describe *both* the music *and* its cultural background as interrelated parts of a total system."[24]

The ultimate desideratum, as formulated by Professor Blacking, is the following: "We need a unitary method of musical analysis which can not only be applied to *all* music, but can explain both the form, the social and emotional content, and the effects of music, as systems of relationships between an infinite number of variables."[25] It should be possible to apply such a method "to the music of Beethoven and Mahler, as well as to the music of the Venda or the Zulu."

This, then, is the challenge that "the anthropology of music" presents to traditional musicology. There is increasing evidence that current thought in musicology is preparing to meet this challenge. Perhaps the preliminary model that I have proposed may help to carry the current of musicological thought a little further in this direction.

Gilbert Chase

Notes

1. See in particular Claude Lévi-Strauss, *Structural Anthropology*, trans. Claire Jacobson and Brooke Grundfest Schoepf (New York: Basic Books, 1963). (This is a collection of papers written between 1944 and 1957. The book was first published in France in 1958.)

2. Frank Ll. Harrison, Mantle Hood, and Claude V. Palisca, *Musicology* (Englewood Cliffs, N.J.: Prentice-Hall, 1963).

3. Glen Haydon, *Introduction to Musicology* (New York: Prentice-Hall, 1941), p. 9.

244

4. Claude Lévi-Strauss, *La Pensée sauvage* (Paris: Librairie Plon, 1962) was "deflowered" in the English translation because the title in French means both "savage thought" and the wild pansy.

5. Claude Lévi-Strauss, *The Savage Mind* (Chicago: University of Chicago Press, 1966), p. 260.

6. Ibid.

7. Ibid., p. 256.

8. Charles Seeger, "Preface to the Description of a Music," in *Report of the Fifth Congress of the International Society of Musical Research, Utrecht, 3–7 July 1952* (Amsterdam: G. Alsbach, 1953), p. 366.

9. Lévi-Strauss, *Structural Anthropology*, pp. 16–17.

10. Alan P. Merriam, *The Anthropology of Music* (Evanston, Ill.: Northwestern University Press, 1964), p. 7.

11. Harrison, Hood, and Palisca, *Musicology*, p. 79.

12. Ibid., pp. 79–80 (italics added).

13. Ibid., p. 83.

14. Ibid., p. 116 (italics added).

15. Ibid., p. 108 (italics added).

16. Ibid., p. 282.

17. François Lesure, "Un Moteur pour la Musicologie," *International Review of Aesthetics and Sociology of Music* 1, no. 1 (June 1970): 91. My translation.

18. See Lévi-Strauss, *Structural Anthropology*, chap. 2, "Structural Analysis in Linguistics and in Anthropology."

19. See *Sémiologie de la Musique, Musique en Jeu* 5 (1971).

20. Jan La Rue, ed., *Report of the Eighth Congress of the*

International Musicological Society, New York, 1961, 2
vols. (Kassel: Bärenreiter, 1961), 1:334.

21. Cf. Thomas S. Kuhn, *The Structure of Scientific Revolutions* (Chicago and London: University of Chicago Press, 1962).

22. Charles Seeger, "Toward a Unitary Field Theory for Musicology," Institute of Ethnomusicology of the University of California at Los Angeles, *Selected Reports*, vol. 1, no. 3 (1970). The statement I quote is from an illustrative chart, "Conspectus of the Resources of the Musicological Process," a quadrifold insert attached to the back cover of the issue.

23. John Blacking, *Venda Children's Songs* (Johannesburg: Witwatersrand University Press, 1967).

24. John Blacking, "Deep and Surface Structures in Venda Music," *Yearbook of the International Folk Music Council* 3 (1971): 93.

25. Ibid., p. 92.

Gilbert Chase

The Prospects for Research in Medieval Music in the
1970's
Gilbert Reaney

Eight

Let me start by saying that the prospects are still extremely good. Statistics suggest that, next to the Renaissance,
the Middle Ages is the most popular period for research
at the present time. The reasons are not far to seek. Both
these periods were neglected for centuries, though the
sources, printed and manuscript, were available to the
scholar. The Middle Ages, in particular, because of its notational difficulties, was musically unknown until the
twentieth century. Even now, although it may have a
novelty appeal, the music of this period is still "caviare
to the general," though it attracts an ever-increasing number of devotees. One of the big attractions for the scholar has been the possibility of unveiling hidden monuments
of ancient music. And especially during the last twenty-
five years or so, since the end of World War II, the
amount of medieval and Renaissance music published has
been enormous. Are we in fact coming to the end of the
fund of sources, the supply of which is not unlimited?
Are we in the same situation as the antique dealer who
has to produce second-rate articles when he runs out of
his best stock?

I think this can be true only if we think in a very limited way. There is only one Montpellier motet manuscript[1] and only one Florence Notre Dame manuscript.[2]
Such prizes cannot be transcribed every day. And when
they are, scholars have a tendency to preempt them for
their own use,[3] which, I must say, has always seemed a
most unscholarly thing to do, as far as I am concerned.
Under these circumstances, it is perhaps surprising that
good editions of all the music in the Florence manuscript
are not yet available in print, though much more can be
found in unpublished dissertations.[4] While these dissertations are often of the utmost value, we cannot usually
consider them the equivalent of a published edition. For
one thing, they may well represent the first rather than
the mature work of a scholar, and, second, it remains
true that the clausulas, conductus, some organa, and

247

even some motets are not available in print from the Florence source.

We have, of course, overstressed polyphony, and I hardly need to point out once again that monophonic music was the rule in the Middle Ages, polyphony the exception. And yet we continue to disregard this fact and put polyphony in the forefront just because we like it. A glance at some modern editions will show to what extent we have done this. The motets from the Roman de Fauvel have all been published, but not the lays or the conductus. Similarly, we know little about the sixty rondelli from the Florence Notre Dame manuscript, just because they are monophonic.[5] And no one has yet published the fifteen monophonic motets from the trouvère manuscript Paris, Bibliothèque nationale, fonds français 845. But since I am unlikely to shake anyone's ultimate enthusiasm for polyphony, let me say a few words about the unpublished sources.

Many researchers turn to other areas because they feel that practically all medieval polyphonic music has been published, as if, once the music is available, we can forget about it. But, in fact, much has not been published. We are badly in need of a complete edition of the earliest polyphonic pieces, many of which are quite short. Several were discussed in Marion Gushee's dissertation "Romanesque Polyphony"[6] and previously in Marius Schneider's controversial *Geschichte der Mehrstimmigkeit*.[7] Some early sources deter the researcher because of certain difficulties that seem almost insuperable. An obvious case is the Cambridge manuscript of the so-called Winchester Troper, with its 160 two-part organa from as early as the eleventh century. The staffless neumes of the second voice can only be approximately deciphered, though the plainsong can be rendered fairly accurately.[8] One of the difficulties is knowing what interval occurs between the two parts at the very outset, but we may be rather sure that perfect consonances predominated for the rest. Armand Machabey transcribed most of the pieces, and we may be sure others will make the attempt, too. However approximate the results, it soon becomes clear that there are many things one cannot do, and therefore a solution becomes clearer.

A more frequent problem previous to the Notre Dame school is that of rhythm, and it remains a problem in such

Notre Dame pieces as the conductus and the two-part organa. Scholars such as Gordon Anderson, Robert Falck, Ethel Thurston, Fred Flindell, and Janet Knapp have done much work on the conductus, but, until they commit their transcriptions to print, we cannot come to more definite conclusions ourselves.[9] Since William Waite published the two-part organa of the MS W_1,[10] other scholars, such as Theodore Karp,[11] have improved on the rhythmic organization, though Waite was unfortunate in being unable to publish the other Notre Dame works he had transcribed in his dissertation. We still need the remaining two-part works and the enormous body of clausulas in print. The prevalence of modal rhythm in conductus and organa can hardly be doubted, but more needs to be and will be written on this question. Many people feel that such rhythms should also be applied to the St. Martial repertory,[12] and, indeed, a comparison with similar pieces from the Notre Dame conductus collections reveals many points in common. Both Bruno Stäblein and Theodore Karp have undertaken transcriptions of the entire St. Martial and Compostela polyphonic repertories, but as yet nothing has been published. Some other areas have been neglected, however, such as the sequences in the late thirteenth-century British Museum MS Egerton 945. These pieces are in definite mensural notation, like other sequences of this period, and the whole area, monophonic or polyphonic, requires more investigation.

One point is often forgotten, namely, the rather haphazard way in which editions of medieval music have originated; and it is a curious fact that we are cataloguing the sources, for instance in the Répertoire International des Sources Musicales (RISM), after many sources have been published. The motet repertory of the thirteenth century is a case in point. The Bamberg manuscript was published years ago by Pierre Aubry—in 1908, to be exact[13]—while the Montpellier Codex had to wait another thirty or forty years for its publication. And yet neither of these editions, in spite of their great merits, will entirely stand up to modern demands. Aubry used old clefs and long notes in his transcriptions, while Yvonne Rokseth failed to give a full critical apparatus. Fortunately, the two-part motets from the Montpellier Codex received a full critical treatment in Georg Kuhlmann's dissertation, published in 1938.[14]

This question of critical apparatus is rather important, especially since our rights in this respect are eroded by publishers who refuse to give the space necessary to such apparently extraneous material. In most cases, however, it is only by sifting through the entire evidence and listing it that a really good critical version of the music and its accompanying text will be obtained. We may not, of course, wish or be able to go to the extent of publishing so many parallel versions of one text as Kuhlmann did, but it can be a good method, especially when the number of versions is limited to three or four and when variants are frequent. It would be easy to spend hours discussing critical apparatus, but let me just mention one or two points of importance. In some cases there may be an inordinate number of sources for a composition. It may be necessary to omit some of the less important ones, in such a case, from the critical notes. But it is essential to give consideration to these other sources in the discussion of sources, which should precede the edition or the critical apparatus. In other words, it is insufficient to take one or two important sources as a basis for the edition and neglect any others. It may, of course, turn out that these other sources are not of great value—perhaps they are just copies of the principal sources—but this has to be determined in the first place. When we look at the various editions of medieval music, it becomes clear that very few editors have provided ample critical notes. If we examine, for instance, the two editions of Guillaume de Machaut's complete works,[15] it is evident that Leo Schrade's edition has far more comprehensive notes than Friedrich Ludwig's. Also, Schrade uses modern clefs, making his version much more usable for both study and performance. However, a recent article suggests that neither edition is without flaws, for a checkup revealed that variants were incorrectly recorded in both.[16]

Similarly, if we consider the editions of thirteenth-century motets, it cannot be said that we are as well off as we seem to be. Better than editions of separate manuscripts, involving numerous duplications, would be a complete corpus of the thirteenth-century motets, which is a job needing the collaboration of several scholars. Dr. Hans Tischler has edited the earliest motets in the manuscripts F and W_2, but it remains to be seen how comprehensive his projected edition will be when it finally gets into print. In any case, in spite of the existing editions of the Bamberg, Montpellier, Turin, and Las Huelgas manuscripts,[17] a curious exception has been the ninety-one motets of the Chansonnier Noailles, for which there are, admittedly, many concordances. If they have not been published as a whole, however, Friedrich Gennrich published nineteen in his *Rondeaux, Virelais, und Balladen*.[18] The St. Victor manuscript, too, although it has appeared in facsimile, has only just received a study of the forty clausulas,[19] which have long been considered as rather mysterious reversions to clausula form from motets. Normally, of course, the thirteenth-century motet was itself based on a clausula, unless it was newly composed.

In many ways one of the best editions, though it contains only a selection of fifty-nine motets, is Higini Anglès's three-volume publication of the Las Huelgas Codex. For one thing, he gives many concordant versions, though with the motets these are often less necessary than with organa and conductus. A particularly valuable task awaits the scholar in publishing parallel versions of twelfth-century tropes and sequences in the way Anglès has done. For example, a piece like the Kyrie trope *Rex virginum*, which opens the Las Huelgas Codex, not only shows interesting developments in the process of composition but also is of assistance in understanding the rhythm of such an early piece. The Las Huelgas version opens in a similar way to the somewhat later Munich Codex, 23286 of the Staatsbibliothek, but especially interesting is the parallel text *Cunctipotens* according to the Milan treatise and the Compostela MS.[20] Both versions are well known from the *Historical Anthology of Music*,[21] but, whereas Milan is completely syllabic, the Compostela composition has an extremely florid upper part. A comparison of the two versions suggests that the Compostela writer may have known the Milan source and composed his far more florid piece on the Milan basis.

The student looking for music to transcribe from the fourteenth century may well feel that everything has or is being done. There are two Machaut editions, two editions of the Italian Trecento music,[22] two editions of the Chantilly motets,[23] and now two editions of the Old Hall manuscript.[24] There is an edition of most continental mass music,[25] though English masses and motets are still lacking. Here again, however, the majority of compositions will be published soon in the corpus *Early English Church Music*. The Worcester fragments have, of course, been published in an edition that deserves great praise for its time,[26] but we can, I have no doubt, look forward to a new edition of this difficult source. On the continent, there have been a few new discoveries in Holland, and it appears that the Utrecht and Leiden fragments[27] will be published by the Musicological Institute of the University of Utrecht. The much-damaged Cambrai fragments have been tackled by a graduate student of UCLA, Barbara Barclay, and I hope these will eventually be published.[28] Finally, the Nuremberg fragments,[29] which I was one of the first to use, augment this corpus of relatively unknown works. We cannot, as I said earlier, expect to find further large sources of medieval polyphony, but such small sources as those I have just mentioned all show new traits. The Cambrai fragments reveal that the virelai was more important than we often think, the Utrecht and Leiden fragments contain several Dutch pieces in Ars Nova style, and the Nuremberg fragments contain an instrumental piece in virelai form, a *Deo gratias* substitute in madrigal form, and a unique nonisorhythmic, motetlike work in honor of the Count of Flanders.

I mention these pieces because new music will turn up, and we should continue to be on the lookout for it. But sometimes existing music is neglected because it does not fall into a pattern. The fifteenth-century Shrewsbury MS VI of the School Library[30] is perhaps the earliest part book we know. It dates from about 1450 and parallels the Egerton 3307 collection of Holy Week music in the British Museum.[31] But because it is a single part book, no one has yet studied it thoroughly. A transcriber needs familiarity with the style of the period, but this is fairly conventional, and a keen researcher might find it easier than he thinks to complete the two- or three-part texture, especially if a cantus firmus is involved.

Another example of neglect is German polyphony of the fourteenth and fifteenth centuries. Because it is not as forward looking as French, Italian, or even English polyphony of the period, it has been largely neglected, and it is time a systematic study was made of such sources as British Museum Additional 27630, Engelberg Stiftsbibliothek 314, Munich Staatsbibliothek cgm. 716, and others.[32] Dr. Theodor Göllner has made an impressive study of a special field in his *Die mehrstimmigen liturgischen Lesungen*,[33] but more attention needs to be given to polyphonic settings of the more regular liturgical music, such as antiphons, responds, and *Benedicamus* tropes.[34] The notation is a difficulty, but although not so obviously mensural as that of France or Italy, it is a challenge that should be met, and its rhythm should be worked out in a reasonable, modern transcription. These sources also have what Jacques Handschin would call a "peripheral" motet repertory, which still needs thorough investigation.[35]

The Prospects for Research

The time has come, of course, when complete repertories of polyphonic music can be studied. A good example is the recent two-volume survey of medieval settings of the Mass Ordinary, complete with valuable transcriptions, using a very sensible rhythmic method for the nonmensural notation of the earliest pieces. I am speaking of Max Lütolff's *Die mehrstimmigen Ordinarium Missae sätze*.[36] One of my own students is working on a complete transcription and study of the untroped *Benedicamus domino* settings from the early Middle Ages to the fifteenth century. And the troped *Benedicamus* offers even more possibilities, interlocking as it does with so many other forms, such as the conductus and motet, to mention only two. And, if it is impossible as yet to make a survey of the entire conductus repertory because of the lack of transcriptions, it is surely time the motet was more fully covered, in spite of the many articles and commentaries on single sources.

I have spoken enough about editions of music. Another area still having some scope for work is that of music theory. The editions of musical treatises, published in large number by C. E. H. de Coussemaker and Martin Gerbert,[37] long ago ceased to satisfy modern critical standards. But, even in this field, the principal treatises are being republished in the *Corpus Scriptorum de Musica* and other individual editions, such as Fritz Reckow's edition of the well-known Anonymous IV.[38] Thus, scholars are turning to lesser-known works, particularly anonymous ones. One of my own students, Cecily Sweeney, has edited the musical treatise attributed to John Wylde.[39] This is preserved in a fifteenth-century manuscript—London, British Museum, Lansdowne 763—but may well date from the early fourteenth or late thirteenth century. Moreover, it is probably anonymous, Wylde being the copyist rather than the author. Its importance lies in its clear exposition of mode in plainsong, a topic that is being exploited in independent studies. Whether the subject will ever be exhausted is doubtful, since there is an inevitable vagueness about even the clearest discussion, and, of course, much depends on the limits of the subject and the period and forms covered.

A list of treatises at present being edited or in course of publication for the Corpus is given in *Musica Disciplina* 25 (1971): 250-251. The stress is on the music of the later Middle Ages, but such important earlier treatises as those of Aurelianus Reomensis and Willehelmus Hirsaugensis are not neglected. Similarly, the series takes in Renaissance treatises if they are unpublished or unavailable in a good edition. It is, in any case, difficult to know where the Middle Ages ends in the field of music theory, for such popular medieval subjects as plainsong modality and mensural notation continued to be treated throughout the Renaissance and later. The question is often asked what value these medieval treatises have. My answer would be that they are the only direct word of the period on musical thought, however much it may sometimes be bound up with traditional material, often going back to Boethius and the Greeks.

Many people feel that an edition of a Latin treatise should always be coupled with an English translation, and, certainly, for class use and speed of reading, a translation can be very valuable. However, it does seem that we should continue to strive for a reliable critical edition before attempting a translation. In any case, the field is at present wide open, for few treatises have appeared in translation.[40] For the student, a translation can be a worthwhile Ph.D. assignment, but, like an edition of music, it needs to be combined with an exhaustive study to satisfy the examiners. And with some reason, because in this way the student not only shows how well he can handle language but also proves his worth as a scholar of insight. When it comes to publication, some paring down may be needed, but at least we can say today that outlets for the publication of treatises in translation are on the increase; and I hardly need to mention names like

Gilbert Reaney

Armen Carapetyan, Albert Seay, and Luther Dittmer.

Even now, however, we have hardly begun to discuss the topics for study that still await the scholar's attention. It goes without saying, however, that even editions that do seem to be comprehensive and well produced have scarcely been examined in a thorough fashion. A good example is the substantial corpus of masses, motets, ballades, rondeaux, and virelais to be found in the early fifteenth-century Cyprus manuscript.[41] We know that this music has ties with Machaut and the transitional composers of about 1400, such as Johannes Carmen and Johannes Tapissier,[42] but much work remains to be done on the complete output of these anonymous Cypriot composers. Another corpus that has never been properly treated is the body of Trecento music, much of which is now available in the two editions of Marrocco and Pirrotta. It may seem rather picayune to come to terms with every piece in an edition, as one usually does in a commentary, but where would we be without Anglès's commentary to his Las Huelgas edition[43] and Rokseth's to her Montpellier edition?[44] One of these days, we will have a complete corpus of St. Martial polyphony, complete with commentary, with the transcriptions perhaps in two versions, facing each other, one mensural, the other not. Incidentally, in this area of the commentary, the computer can come into its own. Dr. Karp, for example, has processed the entire Notre Dame organa *dupla* repertoire and made it possible to locate 371 motifs in 100,000 citations.[45] In choosing this group of compositions, he was well aware that certain variants appear time and time again, even at the beginning of a composition or its verse. The same procedure would be well worth carrying out with the organa *tripla*.

In the monophonic field, we have barely begun to scratch the surface of the many existing sources. Plainsong, as everyone knows, is an immense field, and facsimile editions, such as the *Paléographic musicale*, are just a drop in the ocean. They scarcely provide us with more than one example of the main types of plainsong notation. From the researcher's point of view, we seem to have few antiphonals and many graduals. This is, of course, because the mass repertory, while it may require detail work, was much more settled already in the Middle Ages, while plainsong offices continued to be written.

Thus, we often need to search for antiphons and responsories in such valuable sources as the Worcester and Sarum
antiphonals. There is still much scope for the publication
of complete offices with all texts and a critical edition
of the music. Even such a popular saint as St. Nicholas is
still without an edition of the music to his office, though
the liturgy itself has been edited.[46] Similarly, in spite of
a handful of studies dealing with individual sources, the
main body of tropes and sequences is still unpublished
in a modern edition.[47] To be sure, the further we go
back in time, the more notational problems occur, but
these are meant to be grappled with and can often be
overcome by more recent versions of the same music in
a more modern notation. In any case, it is little short of
amazing that there is still no facsimile edition of the
Winchester Troper, though there have been several substantial studies of the Codex.[48] In spite of the name, it
should be mentioned that this manuscript is really a Can-
tatorium, containing solo chants of the mass, but it does
contain also a few tropes and sequences. Also, there are
in fact two manuscripts, one at Oxford—the earlier one—
and one at Cambridge that contains the polyphony. The
two sources, though independent, overlap and complement each other. In fact, we tend not only to overstress
polyphony in our studies but also to separate monophony and polyphony in an unrealistic fashion. There are
few medieval manuscripts that do not contain one-line
melodies as well as part music. In many, the polyphony
is the exception, monophony the rule. And this applies
to secular as well as sacred music. Even some of the great
monuments of polyphonic music, such as the Notre
Dame organa, alternate plainsong with polyphony, and
only by the fourteenth century does accompanied secular song become the rule, though we assume some sort
of improvised accompaniment earlier, but only when
the occasion arose.

Attention has recently centered on pre-Gregorian chant
and such variant forms of chant, whether preexistent or
coexistent, as Ambrosian and Mozarabic chant. Cistercian chant was a reformed chant, which eliminated what
were thought to be superfluities and corruptions in the
existing chant, under St. Bernard of Clairvaux's rather
ascetic influence. Much research remains to be done on
this chant, but publication of the Antiphonal, Gradual,

Psalter, and Hymnary has been carried out in recent years at Westmalle in Belgium.[49] The question of importance in the reform, namely, what type of chant was in fact being reformed, is in the process of research by Father Waddell of Gethsemani Abbey in Kentucky. A new edition is needed of the treatise *Regulae de arte musica* by St. Bernard's principal theorist, Guy de Cherlieu.[50] A particularly controversial issue, however, has been that of the Old Roman chant. Opinion has varied as to how it was related to what we call Gregorian chant. Most people thought it was an early form of Gregorian chant,[51] either localized in Rome or originally more generalized, but with its remaining vestiges preserved in Rome. Others, including Walther Lipphardt and Paul Cutter,[52] especially in view of the late dissemination of Old Roman chant in the manuscripts, feel that Gregorian chant was the original chant of Rome and that Old Roman chant was the result of two centuries more of oral transmission, the earliest sources being from the eleventh century. It seems that, once again, the only solution is to study the various sources of Old Roman chant and compare them with Gregorian versions. Cutter tends to oppose documentary evidence of the early Middle Ages as being worthless, and certainly it often has the character of legend.

Ambrosian chant has suffered from the same diversity of opinion, even though it has been performed from the Middle Ages to the present day. Because it was associated with St. Ambrose, musicologists thought of it as an earlier, rather more roughly formed, chant than Gregorian,[53] but again, the sources are late, the three main ones being from the twelfth and fourteenth centuries. Michel Huglo has discussed the sources of both Old Roman and Ambrosian chant.[54] Editions of the Old Roman chants are particularly needed, though there are editions of Ambrosian chants for the mass and for vespers.[55] Much more of a problem is the Mozarabic chant, with its cryptic notation, whose significance has not yet been discovered. The staffless neumes cannot be deciphered, but Clyde W. Brockett, in his study *Antiphons, Responsories, and Other Chants of the Mozarabic Rite*,[56] suggests that, as in the Byzantine chant, the determination of mode may help. He catalogues the chant sources and rejects the idea of an early notation dating from before the ninth century, which Anglès had put forward.[57] There is ob-

The Prospects for Research

viously much scope for research in this field. Apart from individual manuscripts to be studied, there are more antiphons than in the Gregorian repertory, including the type with refrain, and a large number of responsories. Moreover, there are unique forms like the *vespertinum* and *sono*, the latter sung sometimes with sequences in the melismata. Don Randel's service,[58] on the other hand, was to show that there are two distinct traditions in the responsorial psalm tones of the Mozarabic office, the León and the Rioja traditions, which are nevertheless linked with the same responsory melodies. In this connection, he is inclined to doubt any very clear system of mode. Here, then, is a topic to follow up, it seems to me: the concept of mode in Mozarabic chant. The result is likely to be the same as with other non-Gregorian repertories, such as Ambrosian chant,[59] namely that mode is much less evident and certainly less systematized, possibly due to the powerful influence of Greek theory as handed down by Boethius on Gregorian chant. I notice that one of the dissertations formerly listed as in progress at the University of Michigan, but now dropped, was called *Modality in Continental Liturgical Polyphony from the Ninth through the Fourteenth Century*. This in itself is a big period of time to cover, but, in any case, an assessment of mode in polyphonic music can only be arrived at by working from plainsong modality.[60] And it is a measure of the duration of this principle that, even at the time of Johannes Tinctoris in the second half of the fifteenth century, the modality of a piece as a whole was still judged from the tenor.[61] This is quite a remarkable fact when we consider that the tenor was generally no longer the lowest voice in a composition at this time. It might be expected that monophonic secular music would show a different system, for instance, in the songs of the trouvères, especially in the light of Johannes de Grocheo's statement that "we do not recognize secular song by mode, for example, in cantilena, ductia, or estampie."[62] However, a great many melodies seem to fit into the categories of plainsong modality, such as the Dorian and Mixolydian modes. There are fewer songs that suggest C major, like the well-known rondeau *En ma dame ai mis mon cuer*.[63] The melodic line, with its broken triads and ornamented leading tone proceeding to the final, might be out of one of the lyric lays, but, as Ursula Aarburg has pointed out,[64] the final is often on G here. Nevertheless, as in the opening phrase of the *Lay des Pucelles*, which also happens to be the melody of Pierre Abelard's planctus *Ad festas choreas*,[65] what we appear to have is a kind of Hypoionian mode, so that, if the final is on G, the octave tends to be divided into an upper fifth and lower fourth rather than the reverse. In any case, a thorough survey of the modality of secular melodies is overdue. With plainsong, of course, the situation is different in that even quite early sources indicate what they feel is the mode of a piece.[66] The relation of the eight Byzantine echoi to the eight modes of Gregorian chant is another question that still needs research. We are told that, while the Gregorian modes are scales, the Byzantine echoi are defined by melodic formulae,[67] and certainly Hucbald of St. Amand, one of the earliest important plainsong theorists writing in the ninth or early tenth century, gives a very scalar interpretation of mode.[68] Even so, it is quite clear that melodic structure also defines the Gregorian modes, as the various formulas called *neumae* discussed by theorists from the ninth to the fifteenth centuries indicate.[69]

The Prospects
for Research

The question of performance is a difficult one for medieval music as a whole. For plainsong, at least, the various liturgical books and manuscripts can give a lead and, incidentally, also help to show where some polyphonic pieces might be used. Frank Harrison's *Music in Medieval Britain*[70] is a mine of information on this subject, and musicians could well use more of these discussions involving both liturgy and music. And yet Harrison is using only the published liturgical books, such as *The Use of Sarum*[71] and the Exeter Ordinal,[72] together with some manuscript sources. Particularly valuable are such books as the customaries,[73] which define the people taking part in the service. A good example is the description of the Palm Sunday procession in Salisbury.[74] Without going into the full ceremony, we learn that the antiphon *En rex venit* was sung by three clerks turning to the people, and they alternate with the officiant and the choir throughout the piece. For instance, *Salve quem Jesum* is sung by the officiant while turning to the relics; the continuation *Testatur plebs* is taken by the choir, with a genuflection to the relics; the verses *Hic est qui de Edom* and *Hic est ille* go to the clerks again; and each is followed by another *Salve* begun by the officiant and continued by the choir. We also learn that the processional hymn *Gloria, laus et honor* was sung by seven boys in a high place, alternating with the choir, who sang the repeat of the refrain as well as the intermediate refrains between the verses. The verse *Unus autem ex ipsis* from the processional antiphon *Collegerunt* was sung by three from the senior stalls turning to the people. No wonder we have three-part polyphonic settings of Holy Week music[75] when there are so many references to groups of three singers, who, of course, mainly sang plainsong. One factor that governs both plainsong and secular monophony in performance is a large amount of repetition. A typical example is the sequence, which I am sure is rarely sung as it should be, with a repeat of the melody of each versicle sung to the vowel *a*.[76]

The performance of polyphonic music is not basically different from that of monophonic music. In church music it is often a question of knowing where the piece fits liturgically, simply because the big collections of medieval music tend to consider musical rather than liturgical categories. We know where the Notre Dame organa fit, because they have regular gradual, alleluia, or responsory texts, but the conductus nearly always have new texts as well as new music. These texts can just as well be sacred as secular, but even the sacred texts may be what has often been called paraliturgical. They are often moralizing texts, to be sure, but perhaps more sung in the refectory than in the chapel. Fifteenth-century English carol texts have the same semireligious, nonliturgical character, and we certainly know they were sung in the dining hall—for instance, at Winchester College in 1487 before the king.[77] Even so, it does seem likely that a text commemorating a saint and at the same time ending with the word *domino*, or having the words *Benedicamus domino* near the end like the two-part conductus *Nicholai sollempnia*,[78] may be a *Benedicamus* substitute—in other words, a piece to replace the plainsong *Benedicamus* or to complement it. There is much scope for study of the possible place of conductus and motets in the liturgy, though many secular motets of the thirteenth century must have been simply a polyphonic counterpart to monophonic song in spite of their frequent use of a plainsong tenor. We do not need to infer, therefore, that the work was performed in church, though we should probably also not exclude the many Latin motets that could be performed in church. It is often forgotten that there are monophonic motets with French texts that surely were never performed in church, such as the fifteen in the trouvère *chansonnier* Paris, Bibliothèque nationale, français 845. Thus, we once again have to separate the sheep from the goats, if we can, as in that wonderful English motet *Balaam de quo vaticinans*, which clearly formed one section of the sequence *Epiphaniam domino* in performance at mass.[79]

In reality, it becomes almost as difficult to know when secular music was performed as liturgical. There are obvious cases of rondeaux that were meant for dancing, like the one I mentioned: *En ma dame ai mis mon cuer*. But were the polyphonic ballades of Guillaume de Machaut used for dancing? Probably they were more in the nature of after-dinner music for the nobility, and we know that much fourteenth-century secular music was performed in the banqueting hall. Such problems are worth considering, and there is more realistic discussion of court life in the *romans* of the time than is often understood.[80]

The question, however, that perhaps excites the musician most of all is that of the actual sound of the music. Again, this is a rather wide-open field. There are individual studies, such as Werner Bachmann's *The Origins of Bowing*,[81] that are remarkably useful, but many more studies are required of all kinds of instruments. For the Middle Ages, one of the problems is the lack of discussion of performance in contemporary sources and, beyond that, the lack of treatises on instruments, or even treatment of vocal technique. So often it becomes necessary to fall back on iconography, which has so many snags. A colleague of mine, Mary Remnant, is making a very exhaustive study of medieval stringed instruments as they appear in paintings, carvings, and, in fact, reproductions of all kinds. But it is necessary to weed out poorly restored reproductions, such as the medieval violins in Peterborough Cathedral,[82] deliberate distortions, and impossible situations, not to mention such less-obvious errors as pure musical symbolism, which, in the depiction of musical performance, has nothing to do with performance as such. This is often the case in the Psalms[83]— for example, David holding a psaltery (*psalterium* in Latin) may be a reference to the Psalter (also *psalterium*).

The lack of standardization in instruments is, of course, one factor militating against a satisfactory realization of such features as compass, tone quality, and playing methods. Fortunately, we have at least a clue in the clearly contemporary fourteenth-century illustrations of instruments, complete with ranges, in the important Berkeley theory manuscript edited by Oliver Ellsworth for his dissertation.[84] Frank Harrison has tried to show what instruments belonged in what areas of society and at what times.[85] He is perhaps a little too restrictive in his application of wind instruments to the performance of existing pieces, for it is always dangerous to assume that men of earlier times had less ability than those of today, and I have little doubt that a sackbut was available to play the *trompette* part of Pierre Fontaine's *J'ayme bien*.[86] Even so, his survey is commendably constructive, and many of his suggestions refreshingly novel. However, there are contradictions, since, although he can understand a clausula tenor being played on the organ just as he can an isorhythmic motet tenor, he seems to feel that late medieval sacred music in chanson style had vocalized tenors and contratenors.[87]

Instruments alone, however, are only part of the problem of medieval performance practice. Noah Greenberg touched on a few of the difficulties in his article in the Reese Festschrift.[88] Unless we have some precise information, we may well be performing a composition in a way that does not correspond to the original method. There is much scope for research into vocal and instrumental methods of performance that are not obviously wrong for the time. I was happy to see that the University of Texas Collegium Musicum has experimented with the use of ornamentation in fifteenth-century pieces. We do not, of course, have treatises on ornamentation from the Middle Ages, but it seems to me that later treatises from the Renaissance and baroque periods use much the same methods as medieval compositions.[89] Keyboard ornamentation of originally vocal compositions, such as we find in the Faenza Codex,[90] can be of great value as living examples of the medieval method. And, by a comparison with practical music of the Middle Ages, it is usually easy to eliminate types of ornament discussed in later treatises that were not used in the Middle Ages. The *trillo*, for example, would not be found, though I do be-

lieve groups of two or three repeated unisons were employed, in the manner of the bistropha and tristropha of
plainsong. Examples can be found, for instance, in the
lays of the Roman de Fauvel.[91]

Instrumental accompaniment is a thorny question. It
seems to me that references in both the Middle Ages and
the Renaissance suggest much more alternation between
vocal and instrumental ensembles than the combination
of voices and instruments that seems obvious to us today.[92] And in church music the organ was the only really welcome instrument. Strings were in any case more acceptable than wind instruments, even as late as the seventeenth century, probably because they kept in tune better
as well as being less raucous.[93] Experimentation and
study of documents is also worthwhile in another matter
brought up by Greenberg: the size of ensembles.[94] A
great deal of polyphonic music will be found to be intended for small groups, if not soloists, and, indeed, it is
only during the fifteenth century that the alternation of
soloists and chorus is marked in some manuscripts.[95]
Greenberg also asks what kind of sounds singers produced
in the Middle Ages and Renaissance.[96] Here, again, there
is scope for study, and I believe the idea that all voices
sounded reedy and strained is rather too one-sided, especially in view of the constantly stressed sweetness of
many instruments.[97]

The application of accidentals and, indeed, the normal
structure of the scale used in both monophonic and polyphonic music are topics that concern both the scholar
and the performer.[98] Articles and longer studies continue to be needed on smaller or larger areas so that we can
at least approach the correct melodic contours of medieval music. And, here again, the field of music theory can
be very helpful because of the many discussions of hexa-
chords[99] and the incidental use of accidentals. Monophonic music, both sacred and secular, needs even more
study from this angle of accidentals, because it is more
difficult to know when monophonic pieces need or do
not need sharps or flats. Many troubadour songs seem to
require flats, either partially or throughout,[100] and the
cadences of many trouvère songs seem to require F-sharp,
as suggested by the movement to the final G. In cases in
which the final is C or F, the semitone B or E is automatically present. Important results could be derived by con-

sidering such parallel cases. Fortunately, there is a corpus of troubadour melodies,[101] but the much larger body of trouvère melodies[102] still awaits systematic edition in spite of the valiant efforts of Gennrich and Jean-Baptiste Beck.[103] A field in which Gennrich has also been very active is that of contrafacta,[104] and much more can be done in this area, for the concept permeates the whole of medieval music.

There are still many more aspects of research that I ought to discuss, but let me mention briefly the burgeoning field of Slavonic medieval music, within which I must include Hungary.[105] The problems and evaluation of musical style cover the whole field of medieval music, and, curiously enough, studies of such basic matters as harmony are still rare.[106] Even melody has many secrets to yield,[107] and it would seem that attention has been focused on rhythm and form. But these areas, too, still have much to offer, and I would like to end as I began, by saying the prospects are bright. Indeed, the study of individual manuscripts has scarcely begun, and many preconceptions have to be put right about even the best-known sources. It will, I suspect, be true of research as of art that it is of much longer duration than human life.

Notes

1. Montpellier, Faculté de Médicine, H 196, completely transcribed in Yvonne Rokseth, ed., *Les Polyphonies du XIIIᵉ siècle*, 4 vols. (Paris: Editions de l'Oiseau Lyre, 1935–1939).

2. Florence, Biblioteca Laurenziana, Pluteus 29.1.

3. Sometimes the very fact that a scholar indicates that he is working on an edition of a particular source may suggest this, though the scholar himself may have no intention of putting a wall around the source.

4. For example: Janet E. Knapp, "The Polyphonic 'Conductus' in the Notre Dame Epoch: A Study of the Sixth and Seventh Fascicles of the Manuscript Florence, Biblioteca Laurenziana, 'Pluteus 29.1,' " 4 vols. (Ph.D. diss., Yale University, 1961), has transcriptions of all three- and two-part conductus from this MS in vols. 2 and 3; Nor-

man E. Smith, "The 'Clausulae' of the Notre Dame
School: A Repertorial Study," 3 vols. (Ph.D. diss., Yale
University, 1964), contains a transcription of the clausu-
las from MS W_1 (MS abbreviations will be as used in the
Répertoire International des Sources Musicales [RISM]
B IV, vols. 1 and 2); and William G. Waite, "The Rhythm
of the Twelfth Century 'Organum' in France," 3 vols.
(Ph.D. diss., Yale University, 1951), contains transcrip-
tions of all two-part organa and most of the clausulas
from F.

5. Leo Schrade, ed., *The Polyphonic Music of the Four-
   teenth Century* (Monaco: Editions de l'Oiseau Lyre,
   1956-), 1:2-71, contains the Fauvel motets. The mono-
   phonic works have been edited in Gregory A. Harrison,
   "The Monophonic Music in the Roman de Fauvel"
   (Ph.D. diss., Stanford University, 1963). Concerning the
   Florence *rondelli*, see Robert A. Falck, "*Rondellus*,
   Canon, and Related Types before 1300," *Journal of the
   American Musicological Society* 25 (1972): 38-57. A
   similar discussion appears in F. Reckow, "Das Handwör-
   terbuch der musikalischen Terminologie," *Archiv für
   Musikwissenschaft* 25 (1968): 241-277.

6. Marion Gushee, "Romanesque Polyphony" (Ph.D. diss.,
   Yale University, 1965). See also Sarah A. Fuller, "Aqui-
   tanian Polyphony of the Eleventh and Twelfth Centuries"
   (Ph.D. diss., University of California at Berkeley, 1969).

7. Marius Schneider, *Geschichte der Mehrstimmigkeit*, 2
   vols. (Berlin: J. Bard, 1934-1935); see vol. 1.

8. Cf. Armand Machabey, "Remarques sur le Winchester
   Troper," in *Festschrift Heinrich Besseler* (Leipzig: VEB
   Deutscher Verlag für Musik, 1961), pp. 67-90, and
   Andreus Holschneider, *Die Organa von Winchester*
   (Hildesheim: Georg Olms, 1968).

9. We have at least Janet Knapp's edition of *Thirty-five
   Conductus*, Collegium Musicum, vol. 6 (New Haven,
   Conn.: Yale University, Department of Music, 1965).

10. MS W_1 (Wolfenbüttel, Herzog-August-Bibliothek, MS
    628) in William G. Waite, *The Rhythm of Twelfth Cen-*

tury Polyphony (New Haven, Conn.: Yale University Press, 1954).

11. Theodore Karp, "Towards a Critical Edition of Notre Dame Organa Dupla," *Musical Quarterly* 52 (1966): 350-367. See also Raymond F. Erickson, "Rhythmic Problems and Melodic Structure in Organum Purum: A Computer-Assisted Study" (Ph.D. diss., Yale University, 1970).

12. Theodore Karp, "St. Martial and Santiago de Compostela: An Analytical Speculation," *Acta Musicologica* 29 (1967): 44-60; and Gilbert Reaney, "A Note on Conductus Rhythm," in *Kongressbericht Köln 1958*, ed. Gerald Abraham et al. (Kassel: Bärenreiter, 1959), pp. 219-221. See also Bruno Stäblein, "Modale Rhythmen im Saint-Martial-Repertoire," in *Festschrift Friedrich Blume*, ed. Anna Amalie Abert and Wilhelm Pfannkuch (Kassel: Bärenreiter, 1963), pp. 340-362.

13. Pierre Aubry, *Cent Motets du XIIIe siècle*, 3 vols. (Paris: Rouart & Lerolle, 1908).

14. Georg Kuhlmann, *Die zweistimmigen französischen Motetten des Kodex Montpellier, Faculté de Médecine H 196*, 2 vols. (Würzburg: Triltsch, 1938); see vol. 2.

15. Guillaume de Machaut, *Guillaume de Machaut: Musikalische Werke*, ed. Friedrich Ludwig, 4 vols. (Leipzig and Wiesbaden: Breitkopf and Härtel, 1926-1954); and Schrade, ed., *Polyphonic Music*, vols. 2-3.

16. Wolfgang Dömling, "Zur Überlieferung der musikalischen Werke Guillaume de Machauts," *Die Musikforschung* 22 (1969): 190-191.

17. For Bamberg and Montpellier, see nn. 13 and 1. The Turin and Las Huelgas sources are transcribed respectively in Antoine Auda, ed., *Les "Motets Wallons" du manuscrit de Turin: Vari 42*, 2 vols. (Brussels: Privately published, 1953); and H. Anglès, *El Còdex musical de Las Huelgas*, 3 vols. (Barcelona: Institut d'Estudis Catalans, 1931). Gordon Anderson is at present in the process of publishing editions of the W$_2$ Latin motets and con-

ductus and the motets from the La Clayette Codex for the Institute of Medieval Music and the American Institute of Musicology respectively.

18. Friedrich Gennrich, *Rondeaux, Virelais, und Balladen aus dem Ende des 12., dem 13. und dem ersten Viertel des 14. Jahrhunderts*, 2 vols. (Dresden: Niemeyer, 1921; Göttingen: Niemeyer, 1927), pieces 28-33, and 35, 1: n.p.; 2:21-23.

19. Jürg Stenzl, *Die vierzig Clausulae der Handschrift Paris, Bibliothèque nationale, Latin 15139* (Bern and Stuttgart: Paul Haupt, 1970).

20. Milano, Biblioteca Ambrosiana, MS M.17 sup., fol. 56, and Compostela, Biblioteca de la Catedral, Codex Calixtinus, fol. 190.

21. Archibald T. Davison and Willi Apel, eds., *Historical Anthology of Music*, 2 vols. (Cambridge, Mass.: Harvard University Press, 1946, rev. 1949), pieces 26*a* and 27*b*, 1 (rev.):22 and 23.

22. Nino Pirrotta, *The Music of Fourteenth Century Italy*, 5 vols. (Rome: American Institute of Musicology, 1954-1964); W. Thomas Marrocco, ed., *The Polyphonic Music of the Fourteenth Century*, vols. 6-7; and Schrade, ed., *Polyphonic Music*, vol. 4.

23. Ursula Günther, *The Motets of the Manuscripts Chantilly, Musée Condé, 564 (olim 1047) and Modena, Biblioteca Estense, α .M.5, 24 (olim lat. 568)* (Rome: American Institute of Musicology, 1965); and Frank Ll. Harrison, ed., *The Polyphonic Music of the Fourteenth Century*, vol. 5.

24. Alexander Ramsbotham, Dom Anselm Hughes, and H. B. Collins, *The Old Hall Manuscript*, 3 vols. (Nashdom Abbey, Burnham, Bucks.: Plainsong and Medieval Music Society, 1933-1938); and M. Bent and A. Hughes, *The Old Hall Manuscript*, 3 vols. (Rome: American Institute of Musicology, 1969).

25. Hanna Stäblein-Harder, *Fourteenth-Century Mass Music in France* (Tübingen: American Institute of Musicology, 1962).

26. Luther A. Dittmer, *The Worcester Fragments: A Catalogue Raisonné and Transcription* (Nijmegen: American Institute of Musicology, 1957).

27. Cf. Gilbert Reaney, "New Sources of Ars Nova Music," *Musica Disciplina* 19 (1965): 59-61; and H. Wagenaar-Nolthenius, "De Leidse Fragmente," in *Renaissance-Muziek 1400-1600 (Donum Natalicium René Bernard Lenaerts)*, ed. Jozef Robijns et al. (Louvain: Katholieke Universiteit, Seminarie voor Muziekwetenschap, 1969), pp. 303-315.

28. See also M. P. Hasselman, "The French Chanson of the Mid-Fourteenth Century," 2 vols. (Ph.D. diss., University of California at Berkeley, 1970).

29. Cf. Gilbert Reaney, "The Performance of Medieval Music," in *Aspects of Medieval and Renaissance Music*, ed. Jan La Rue (New York: W. W. Norton and Co., 1966), pp. 710 and 714-715.

30. Cf. Karl Young, *The Drama of the Medieval Church*, 2 vols. (Oxford: Clarendon Press, 1933), 2:514-520.

31. Transcribed in Gwynn S. McPeek, *The British Museum Ms Egerton 3307* (London: Oxford University Press, 1963); and A. Hughes, *Fifteenth-Century Liturgical Music* (London: Stainer and Bell, 1968), pp. 44-158.

32. The first and second source are discussed in some detail in Theodor Göllner, *Formen der frühen Mehrstimmigkeit in deutschen Handschriften des späten Mittelalters* (Tutzing: Hans Schneider, 1961), pp. 15-59, and Jacques Handschin, "Angelomontana polyphonica," *Schweizerisches Jahrbuch für Musikwissenschaft* 3 (1928): 64-95, respectively.

33. Theodor Göllner, *Die mehrstimmigen liturgischen Lesungen*, 2 vols. (Tutzing: Hans Schneider, 1969).

Gilbert Reaney

34. Cf. Arnold Geering, *Die Organa und mehrstimmigen Conductus in den Handschriften des deutschen Sprachgebietes* (Bern: P. Haupt, 1952), pp. 25-27, 36, 65-69, 71-73.

35. Ibid., pp. 6-20, 37-38.

36. Max Lütolff, *Die mehrstimmigen Ordinarium Missaesätze*, 2 vols. (Bern: P. Haupt, 1970).

37. C. E. H. de Coussemaker, ed., *Scriptorum de musica medii aevi nova series*, 4 vols. (Paris: Durand, 1864–1876); and Martin Gerbert, ed., *Scriptores ecclesiastici de musica*, 3 vols. (Sankt Blasien: Abbey of Sankt Blasien, 1784).

38. Fritz Reckow, *Der Musiktraktat des Anonymus 4*, 2 vols. (Wiesbaden: Franz Steiner, 1967).

39. Cecily P. Sweeney, "The Musical Treatise Formerly Attributed to John Wylde and the Cistercian Chant Reform," 2 vols. (Ph.D. diss., University of California at Los Angeles, 1972). The treatise is given in vol. 2.

40. Aurelian of Réomé, *Musica Disciplina*, ed. and trans. Joseph Ponte, Colorado Music Press Translations, no. 3 (Colorado Springs: Colorado College, 1968), is one that has appeared in translation.

41. Richard H. Hoppin, *The Cypriot-French Repertory of the Manuscript Torino, Biblioteca Nazionale, J.II.9*, 4 vols. (Rome: American Institute of Musicology, 1960–1963).

42. Richard H. Hoppin, "The Cypriot-French Repertory of the Manuscript Torino, Biblioteca Nazionale, J.II.9," *Musica Disciplina* 11 (1957): 79-125.

43. Anglès, *El Còdex musical de Las Huelgas*, vol. 1.

44. Rokseth, ed., *Les Polyphonies du XIIIe siècle*, vol. 4.

45. Theodore Karp, "A Test for Melodic Borrowings among Notre Dame *Organa Dupla*," in *The Computer and Mu-*

sic, ed. Harry B. Lincoln (Ithaca, N.Y.: Cornell University Press, 1970), pp. 293–295. See also Raymond Erickson's review of this book in *Journal of the American Musicological Society* 25 (1972): 102–107.

46. C. W. Jones, *The St. Nicholas Liturgy (with an Essay on the Music by Gilbert Reaney)* (Berkeley and Los Angeles: University of California Press, 1963).

47. Tropes from MS Paris, Bibliothèque nationale, fonds latin 1121 are published in Paul Evans, *The Early Trope Repertory of Saint Martial de Limoges* (Princeton: Princeton University Press, 1970). Aquitanian tropes are published by Günther Weiss in vols. 3 (1970), 6 (in preparation), and 11 (in preparation) of the series Monumenta Monodica Medii Aevi (Kassel: Bärenreiter).

48. W. H. Frere, *The Winchester Troper* (London: Henry Bradshaw Society, 1894); Jacques Handschin, "The Two Winchester Tropers," *Journal of Theological Studies* 37 (1936): 34–49 and 156–172; see also n. 8.

49. 1946, 1934, 1925, and 1941 respectively.

50. The old edition in Coussemaker, ed., *Scriptorum de musica*, 2:152–191, is still serviceable.

51. For example, Robert Snow in Willi Apel, *Gregorian Chant* (Bloomington, Ind.: Indiana University Press, 1958), p. 503.

52. Walther Lipphardt, "Gregor der Grosse und sein Anteil am römischen Antiphonar," in *Atti del congresso internazionale di musica sacra 1950* (Tournai: Desclée, 1952), pp. 248–254; and Paul F. Cutter, "The Old Roman Chant Tradition: Oral or Written?" *Journal of the American Musicological Society* 20 (1967): 167–181. On the repertory of Old Roman chant, see also Thomas H. Connolly, "Introits and Archetypes: Some Archaisms of the Old Roman Chant," *Journal of the American Musicological Society* 25 (1972): 157–174.

53. Gustave Reese, *Music in the Middle Ages* (New York: W. W. Norton and Co., 1940), pp. 106–107.

54. Michel Huglo, "Le Chant 'vieux-romain': Liste des manuscrits et témoins indirects," *Sacris erudiri* 6 (1954): 90–
124; idem, *Fonti e paleografia del canto ambrosiano*,
Archivio Ambrosiano, vol. 7 (Milan: Scuola Tipografica
San Benedetto, 1956).

55. Gregorio Suñol, ed., *Antiphonale missarum juxta ritum
Sanctae Ecclesiae Mediolanensis* (Rome: Desclée, 1935);
Liber vesperalis juxta . . . Mediolanensis (Rome: Desclée,
1939).

56. Clyde W. Brockett, *Antiphons, Responsories, and Other
Chants of the Mozarabic Rite* (Brooklyn, N.Y.: Institute
of Mediaeval Music, 1968).

57. Higini Anglès, "Gregorian Chant," *New Oxford History
of Music*, 11 vols. (London: Oxford University Press,
1954-), 2:107–109.

58. Don M. Randel, *The Responsorial Psalm Tones for the
Mozarabic Office* (Princeton: Princeton University Press,
1969).

59. Roy Jesson, "Ambrosian Chant," in Apel, *Gregorian
Chant*, p. 480.

60. Cf. Frederick S. Andrews, "Mediaeval Modal Theory"
(Ph.D. diss., Cornell University, 1935) for this area.

61. Johannes Tinctoris, "Liber de natura et proprietate to-
norum," in Coussemaker, ed., *Scriptorum de musica*,
4:29.

62. Ernst Rohloff, *Der Musiktraktat des Johannes de Grocheo*
(Leipzig: Gebr. Reinecke, 1943), p. 60. My translation.

63. Davison and Apel, *Historical Anthology of Music*, piece
19*d*, 1 (rev.): 17.

64. Cf. Ursula Aarburg, "Lay," in *Die Musik in Geschichte
und Gegenwart*, ed. Friedrich Blume, 14 vols. (Kassel
and Basel: Bärenreiter, 1949–1968), vol. 8, col. 84.

65. Giuseppe Vecchi, *Pietro Abelardo: I "Planctus"* (Modena: Società Tipografica Modense, 1951), pp. 48-55, and musical appendix, pp. vii-xiv.

66. For example, Sankt Gallen, Stiftsbibliothek, MS 390-391.

67. Reese, *Music in the Middle Ages*, pp. 86-87.

68. Gerbert, ed., *Scriptores ecclesiastici*, 1:119-121.

69. Ibid., 1:214-216.

70. Frank Ll. Harrison, *Music in Medieval Britain* (London: Routledge and Kegan Paul, 1958).

71. W. H. Frere, *The Use of Sarum*, 2 vols. (Cambridge: Cambridge University Press, 1898 and 1901).

72. J. N. Dalton, *Ordinale Exoniense*, 4 vols. (London: Henry Bradshaw Society, 1909-1940).

73. Cf. K. Hallinger, ed., *Corpus Consuetudinum Monasticarum*, 4 vols. (Siegburg: F. Schmitt, 1963-1967).

74. W. G. Henderson, *Processionale ad usum Insignis ac Praeclarae Ecclesiae Sarum* (Leeds: McCorquodale, 1882), n. p.

75. In MS Egerton 3307, for instance; see Frere, *The Use of Sarum*, 1:59-61; 2:161-162.

76. Joseph Smits van Waesberghe, "Zur ursprünglichen Vortragsweise der Prosulen, Sequenzen und Organa," in *Kongressbericht Köln 1958*, ed. Gerald Abraham et al. (Kassel: Bärenreiter, 1959), pp. 251-254.

77. J. Leland, *J. Lelandi antiquarii de rebus Britannicis Collectanea* (London: B. White, 1774), 4:237.

78. Oxford, Bodleian Library, Lat. liturg. d.5, fol. 104 (transcribed in Geering, *Die Organa und mehrstimmigen Conductus*, appendix, no. 7.

79. Both sequence and motet in Denis Stevens, *Treasury of English Church Music*, 5 vols. (London: Blandford Press, 1965), piece 5, 1:11-18.

80. For instance, see Guillaume de Machaut's *Remède de Fortune*, in *Oeuvres de Guillaume de Machaut*, ed. Ernest Hoepffner, 3 vols. (Paris: Firmin Didot, 1908-1921), 2:1-57; and Jean Froissart's *Meliador*, 3 vols. (Paris: Firmin Didot, 1895-1899).

81. Werner Bachmann, *The Origins of Bowing*, trans. Norma Deane (Oxford: Oxford University Press, 1970).

82. Mary Remnant, "Rebec, Fiddle, and Crowd in England," *Proceedings of the Royal Musical Association* 95 (1969): 16.

83. James W. McKinnon, "Musical Instruments in Medieval Psalm Commentaries and Psalters," *Journal of the American Musicological Society* 21 (1968): 13-18.

84. Oliver B. Ellsworth, "The Berkeley Manuscript (olim Phillipps 4450): A Compendium of Fourteenth-Century Music Theory," 2 vols. (Ph.D. diss., University of California at Berkeley, 1969). For the illustrations, see 1:66-72.

85. Frank Ll. Harrison, "Tradition and Innovation in Instrumental Usage, 1100-1450," in *Aspects of Medieval and Renaissance Music*, ed. La Rue, pp. 319-335.

86. Transcription in Guillaume Dufay, *Opera Omnia*, ed. Heinrich Besseler, 6 vols. (Rome: American Institute of Musicology, 1970), piece 86, 6:102.

87. Harrison, "Tradition and Innovation in Instrumental Usage," p. 331.

88. Noah Greenberg, "Early Music Performance Today," in *Aspects of Medieval and Renaissance Music*, ed. La Rue, pp. 314-318.

89. Cf. Imogene Horsley, "The Diminutions in Composition and Theory of Composition," *Acta Musicologica* 35 (1963): 124–153.

90. Cf. Dragan Plamenac, "Keyboard Music of the 14th Century in Codex Faenza 117," *Journal of the American Musicological Society* 4 (1951): 190–192.

91. Examples in Jean Maillard, *Evolution et esthétique du lai lyrique* (Paris: Centre de Documentation Universitaire, 1961), p. 331.

92. An obvious case is the alternation of plainsong and organ in the organ mass, but the variety of performing media used at the Duke of Burgundy's Peacock Feast also shows very little simultaneous use of voices and instruments. Cf. J. Page-Phillip and Thurston Dart, "The Peacock Feast," *Galpin Society Journal* 6 (1953): 9.

93. Cf. Charles Butler, *The Principles of Musick in Singing and Setting* (London, 1636), p. 118; also Robert Donington, *The Interpretation of Music* (London: Faber and Faber, 1963), pp. 482–484.

94. Greenberg, "Early Music Performance," in *Aspects of Medieval and Renaissance Music*, ed. La Rue, p. 317.

95. Cf. Manfred F. Bukofzer, *Studies in Medieval and Renaissance Music* (New York: W. W. Norton and Co., 1950), pp. 177–189.

96. Greenberg, "Early Music Performance," in *Aspects of Medieval and Renaissance Music*, ed. La Rue, p. 318.

97. Paul Henry Lang, *Music in Western Civilization* (New York: W. W. Norton and Co., 1941), p. 159.

98. Cf. Marie Louise Martinez-Göllner, "Marchettus of Padua and Chromaticism," in *L'Ars Nova Italiana del Trecento*, ed. F. Alberto Gallo (Bologna: Forni, 1970), pp. 187–202; Gilbert Reaney, "Accidentals in the Music of the Fifteenth Century," in *Renaissance-Muziek 1400–1600*, ed. Robijns et al., pp. 223–231.

99. Martin Ruhnke, "Hexachord II," in *Die Musik in Geschichte und Gegenwart*, ed. Blume, vol. 6, cols. 352-358; Albert Seay, "The 15th Century Coniuncta: A Preliminary Study," in *Aspects of Medieval and Renaissance Music*, ed. La Rue, pp. 723-737.

100. E.g., *Lancan vei la folha* by Bernart de Ventadorn; see Friedrich Gennrich, *Der musikalische Nachlass der Troubadours*, 2 vols. (Langen: Privately published, 1958), 1:39.

101. Gennrich, *Der musikalische Nachlass der Troubadours*.

102. For a bibliography of sources, see the article by Gennrich, "Troubadours, Trouvères," in *Die Musik in Geschichte und Gegenwart*, ed. Blume, vol. 13, col. 835 ff.

103. Jean-Baptiste Beck began a *Corpus cantilenarum medii aevi* but only completed editions of the Chansonnier Cangé and the Chansonnier du Roi, each in two vols. (Paris: Librairie Honoré Champion, 1927; and Philadelphia : University of Pennsylvania Press, 1938).

104. See especially Friedrich Gennrich, *Die Kontrafaktur im Liedschaffen des Mittelalters* (Langen: Privately published, 1965).

105. To list a comprehensive bibliography for this field would be beyond the scope of this article, but a good beginning may be made by consulting the following articles in *Die Musik in Geschichte und Gegenwart*, ed. Blume: "Jugoslawien," vol. 7, cols. 314-315, 324, 331-332; "Polen," vol. 10, cols. 1411-1414; "Tschechoslowakei," vol. 13, cols. 906-907; "Ungarn," vol. 13, cols. 1067-1068.

106. Joseph Wouters, *Harmonische Verschijningvormen in de Muziek* (Amsterdam: Privately published, 1954); Gilbert Reaney, "Fourteenth Century Harmony and the Ballades, Rondeaux, and Virelais of Guillaume de Machaut," *Musica Disciplina* 7 (1953): 129–146, and "Notes on the Harmonic Technique of Guillaume de Machaut," in *Essays in Musicology (A Birthday Offering for Willi Apel)*, ed. Clare Rayner (Bloomington, Ind.: Indiana University Press, 1968), pp. 63–68.

107. Joseph Smits van Waesberghe, *A Textbook of Melody* (Rome: American Institute of Musicology, 1954); Bence Szabolcsi, *A History of Melody* (London: Macmillan & Co., 1965).

Gilbert Reaney

The Library of the Mind:
Observations on the Relationship between Musical
Scholarship and Bibliography
Vincent Duckles

Nine

The traditional image of the humanist scholar is of an individual working in the privacy of his own study, surrounded by his books and files, having at his fingertips all the information that has bearing on his investigation. He sifts and sorts that information, bringing it into focus through the power of his imagination much as a burning glass gathers and intensifies the heat of the sun; and as the concentration of heat brings about a transformation of matter, so the scholar's imagination creates new patterns and insights out of facts at hand. The picture may be somewhat romantic, even archaic, by twentieth-century standards, but it still carries the ring of truth.

There is another image current in the folklore of scholarship, an image that reflects more realistically the frustration an investigator must feel when confronted with the vast network of documentation that separates him from his objective, and which he must bring under control before he is in a position to make a fresh contribution to knowledge. The documents are multiplying every day, almost every hour, so that in his less inspired moments the scholar is impressed by nothing so much as the thought of miles of library shelves through which he must search to find material relevant to his study: periodical articles buried in obscure journals, monographs in unanalyzed series, all of which contribute to the haunting fear that the subject of his investigation may already have been treated by somebody else. An awareness that the world is full of recorded knowledge on every conceivable subject can be both an inspiration and a source of discouragement. The problem of how to gain mastery over bibliography is one of the perpetual concerns of scholarship. It is particularly acute in the humanities, where boundaries between disciplines are ill defined and there is much overlapping of interests. The two images I have suggested, that of the creative scholar and of the bibliographical drudge, represent two phases in the profile of research activity: the phase of assimilation, on the one hand, and of productivity on the other. Both are essential elements in the process: but at some point in his investigation the scholar must free himself of the library—must undergo a shift in emphasis from intake to output.

Charles Burney has given vivid expression to that crucial change in direction in the preface to his *General History of Music* (1776). He is talking about his efforts to find his way through the maze of literature on "the music of the Ancients":

Vincent Duckles

After reading, or at least consulting, an almost innumerable quantity of old and scarce books, of which the dulness and pedentry were almost petrific, and among which, where I hoped to find the most information, I found but little, and where I expected but little, I was seldom disappointed: at length, wearied and disgusted at the small success of my researches, I shut my books, and began to examine myself as to my musical principles; hoping that the good I had met with in the course of my reading was by this time digested, and incorporated in my own ideas; and that the many years I had spent in practice, theory, and meditation, might entitle me to some freedom of thought, unshackled by the trammels of authority.[1]

"I shut my books"! This is the moment the scholar has been waiting for. It signifies an act of courage as well as an expression of satiety. It marks the throwing away of crutches, of all external supports, a readiness to proceed on one's own. It is also a moment that the overcautious investigator never experiences. How often one reads dissertations, or monographs, or research papers that never move beyond the preliminary, accumulative stages—like a dissonance that is prepared but not resolved. At the same time, we all know of people who have shut their books too soon, who venture to speak with authority before they have earned the right to do so, who have failed to make themselves masters of the literature of their field.

My purpose in this paper is to explore some of the relationships between creative scholarship in music and its bibliographical foundations. My aim, to put it another way, is to consider how the scholar links himself with the power contained in books. From our position in the latter part of the twentieth century, we can make use of a number of resources not available to musicologists of earlier eras; the computer—with its applications to music bibliography—comes first to mind. I shall return to a consideration of this mixed blessing later in the discussion. Suffice it to say that the innovations of computer technology are not as far-reaching as many would have us believe. Humanistic scholarship is firmly rooted in tradition. Our patterns of investigation do not differ materially from those of our predecessors. For example, we hold fast to the belief that musical learning is to be identified with the knowledge of books. This is an eighteenth-century concept, a view we inherited from the Enlightenment, a time in which Reason was elevated above all other human faculties. Our eighteenth-century forerunners went so far as to believe that, if they produced a book voluminous enough and compiled by the world's leading experts, it could contain all the knowledge worth knowing. The great French *Encyclopédie* exemplifies that ideal. Perhaps we do not challenge the belief in the supremacy of book learning or admit other kinds of knowledge into the temple of scholarship as often as we should. In the eighteenth century a sharp distinction came to be made between musical *Fachlehre*, the "know-how" of the professional musician, and *Musikalische Wissenschaft*, the kind of scientific knowledge that could only be gained from reading. One can trace this literary emphasis in such works as Jacob Adlung's *Anleitung zu der musikalischen Gelehrtheit* (1758), which is essentially an annotated bibliography of books indispensable to the learned musician. Johann Adam Hiller's "Kritische Entwurf einer musikalischen Bibliothek," published serially in his *Wochentliche Nachrichten* beginning in 1768, is the description of a model music library designed for the cultivated amateur who wished to penetrate beneath the surface of his experience and gain a deeper understanding of the nature of his art. Hiller and many of his contemporaries deplored the fact that musicians did not read books, and for that reason the art of music had come to be regarded as a craft rather than as a science. The outcome of the practicing musician's reluctance to read and think about music is the fact that musicology, when it began to emerge as a valid discipline toward the

Vincent Duckles

end of the eighteenth century, took its character from the interests of the dilettante rather than those of the composer or performer. The traces of that lineage are all too evident in musical scholarship today, particularly in the wide gap that usually separates those who study music from those who make it. In any case, the Age of Reason, which gave birth to modern musical scholarship, also witnessed the beginnings of music bibliography.

It is not my intention here to discuss music bibliography in all its aspects. It has somewhat different connotations for the scholar, the librarian, and the music collector. Instead, I should like to give the term a metaphorical twist by suggesting that *bibliography is the library of the mind*. A catalogue is the record of the holdings of some existing collection; a bibliography, on the other hand, is made up of documents that have no inherent connection apart from the mind of the individual who selected, rejected, or otherwise organized them. The physical components of a bibliography may be scattered over the face of the earth.

There are at least three avenues of approach to music bibliography, leading to three different kinds of musical knowledge (no hierarchy is intended here; each bears its own justification): (1) the analytical, or descriptive, approach; (2) the functional, or applied, approach; and (3) the systematic, or subject, approach. Since I intend to direct my remarks chiefly to the third of these approaches, let me dispose briefly of the first two. Analytical, or descriptive, bibliography is the province of a few dedicated specialists whose interests and training lie in the direction of printing techniques or in the history of printing and publishing. In the field of literature this approach has fostered a high degree of technical complexity and has produced some spectacular results, for example, in establishing the chronology of early Shakespeare editions or in identifying and organizing the corpus of books printed before 1501. Few studies of music printing have reached this level of sophistication. As far as music is concerned, descriptive bibliography is a comparatively unexplored territory, although we have an increasing number of useful works on individual music printers from the sixteenth through the eighteenth centuries. An exemplary blend of musical and typographical knowledge is found in Professor Daniel Heartz's study of *Pierre Attaingnant: Royal Printer of Music*.[2]

Functional, or applied, bibliography serves the immediate purposes of the research scholar. It provides a means to an end, that end determined by the range and scope of a specific investigation. There is no recipe for gaining mastery over bibliography through this approach save continuing research experience. There are, of course, a number of standard tools and aids that every musical scholar must become acquainted with: the basic music dictionaries and encyclopedias, indexes to periodical literature, listings of primary source materials, such as Robert Eitner's *Quellen-Lexikon*, the *British Union Catalogue of Early Music*, or the volumes of the *International Inventory of Musical Sources*. But the acquisition of such knowledge is incidental. There is no point in cluttering the mind of a young musicologist with the memorized titles of hundreds of music reference books. He will learn what he needs to know about music bibliography through the necessarily tedious but often exciting progression from footnote to footnote. This is a time-consuming process but rewarding in the long run. Every pebble tossed into the pool of learning creates widening circles of relevance so that, no matter where a start is made, a full command of bibliographical knowledge will eventually result. What began as applied bibliographical knowledge will begin to reveal the lineaments of a systematic structure. The materials will organize themselves through the natural processes of being used. This, incidentally, is the basis for the criticism that many practicing musicologists level against formal courses in music bibliography. They take the position that there is no substitute for learning by doing, and there is much to be said for this view.

But such critics overlook the fact that bibliography can serve as an approach to knowledge in its own right. The interest in documentation, which is a by-product of research, can come to occupy the center of the stage. In most diagrams of the field of musicology, from Guido Adler to the present day, bibliography is relegated to the status of a *Hilfswissenschaft*, an auxiliary discipline; but it is quite possible to construct a schematic outline of musical knowledge in which the literature of music itself occupies the apex of the pyramid. Systematic, or subject, bibliography provides its own rationale. Closely allied to the study of the history of ideas, it is concerned with the shape of musical learning as reflected in the innumerable documents that record man's involvement with the art. Insofar as it treats the history of those documents and the changes in meaning they have conveyed in the past, it falls within the domain of historiography. When I suggested that the eighteenth century marked the beginnings of modern music bibliography, this was the approach I had in mind.

Vincent Duckles

The Age of Reason was an age of system building. The scholars of the Enlightenment were important, above all, for their contributions to the organization of knowledge; they excelled in making maps of learning. Their preoccupation with the structure of knowledge is reflected in the above-mentioned French *Encyclopédie* of Denis Diderot and Jean Le Rond d'Alembert, and, with a somewhat different emphasis, in the work of the so-called universal historians at Göttingen during the latter part of the century. These men were the founders of what we know as *cultural history*.[3] They insisted on viewing the world and its parts as a whole. Their studies took them far beyond the familiar domain of the political or military historian, into the comparatively little-known territories of the history of law, religion, customs, and the arts. Nothing in human experience was remote from their concern.

One of the earliest exemplars of the systematic approach to music bibliography is furnished by the Frenchman Sébastien de Brossard.[4] He began with the intention of compiling a list of Greek, Latin, and Italian terms with their French equivalents to be appended to the second edition of his two-part motets, *Prodromus Musicalis* (1702). In the process of putting this modest list together, he became involved in an enterprise far greater than he may have envisaged. It led him beyond a simply polyglot lexicon to a full-scale dictionary of musical terms, the first since Johannes Tinctoris's *Terminorum Diffinitorium* of the late fifteenth century. It sometimes happens that the initial effort in a new direction turns out to be a definitive statement, setting a standard for all future efforts. This was the case in 1501 when Ottaviano dei Petrucci first set polyphonic music in movable type with an artistry and technical skill that has never been surpassed. The same could be said, in another sense, of Brossard's *Dictionaire*. His accomplishment was not fully realized, but the program he outlined for achieving bibliographical control was far ahead of his time. The substance of that program is contained in an appendix to the dictionary proper, a section headed "a catalogue of those authors who have written in all languages, times, and countries, on music in general or in particular." He is quite frank in confessing the limitations of his work as measured against the ideal:

For more than ten years I have been collecting materials to form a catalogue, not only of authors who have written about music, but also of those who as composers have given their creations to the world, and finally of those who have become distinguished in performance and practice: a *catalogue historique et raisonné* in which an attempt is made to give exactly not only the names and surnames of the illustrious, their lives, their times, their principal employment, but also the titles of their works, the language in which they wrote, the translations and different editions that have appeared, the places, dates, printers, and the form of the editions; even the locations, that is to say, the bookshops and libraries where copies may be found, whether manuscripts or printed books, and finally (that which to me seems not only the most difficult but also the most important) the good and bad judgements which the most judicious critics have uttered either vocally or in writing. But I must admit that, in spite of all my efforts, my materials are not extensive enough to complete a work of this nature with the necessary exactitude.[5]

What Brossard intended in his "catalogue . . . of authors" was to demonstrate a method of bibliographical research, to whet the appetites of his readers, and to enlist their aid in bringing his ambitious project to completion. He lists the names of some 900 writers on music from ancient times to his own day, without reference to any specific titles of works, and separates these names into three groups classified according to his own degree of familiarity with the authors. Only 230 of the 900 writers had been consulted by Brossard himself. Another 100 were accessible to him and were to be examined as time permitted, but the largest group, 600 or more, were listed on the basis of incomplete, indirect knowledge. They were reputed to have written on music, but he had neither the time nor the opportunity to verify this surmise. At this point he was forced to call upon his readers for assistance, giving them precise instructions as to the kind of information he needed and the form it should take. He solicited, first of all, an exact transcription of the title page and imprint; next, he gave instructions for transcribing titles in unfamiliar languages, and, further, he explained how to treat volumes with multiple authorship and how to handle special problems in bibliographical description. Finally, he requested that all the information be sent to him care of his publisher, Christophe Ballard, or to his own home at Meaux en Brie. Undoubtedly, the public's response to this appeal was something less than Brossard had anticipated. He did not live to see his great work in print, but we can follow the progress of his magnum opus in entries made in the handwritten catalogue of his library, which he presented to the Bibliothèque du Roy in 1724. These entries indicate that the project that had occupied him for ten years at the time the *Dictionaire* was published had grown by 1724 into an effort of at least thirty-five years duration, all of which was intended to culminate in the creation of a monumental *Dictionaire historique de la musique et des musiciens*. The work was to comprehend "the lives, the qualities, the occupations, the works of the illustrious musicians, theorists as well as practitioners, in all times and conditions, ages, sexes, nationalities, religions, etc."[6] Not until the *Biographie universelle* by François-Joseph Fétis, published more than one hundred years later, was a biobibliographical work of such scope to be achieved.

Brossard is important as one of the first musicians to seek an understanding of his art through a comprehensive study of its documents. We owe to him a significant step toward furnishing the library of the musical mind. Brossard's approach, however, was that of the lexicographer, based on description rather than on the grouping of his materials. To furnish a library, it is necessary to have not only space and shelving, but also, above all, some plan for arranging the material on the shelves. A quantity of books tossed into a bin or sorted arbitrarily by size or shape does not constitute a library. The situation would not be much improved if we arranged them in alphabetical order, such as in an author-title catalogue, or shelved them according to their place in a chronology. Neither of these systems can be said to have a rational basis. They do not represent patterns of meaning that the human mind invents or discovers in order to bring sense out of chaos. What is needed is a system of classification, an organization that reflects the connections between ideas. To know any given subject, at least from a rationalistic point of view, is to break it down into its component parts and to distribute these parts according to higher and lower categories of significance. Here, of course, we are verging on an area that has occupied philosophers from Aristotle to the present day. If time permitted and the resources were available, it would be a fascinating exercise to trace music classification systems from antiquity onward, as Gerhard Pietzsch has done in his study, *Die Klassifikation der Musik von Boetius bis Ugolino von Orvieto*.[7] Renaissance and baroque musical treatises abound in graphic representations of the Temple of Musick, presided over by Frau Musica surrounded by cosmic and mythological symbols of the divisions of the art. One recalls the well-known print from Georg Reich's *Margarita philosophica* (1503) or the elaborate diagram of "The Temple of Speculative Music" in Robert Fludd's *Utrisque Cosmi Historia*, published in 1617. Neither of these projections could satisfy the needs of the Enlightenment, which demanded a structure more clear-cut and practical.

There is an extremely interesting and little-known attempt to diagram the scope of musical learning in a French periodical dating from 1770. It appears in the *Journal de musique historique, théorique, et practique sur la musique ancienne et moderne, les musiciens et les instrumens de tous les temps et de tous les peuples*, in the form of a folding chart headed "Tableau de la musique et de ses branches."[8] It will be noted in this chart that musical practice (*musique practique*) occupies the center of the stage, flanked by music history on one side and musical science on the other. Let us look at the field of music history for a moment. It has two major subdivisions: (1) the history of music itself approached through the various national schools, and (2) the history of musicians. This dichotomy is a familiar one and still separates students of musical styles from those who favor

TABLEAU DE

ET DE SES

MUS

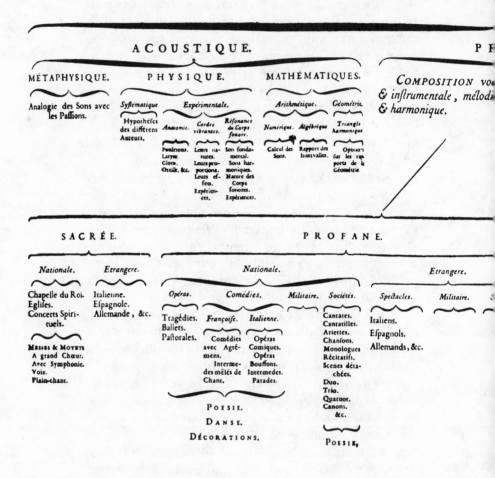

ACOUSTIQUE.				PH
MÉTAPHYSIQUE.	**PHYSIQUE.**		**MATHÉMATIQUES.**	*Composition vo...*
Analogie des Sons avec les Paſſions.	*Syſtématique* — Hypothéſes des différens Auteurs.	*Expérimentale.* — *Anatomie.* Poulmons. Larynx. Glote. Oreille, &c. / *Cordes vibrantes.* Leurs natures. Leurs proportions. Leurs effets. Expériences. / *Réſonance du Corps ſonore.* Son fondamental. Sons harmoniques. Nature des Corps ſonores. Expériences.	*Arithmétique.* — *Numérique.* Calcul des Sons. / *Algébrique.* Rapport des Intervalles. — *Géométrie.* *Triangle harmonique* Opinion ſur les rapports de la Géométrie.	*& instrumentale, mélod... & harmonique.*

SACRÉE.		PROFANE.			
Nationale.	**Etrangere.**	**Nationale.**		**Etrangere.**	
Chapelle du Roi. Egliſes. Concerts Spirituels.	Italienne. Eſpagnole. Allemande, &c.	*Opéras.* Tragédies. Ballets. Paſtorales.	*Comédies.*	*Spectacles.* Italiens. Eſpagnols. Allemands, &c.	*Militaire.*
Messes & Motets A grand Chœur. Avec Symphonie. Voix. Plain-chant.			*Françoiſe.* Comédies avec Agrémens. Intermedes mêlés de Chant. / *Italienne.* Opéras Comiques. Opéras Bouffons. Intermedes. Parades.		
		Militaire.	*Sociétés.* Cantates. Cantatilles. Ariettes. Chanſons. Monologues Récitatifs. Scenes détachées. Duo. Trio. Quatuor. Canons. &c.		
		POESIE. DANSE. DÉCORATIONS.	POESIE.		

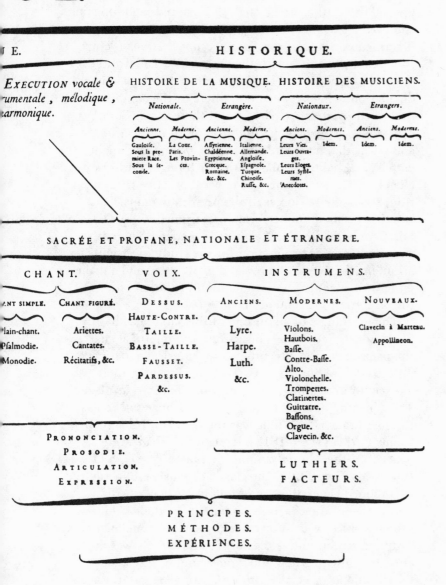

A MUSIQUE

RANCHES.

UE.

| E. | HISTORIQUE. |

| E. | HISTORIQUE. |

EXECUTION vocale &
rumentale, mélodique,
armonique.

HISTORIQUE.

HISTOIRE DE LA MUSIQUE. | **HISTOIRE DES MUSICIENS.**

Nationale.	*Etrangère.*	*Nationaux.*	*Etrangers.*
Ancienne. — *Moderne.*	*Ancienne.* — *Moderne.*	*Anciens.* — *Modernes.*	*Anciens.* — *Modernes.*

Ancienne	Moderne	Ancienne	Moderne	Anciens	Modernes	Anciens	Modernes
Gauloise. Sous la premiere Race. Sous la seconde.	La Cour. Paris. Les Provinces.	Assyrienne. Chaldéenne. Egyptienne. Grecque. Romaine. &c. &c.	Italienne. Allemande. Angloise. Espagnole. Turque. Chinoise. Russe, &c.	Leurs Vies. Leurs Ouvrages. Leurs Eloges. Leurs Systèmes. 'Anecdotes.	Idem.	Idem.	Idem.

SACRÉE ET PROFANE, NATIONALE ET ÉTRANGERE.

| CHANT. | VOIX. | INSTRUMENS. |

CHANT.

NT SIMPLE.	CHANT FIGURÉ.
Plain-chant.	Ariettes.
Psalmodie.	Cantates.
Monodie.	Récitatifs, &c.

VOIX.

DESSUS.
HAUTE-CONTRE.
TAILLE.
BASSE-TAILLE.
FAUSSET.
PARDESSUS.
&c.

INSTRUMENS.

ANCIENS.	MODERNES.	NOUVEAUX.
Lyre.	Violons.	Clavecin à Marteau.
Harpe.	Hautbois.	Appollineon.
Luth.	Basse.	
&c.	Contre-Basse.	
	Alto.	
	Violonchelle.	
	Trompettes.	
	Clarinettes.	
	Guittarre.	
	Bassons.	
	Orgue.	
	Clavecin. &c.	

PRONONCIATION.
PROSODIE.
ARTICULATION.
EXPRESSION.

LUTHIERS.
FACTEURS.

PRINCIPES.
MÉTHODES.
EXPÉRIENCES.

Vincent Duckles

the biographical approach. Further subdivisions distinguish the treatment of the national (French) school from foreign developments and the ancient from the modern worlds as areas of study. *Musique acoustique*, or what we would call the systematic branches of musicology, is given an even more detailed breakdown. Physics, metaphysics, and mathematics are the principal areas considered, and under these headings places are given to experimental studies in the physiology of speech and hearing, the properties of vibrating strings and other sonorous bodies, the mathematical analysis of sounds and intervals, and even a category for the psychology of music, here described as *Analogie des Sons avec les Passions* ("correspondence of sounds with the passions"). The world of musical practice is laid out in generous detail, the major distinction being between the sphere of the composer and that of the performer. The first of these areas (Composition) takes us through all the varieties of musical forms and styles that an eighteenth-century composer might employ: sacred or secular, native or foreign, theater or chamber. The second area of musical practice (Execution) treats the resources of the performing musician, whether his medium be vocal or instrumental. Even certain peripheral areas are taken into account. There is a place under voice production for the study of pronunciation, prosody, articulation, and expression, and a niche under instruments for consideration of the activities of the *luthier*, or instrument maker.

The usefulness of an outline of this kind need hardly be demonstrated. In this beautifully symmetrical chart, the panorama of eighteenth-century musical experience unfolds before our eyes. It was an age in which there was a place for everything, and everything fell into its place. The man who gave bibliographical substance to Nicolas-Etienne Framery's outline was the German, Johann Nicolaus Forkel (1749–1818). Issued more than twenty years after the *Journal de musique*, his *Allgemeine Literatur der Musik* (1792) is the classic of music bibliography. It equipped generations of scholarly musicians with a knowledge of the essential documents of their field. Its primary object was to teach, and the chief beneficiary of that instruction was the author himself. He was in close touch with a new and vital school of historical scholarship at the University of Göttingen, and it was his ambition to apply the methods of that school to the history of music. Forkel was not a sophisticated man of letters as was Charles Burney, nor was he a stuffy antiquarian after the pattern of John Hawkins or Padre Martini. He was a university man, a true academic in the modern sense. He knew better than any of his colleagues that historical insight and judgment depended upon a thorough knowledge of the sources, and he recognized that music was in a poor position to compete with other areas of learning because its source materials were scattered and unorganized. He began the preface to his *Allgemeine Literatur* with the following statement: "When I came to the decision, some fifteen or sixteen years ago, to venture upon a closer examination of the historical nature of my art, it seemed to me to be necessary, above all, to seek out all the pertinent sources, from whatever generation they came, and disclose their contents."[9]

This objective caused him to embark on a period of twelve years of intensive book hunting, during which time there was scarcely any book auction, within Germany or without, in which he did not place bids. If Burney had boasted that he had spent more time and money on music manuscripts and unprinted materials than any other writer on music of his time, Forkel could make the same claim with respect to printed books on the subject. The outcome of these efforts was the creation of a magnificent private music library. We know something of its contents from the catalogue of the auction sale held in 1819 after his death: 465 volumes in folio, 1,730 in octavo, 1,088 volumes of music, to say nothing of an extensive collection of musicians' portraits.

The *Allgemeine Literatur der Musik* was by no means the record of one individual's holdings. Forkel probed every area of musical documentation known to his time in order to build his edifice of musical learning. He gleaned all the information he could from Burney, Hawkins, Martin Gerbert, Brossard, Jean Benjamin de La Borde, Martini, Johann Walther, Johann Mattheson, and many other writers. His efforts marked the beginning of a strong current of philological research, the kind of study that is devoted to the examination, description, and editing of musical source materials. The energy of that approach has continued unabated to the present day, and there is still much work for the source-oriented scholar to do.

Johann Nicolaus Forkel

THE GENERAL LITERATURE OF MUSIC
(*Allgemeine Literatur der Musik*)

I. The Literature of Music History

Origins

Antiquity

The Middle Ages

Modern Music

National Schools   Church Music   Theater Music

Figure 2.

In some respects Forkel's framework for musical knowledge was simpler than that of Framery. His bibliography divides itself into two main streams, the literature of music history and the literature of music theory and practice, foreshadowing that separation of systematic and historical studies that has characterized musicological method to the present day. He was also much aware of the need to bring musical scores under control—an even vaster project than the one devoted to music literature. He went so far as to sketch a plan for score coverage in the *Vorrede* of his *Allgemeine Literatur*. He also projected a large-scale historical anthology of music, a "Geschichte der Musik in Denkmälern von der ältesten bis zur neusten Zeit."[10] His plan called for fifty folio volumes, the first of which was already set up in type when the plates were

II. Literature on the Theory and Practice of Modern Music

Mathematics
Physics

Instrument Making

Musical Practice

Fundamentals

Symbols   Beginners' Methods   Singing

Instrumental Performance
History & Methods

Harmony

Composition

Vocal   Instrumental

Melody

Fantasie

Aesthetics and
Criticism

destroyed in the Napoleonic wars. Forkel never completed his general history of music. Only two volumes appeared, the first in 1788 and the second in 1801. I think it is safe to say that the sheer magnitude of the information he uncovered in his bibliographical investigations discouraged further efforts along that line. The *Allgemeine Literatur der Musik* remains Forkel's greatest contribution, a primary document in the historiography of music and one of the most effective keys to an understanding of the eighteenth-century musical mind.

Some readers may take exception to this reference to the "mind of an age," as if it were something tangible and knowable. I would agree that the attribution of personal characteristics to collective humanity is open to question, but I am convinced (one of the few views I hold

Vincent Duckles

in common with Marshall McLuhan) that a person's mental outlook is conditioned by the media, by the way he receives and stores information. It should be clear from this examination of selected eighteenth-century music bibliographers that the library of the mind is responsive to social influences and pressures, that it is subject to change in content and quality. Our approach to music bibliography has direct bearing on the way we as musicologists acquire a knowledge of our discipline and on the nature and effectiveness of our research.

In reviewing the careers of the musical scholars of the eighteenth and early nineteenth centuries, one cannot fail to be impressed with the breadth of their learning and the thoroughness of their preparation despite their dilettante backgrounds. All of them were literally self-taught, but this holds true of the creative thinkers of any age. Most of them were equipped with splendid private libraries; in addition to the above-mentioned Brossard, Burney, and Forkel, one can cite the collections of Ernst Ludwig Gerber, Adrian de La Fage, Edmund Coussemaker, Raphael Kiesewetter, and François-Joseph Fétis. They were inveterate book collectors, partly by natural inclination, but more often of necessity. Furthermore, they cultivated the field of musical learning with their bare hands. How many hundreds of part books were painstakingly scored by Padre Martini, Raphael Kiesewetter, Carl von Winterfield, or August Wilhelm Ambros! How many early treatises were transcribed or translated, how many manuscripts described, inventoried, or indexed! The voluminous *Nachlässe* of these men in the libraries at Bologna, Vienna, or Berlin give the answer. The Music Library of the University of California at Berkeley holds a substantial collection of the research papers of Alfred Einstein (an even larger body of materials is deposited in the library at Smith College). Einstein died in 1952, which places him well within the orbit of modern musicology, yet his methods had much in common with those of the scholars mentioned above in the patience and precision with which he scored an incredible amount of early music. It was this routine, in some measure, that made him a world-ranking authority in at least two major but separate areas of music research (Mozart and the Italian madrigal) and one of the best generally informed experts our discipline has produced.

It may well be that the kind of universal competence that Einstein possessed is no longer to be expected of musicologists. The field, limited though it is in comparison with other areas in the humanities, is in danger of becoming smothered under the sheer weight of its documentation. Young scholars have every reason to despair at the formidable task that confronts them in keeping abreast of the literature. It is no wonder that many of them give up the effort to contain their field as a whole and retreat toward premature specialization. In this situation it is natural to reach out for the kind of help offered by modern data processing. It is hard to resist the glowing prospect laid before us by Barry Brook in his recent paper "Music Literature and Modern Communication," printed in *College Music Symposium* (1969) and again in *Acta Musicologica* (1970). I do not mean to imply that resistance is in order. Brook's description of his five-phase system for the control and utilization of current musicological literature is a thrilling statement, one that every musicologist, young or old, should read and ponder. Let us by all means accept these innovations and use them to our best advantage, but, at the same time, we should be aware that certain consequences will accrue to the employment of these new methods for advancing knowledge. We should be prepared for the fact that computerized bibliography, data processing, and information retrieval are going to change our patterns of scholarship and research. In some respects that change will be for the good, but we need to guard against the danger of losing certain values we prize very highly. One potential danger lies in the introduction of a new kind of specialist, the data processor, into the research picture. The natural and sociological sciences have long enjoyed the services of this expert, but research in the humanities is particularly sensitive to invasion. The uncritical use of computer technology could result in a situation not unlike that of the sculptor who makes his design on paper or in plaster and turns it over to a craftsman to be executed in bronze. In other words, an important link between the creative thinker and his materials could be broken, and the result might lend some justice to the phrase with which Hans-Heinrich Eggebrecht has characterized much recent computer-oriented research. He calls it "programmed irrelevance."

Vincent Duckles

I recall that the late Thurston Dart, a man who never hesitated to hold unpopular opinions, while he was professor of music at Cambridge, once vetoed the request from a colleague to purchase a new and rather expensive bibliographical tool because he saw no reason why his students should have access to resources that were not available to him when he was a student. Behind this apparently reactionary view, there was at least a grain of reason. He was not so much jealous of a student's access to new resources as he was suspicious of short cuts to knowledge. Dart was honestly convinced that the path he had traversed in gaining mastery of the tools of his trade was, in fact, the most direct and efficient one possible. There are a host of questions prompted by this illustration, questions that require an answer before we can move with confidence into unknown territory. What is the range of effectiveness of the new techniques of documentation, and what are their limitations? What can they do, and what can they not do? What values in the traditional approaches to information control are worth preserving? What articulation can be made between the old and the new? What is the nature of the mentality that will result from the use of the new methods, and how should students be trained to use them?

In evaluating the bibliographical techniques of the future, an important distinction must be kept in mind, the distinction between *information* and *experience*. The data processor is inclined to treat documents (books) primarily as sources of information. The scholar in the humanities, on the other hand, regards such documents as sources of experience. Between these two concepts is a wide gulf that can be bridged only by an effort of the creative imagination. It goes without saying that, in fields in which facts can be isolated and controlled by quantitative methods (such as in the natural sciences and, to a certain extent, in sociology), an information-oriented approach can lead to convincing results. But the experience that is communicated from one mind to another in the reading of a rich and mature piece of scholarship does not lend itself to the techniques of coding and keypunching. The training of musical scholars would be seriously remiss if it did not provide continuing opportunities to deal with documents at the level of experience.

There are two roads to bibliographical mastery of the

kind I have in mind. One is the cultivation of a sense of the shape of the totality of musical knowledge as we know it, an ideological framework that will sustain and support the widening structure of learning. This is an old concept but one that still has value. Just as Brossard, Framery, and Forkel sought to define and diagram the musicological world of their day, so the twentieth-century musicologist should give some thought to the profile of his discipline, to the internal relationships within its parts, and to the links that connect it with the larger world of learning. This is the scaffolding; the structure itself will be made up of books. As for the second road, I would borrow an observation made by my teacher, Manfred Bukofzer. In a seminar on the history of music theory, the discussion turned to the innumerable early treatises on music and the difficulty one had in sorting out the information they contained. Bukofzer's advice was to master three or four such titles thoroughly, for the student would thereby find the keys to unlock the learning in all of them. Thinking along these lines, I would recommend that the young musicologist make a selection of the dozen or more "great books" of his discipline and make them his own by an intensive study and analysis of their content. I would not presume to tell him what those titles should be, although I have my own list. Every individual must make his own choices in this matter. These will be books to which the reader can turn again and again as touchstones of excellence and models of method. They will provide him with much more than data. In fact, the data they contain may be inaccurate or superseded. But, over and above the facts, which can be corrected or verified, they will transmit an experience that is linked directly with the great tradition of scholarship in the humanities.

Notes

1. Charles Burney, *A General History of Music*, 4 vols. (London, 1776–1789), l:vi.

2. Daniel Heartz, *Pierre Attaingnant: Royal Printer of Music* (Berkeley: University of California Press, 1969).

3. The principal Göttingen "universal historians" were

Johann Christophe Gatterer, J. G. Schlözer, and Johann von Müller. Johann Nicolaus Forkel's *Allgemeine Geschichte der Musik*, 2 vols. (Leipzig: Schwikert, 1788–1801), was a direct product of their influence.

Vincent Duckles

4. Sébastien de Brossard, *Dictionaire* [sic] *de musique*, first folio ed. (Paris: Christophe Ballard, 1703). The dictionary is available in a facsimile of this edition (Amsterdam: Antiqua, 1964) and of the second octavo edition (1705) (Hilversum: Fritz Knuf, 1965).

5. Ibid., first folio ed., "Catalogue des auteurs," col. 1 (unpaginated). My translation.

6. Sébastien de Brossard, from the typescript copy of his original handwritten list of his library, offered to the king in 1724 (Paris, Bibliothèque nationale, Rés. Vm^8 20–21, p. 207).

7. Gerhard Pietzsch, *Die Klassifikation der Musik von Boetius bis Ugolino von Orvieto*, Studien zur Geschichte der Musiktheorie im Mittelalter, no. 1 (Halle: Max Niemeyer, 1929).

8. The *Journal de musique* is now available in a reprint edition, preface by Françoise Lesure (Geneva: Minkoff, 1972). Its original editor, and the man presumably responsible for the "Tableau de la musique," was Nicolas-Etienne Framery.

9. Johann Nicolaus Forkel, *Allgemeine Literatur der Musik* (Leipzig: Schwikert, 1792), p. [v]. My translation.

10. See Max Schneider, "Denkmäler der Tonkunst vor hundert Jahren," in *Festschrift zum 90. Geburtstage Sr. Excellenz des wirklichen geheimen Rates Rochus Freiherrn von Liliencron* . . . (Leipzig: Breitkopf and Härtel, 1910), pp. 278–289.

Howard Mayer Brown received his Ph.D. from Harvard University in 1959. From 1960–1972 he taught at the University of Chicago, and from 1972–1974 he was King Edward Professor of Music at the University of London King's College. He recently returned to the University of Chicago, where he is professor of music and director of the Collegium Musicum. He serves on the editorial committee for the new edition of *Grove's Dictionary of Music and Musicians* and as editor of the Early Music series for the Oxford University Press. His most recent books include *Sixteenth-Century Instrumentation* (1974) and *Embellishing Sixteenth-Century Music* (1975).

Elliott Carter, twice awarded the Pulitzer Prize for music and recipient of the Gold Medal for Music from the Institute of Arts and Letters in 1970, teaches at the Juilliard School of Music and is Andrew D. White Professor at Cornell University. He holds honorary degrees from Princeton, Yale, Harvard, Oberlin, and other universities and is a member of the American Academy of Arts and Letters, the American Academy of Arts and Sciences, and the Akademie der Künste (Berlin). In honor of the composer's sixty-fifth birthday, during the winter season of 1973–1974 the New York Public Library presented an exhibition of his manuscripts, photographs, and letters. During the concert season of 1974–1975, the Composers' Quartet gave a concert of his three string quartets at Columbia University, the Whitney Museum devoted a concert to his music, a new Brass Quintet and a Duo for Violin and Piano were premiered, and in the summer of 1975 the New York Philharmonic, under the direction of Pierre Boulez, performed his Concerto for Orchestra at the Edinburgh, Ghent, Paris, and Berlin Festivals.

Gilbert Chase has been appointed visiting professor in comparative studies, history, and music at the University of Texas at Austin for the academic year 1975–1976.

297

During his multifaceted career, he has taught at the University of Oklahoma, Tulane University, Brooklyn College at the City University of New York, and the State University of New York at Buffalo. He has also served as U.S. cultural affairs officer of the American embassies in Lima, Buenos Aires, and Brussels and has frequently been a lecturer for the cultural program of the State Department in Latin America. His main fields of research include American, Latin American, and Spanish musical history, as well as cultural history and the arts. Among his major publications are: *The Music of Spain* (1941, 1959); *A Guide to the Music of Latin America* (1945, 1962); *America's Music* (1955, 1966); and *Contemporary Art in Latin America* (1971).

Vincent Duckles is professor of music and head of the Music Library at the University of California at Berkeley. He is past president of the Music Library Association, has served two terms on the executive board of the American Musicological Society, and is currently chairman of the United States branch of the International Association of Music Libraries. A recipient of Fulbright research grants to Cambridge University in England and Georg August Universität in Göttingen, Germany, his research interests include seventeenth-century English song and the history of musical scholarship. Among his principal publications are *Music Reference and Research Materials: An Annotated Bibliography* (1974) and, with Minnie Elmer, *Thematic Catalog of a Manuscript Collection of Eighteenth-Century Italian Instrumental Music in the University of California, Berkeley, Music Library* (1963).

Charles Hamm has accepted an appointment to become Arthur Virgin Professor of Music and chairman of the Music Department at Dartmouth College in 1976. He holds a Ph.D. in musicology from Princeton University and has taught musicology and theory at the University of Illinois, Tulane University, and the Cincinnati Conservatory of Music. He has served as president of the American Musicological Society, has held Guggenheim and Fulbright grants, and has published books and articles dealing with Renaissance music, the notation of music, American music, opera, and popular music.

Daniel Heartz is professor of music at the University of California at Berkeley and served as chairman of the Department of Music there from 1969 to 1973. He completed his doctoral dissertation, "Sources and Forms of the French Instrumental Dance in the Sixteenth Century," at Harvard University in 1957. Since then, he has published a score of articles on Renaissance topics and has edited works for lute and keyboard originally printed by Attaingnant. His book, *Pierre Attaingnant: Royal Printer of Music* (1969), which he designed himself, has won several prizes, including the Kinkeldey Award of the American Musicological Society for 1971. In 1974 he was elected vice president of the American Musicological Society. His most satisfying achievement is Berkeley's Citation for Distinguished Teaching (1962).

Lewis Lockwood is the Robert Schirmer '21 Professor of Music at Princeton University, where he received his Ph.D. in 1960 and where he has taught in the Department of Music since 1958. His principal fields of study are the Renaissance and Beethoven. Among his publications are *The Counter-Reformation and the Masses of Vincenzo Ruffo* (1970) and a critical edition of Palestrina's *Pope Marcellus Mass* for the Norton Critical Scores series (1975). His article "The Autograph of the First Movement of Beethoven's Sonata for Violoncello and Pianoforte, Opus 69" (1970) won the Alfred Einstein Award of the American Musicological Society for 1970.

Gilbert Reaney, born in Sheffield, England, has been professor of music at the University of California at Los Angeles since 1960. He has received Guggenheim and National Endowment for the Humanities Fellowships and was the first to receive the Dent Medal of the International Musicological Society (New York, 1961). He has been active for many years in the performance of early music, in planning and performing historical concerts for the British Broadcasting Corporation (1952–1975), and as the United States founder and artistic director of the London Medieval Group (1958–1975). He is general editor of the Corpus Scriptorum de Musica series of the American Institute of Musicology and assistant editor of *Musica Disciplina*. His principal publications include: *Early Fifteenth Century Music* (1955–1975);

299

Manuscripts of Medieval Polyphonic Music: 11th Century to c. 1400 (1966–1969); with A. Gilles, *Phillippe de Vitry: Ars Nova* (1964); *Machaut* (1971); and *Franconis de Colonia: Ars Cantus Mensurabilis* (1974).

Charles Seeger is now retired and lives in Bridgewater, Connecticut. Over the years he has been active in many areas of music, including conducting, composition, musicology, and ethnomusicology. He was one of the founders of the American Musicological Society, the Society for Ethnomusicology, the International Music Council, and the International Society for Music Education. He is known as the developer of the melograph, an instrument that has allowed a more scientific study of many aspects of musical sound. Some of his more important articles include: "Systematic and Historical Orientations in Musicology" (1939); "Systematic Musicology: Viewpoints, Orientations, and Methods" (1951); "Preface to the Description of a Music" (1953); "On the Moods of a Music Logic" (1960); "Preface to the Critique of Music" (1965); and "Toward a Unitary Field Theory for Musicology" (1970).

Index

Abelard, Pierre, 259, 272 n. 65
Académie de poesie et musique,
    214-215, 229 n. 58
Accelerando, 80
Adler, Guido, 233, 281
Adlung, Jacob, 279
Aesthetics, 25, 38-39, 233, 241,
    288. *See also* Esthetics
Affections, 193, 214
Age of Reason (Enlightenment),
    279-280
Agricola, Alexander, 89
Air de Cour, 211
Aleatory, 76
Alta, 21
Alternation practices, 263, 274 nn.
    92, 95
Ambros, August Wilhelm, 141, 292
American Anthropological Associa-
    tion, 232
American music, 41-68. *See also*
    American psalmody and
    hymnody; Carter, Elliott
American Musicological Society,
    232
American psalmody and hymnody,
    41-56, 60 nn. 1-4, 61 nn. 5-
    19, 62 nn. 20-22
    instruction books, 44, 45, 46,
    49, 53, 60 nn. 2, 4, 61 nn. 5,
    12, 17, 62 n. 20
    key and mode associations, 46-
    48
    performance practice, 42-43, 54
    psalm books, 44, 45, 46, 50, 51-
    52, 61 nn. 9, 13, 14, 16, 62
    n. 2
    reforms, 43-56
    regular singing (from notes), 43-
    44
    shape note traditions, 54
Ancient Greek music, 193-194,
    210, 212, 254, 258
Anglès, Higini, 251, 255, 257, 266
    n. 17, 269 n. 43, 271 n. 57

Anne of Brittany, queen of France,
    195, 202
Anonymous IV, 253, 269 n. 38
Anthropology, 231-246
    as auxiliary science to musicol-
    ogy, 233
    branches of, 231
    as complementary study to his-
    tory, 235
    cultural, 231-232, 238
    ethnology, 232, 242
    of music, 233, 236-238, 240,
    245
    physical, 232
    social, 238-239, 241-242, 244
    structural, 236
Antimatter, 5
Antiphon, 253, 256-260, 271 n. 56
Antiphonal, 255-256
Antiphony, 76
Aristotle, 6, 285
Arne, Thomas, 55
Arnold, Samuel, 55
Art. *See* Iconography
Attaingnant, Pierre, 129 n. 22,
    197-198, 200-202, 210, 221
    nn. 12-13, 255 n. 37, 280,
    295 n. 2
Aubry, Pierre, 249, 266 n. 13
Auditory time, 64. *See also* Com-
    munication, auditory
Aurelian of Réomé, 254, 269 n. 40
Avant-garde, 67, 73
Axiology, 1, 30

Babbit, Milton, 59
Bach, Johann Sebastian, 139-140
Bagpipe, 131 n. 26, 203
Baïf, Jean-Antoine, 214-215, 216,
    217-218, 229 n. 60, 230 n.
    63
Ballade, 89, 196, 251, 255, 261,
    267 n. 18, 276 n. 106
Ballard, Robert, 207, 212, 218, 284
Ballet de Cour, 193

301

Index

Index

Index